Duncaster

_____

RACE TO THE SKY

RACE TO THE SKY

The Wright Brothers Versus the United States Government

Stephen B. Goddard

McFarland & Company, Inc., Publishers

Jefferson, North Carolina, and London

LIBRARY OF CONGRESS CATALOGUING-IN-PUBLICATION DATA

Goddard, Stephen B., 1941–
    Race to the sky : the Wright brothers versus the United States
government / Stephen B. Goddard.
       p.   cm.
    Includes bibliographical references and index.

    ISBN 0-7864-1594-0 (illustrated case binding : 50# alkaline paper) ∞

    1. Wright, Orville, 1871–1948.   2. Wright, Wilbur, 1867–1912.
3. Aeronautics— Research — United States— History.   4. Government
competition.   5. Research and development contracts, Government—
United States— History.   I. Title.
TL540.W7G596   2003
629.13'007'2073 — dc21   2003011658

British Library cataloguing data are available

Cover photograph: Orville (left) and Wilbur Wright *(©2002 Art Today)*

Manufactured in the United States of America

McFarland & Company, Inc., Publishers
  Box 611, Jefferson, North Carolina 28640
    www.mcfarlandpub.com

To Taegan, Brad and Chelsey,
who have made their dad very proud

Acknowledgments

ANY SCHOLAR WHO HAS DONNED old clothes to rummage through dusty archival storage vaults will recognize the debt that students of early aeronautics owe to historian Marvin W. McFarland. Then director of the Aeronautics Division of the Library of Congress, McFarland compiled two massive volumes in 1953 to honor the 50th anniversary of the Wright brothers' epochal flight at Kill Devil Hills, North Carolina, on December 17, 1903. Those weighty tomes, entitled *The Papers of Wilbur and Orville Wright,* presented the brothers' correspondence from 1899 through 1948, with notes, appendices, and a bibliography. Although it is certainly not an ending point for research into early aeronautics, it is a whale of a beginning point.

A tip of the hat also goes to the Wrights' protagonist Samuel P. Langley and Charles Manly, his chief assistant, who faithfully recorded observations about their activities. Manly, through the Smithsonian Institution, published the weighty *Memoirs of Mechanical Flight* in 1911.

Historians have turned out several fine works about early flight, among them works by Dr. Tom Crouch of the Smithsonian, Fred Howard, official Wright biographer Fred Kelly, Stephen Kirk, Harry Combs, and John Evangelist Walsh. The best one-volume treatment of the subject may be Crouch's *The Bishop's Boys,* published in 1989. Why, then, one might ask, is there a need for yet another work, even with the 2003 centennial of the Wrights' first flight? I believe that, even with all the light thrown into dark corners of early flight by the historians cited, the fascinating story of the American government's creation of a national crusade to achieve first flight remains to be fleshed out. That the story is less well known today than, say, President Kennedy's drive to land a man on the moon, owes less to significance of the mission than to the fact that it occurred in a time of less developed mass media. The participation of President William McKinley, Assistant Secretary of the Navy and later President Theodore Roosevelt, and Charles D. Walcott of the Smithsonian Institution and why they believed a first flight by America was so urgent, politically and strategically, will be a principal consideration of this book.

Before crediting those who have contributed to this work, it is important to say that responsibility for any errors that have crept into it is entirely my own.

Thanks go to the Hartford Public Library and its Hartford Collection, with special thanks to Doreen McCabe and Judith King; Yale University's Sterling Library; the fine specialized library of the New England Air Museum in Windsor Locks, Connecticut; the Trinity College Library in Hartford; the archives of the Library of Congress; Phil Edwards and the Air and Space Museum, Museum of American History, and the Charles D. Walcott Collection of the Smithsonian Institution; the Wright State University Library, especially Dawn Dewey; the staff of the Outer Banks History Center in Manteo, North Carolina; venerable Outer Banks historian David Stick; Louis Carlat and the Thomas Alva Edison archives at Rutgers University; Kitty Hawk mayor and historian Bill Harris; Tom and Suzie Gardner of Kitty Hawk, N.C.; the staff of the Wright Brothers National Memorial at Kill Devil Hills, North Carolina; and Don Weckhorst of the Octave Chanute Aerospace Museum. I would like to also thank Linda Case, Dr. Tom Crouch, Ken Dusyn, Andy Fleischmann, Adrienne Marks, Sue Niedzelski, Wanda Rickerby, Howard Sacks, and Bob Satter.

The family of a person writing a book knows that the work takes up residence in the home, occupies a seat at the dining table, and sometimes acts like a jealous mistress. My wife Patty knows I am at my happiest when writing, but she groans when each new book is undertaken, knowing the price she must pay in competing for my attention. Her sacrifice is a gift of love and makes me love her more. My grown children, to whom this book is dedicated, have been encouraging and helpful throughout.

Stephen B. Goddard
Hartford, Connecticut
July 2003

Table of Contents

Preface

THE INVENTION OF THE AUTOMOBILE transformed Americans' day-to-day life, but the advent of the airplane let people visit far-off places that were heretofore the stuff of dreams. Until the late 1800s, those who dared to seriously contemplate manned flight were considered fools or crackpots. But the history of technology teaches us that when enough intelligent experimenters share ideas and build on each other's results, things start to happen. Such was the case in the last decade of the 19th century. Alexander Graham Bell, renowned inventor of the telephone, and Samuel Pierpont Langley, Secretary of the Smithsonian Institution, set out to make America first in flight. This was no mere sporting competition but a dead serious undertaking, for the winds of colonialism were blowing strong. Building empires meant spilling blood, and victory would go to the nations with the most up-to-date equipment.

European governments took interest in their countrymen's aeronautical experiments, hoping to use aircraft, once developed, for aerial surveillance. Some, like Spain, harbored designs on the western hemisphere. After the U.S. battleship *Maine* was sunk in Havana Harbor in 1898, President McKinley signed on to the Langley-Bell project, and a national race to be first in flight was born.

Langley was probably America's foremost scientist, so it was natural that Wilbur Wright, a Dayton, Ohio, bicycle mechanic, who wanted to read more about aeronautical experiments in 1899, would write to the Smithsonian for information. And so begins the story of the Wright brothers.

The shelves of books written about the Wright brothers have taught generations of schoolchildren that Wilbur and Orville Wright were first in flight. Yet few know that they were up against a national mission backed by money and prestige, that one could liken to President John F. Kennedy's drive to put a man on the moon. That two Midwestern bicycle mechanics, spending a total of $1,000, could be first in flight is amazing. That in so doing they could outpace the collective resources of the American government is nearly unfathomable.

PREFACE

Several fine biographies of the Wright brothers have been written over the years. Their authors tend to be aviation experts themselves, so the books are quite sure-footed technically. As a social historian, I am in debt to them for helping me try to understand the basic principles of flight. What has been missing from the literature on the subject, in my opinion, is a treatment of the dramatic, David-and-Goliath struggle between an entire government and two ordinary men, that came to an exciting end over nine fateful days in December 1903, and why success in this struggle was so important to the geopolitical future of America and Europe.

In fairness, some of the authors cited above limned the competition, but none has put the conflict center stage, where I believe it belongs. The competition was excruciatingly difficult for both the government and the Wrights. Professor Langley, at one point far behind schedule and out of money, practically begged the Wrights, unsuccessfully, to let him in on their plans. The two sides hadn't started out in a race, but as their projects coalesced, each became keenly aware of the other and more determined to be the first to take to the sky.

The Wrights and Professor Langley were noble competitors who demonstrated the best of the American competitive spirit. The same cannot be said for some others, men who devalued means to achieve ends. But the race to the sky is a very important part of the history of American aviation and the industry that changed the world.

The Battle Is Joined

"It is very bad policy to ask one flying machine man about the experiments of another, because every flying machine man thinks that his method is the only correct one."—Wilbur Wright, 1903

A SMALL GROUP OF DISTINGUISHED American scientists approached the fall of 1903 with last-chance intensity, their excitement tempered by trepidation. For nearly a generation, they had cogitated, built, experimented, failed, and regrouped, all several times, in the service of man's nearly-primal desire to fly with the birds. Theirs had become a national crusade, backed by President William McKinley and unprecedented government grants in those days of a do-little federal government. The illustrated magazines of the day lavishly displayed the venture's progress, projecting the same sense of purpose a later generation would feel hearing President John F. Kennedy pledge to put a man on the moon before the end of the 1960s.

The race to the moon would take eight years, but the race to the sky had already dragged on for 17, and public patience was flagging. Back in 1899, sensing government pump-priming had yielded little or no results, officials tightened the purse strings, forcing the project's backers to seek scarce private funding. So as the cool, crisp autumn days began to turn Washington's leaves from green to gold, the scientists had the chilly feeling that the Potomac River trial scheduled for that fall would be do or die.

Samuel Pierpont Langley, the project leader, wasn't used to being on the defensive. Long established as America's leading astronomer and an inventor of note, he projected dignity and rectitude as he neared his 70th birthday. With a patrician nose and a full, graying beard, Langley had the sad, deep-set eyes of a man who knew too much. The Boston Brahmin, accustomed to having the seas part as he approached, conducted inspections of his project wearing a morning coat, tie and vest. With honorary degrees from several Ivy League universities as well as Oxford and Cambridge, Langley had been named Secretary of the Smithsonian Institution in 1887. At his first official dinner in that position, four U.S. Supreme Court justices raised their glasses in a toast to his appointment.

Langley's greatest invention was his own persona of accomplishment, for his highest academic achievement was receiving a high school diploma. An autodidact, he spent years immersing himself in things scientific at the Boston Public Library, then signed on to direct the Allegheny Observatory at the Western University of Pennsylvania. There, he honed his reputation by inventing the bolometer, the most accurate instrument yet to measure heat radiation, and won coveted awards at home and abroad in the process.[1]

Langley's presence alone would have lent the venture an aura of high respect. But among those with whom he associated during this golden age of invention were some of America's best-known applied scientists, men who had harnessed fundamental principles and turned them into cash cows. They included men such as Thomas Alva Edison with whom he had corresponded since 1878 on topics ranging from deafness to heavier-than-air flight; Alexander Graham Bell, whose fame and fortune as the inventor of the telephone gave him the leisure necessary to experiment with the next new thing; and even such transforming industrialists as Andrew Carnegie, who admired Langley from afar, and clamored to meet him.

Langley attended a lecture on aeronautics in 1886, the year before his Smithsonian appointment, and soon dedicated himself to learning what birds already knew. In his new laboratory at the Smithsonian, the carcasses of such creatures as buzzards, an albatross, and a California condor were spun aloft on 30-foot arms at high speeds, so Langley might tease out the first principles of flight.[2] From then until 1891, Langley built more than 100 models of flying crafts, varying the combinations of wing, tail, and propellers, and published his findings in 1891 in *Experiments in Aerodynamics.* His startling conclusion was that "Mechanical flight is possible with the engines we now possess." Using Smithsonian money, Langley perfected a steam-driven model and spent much of the next five years on Washington's Potomac River, but "trial after trial ended with the craft falling into the water off the end of the launch rail."[3]

By 1897, when Langley published his findings in the popular *McClure's Magazine,* he was already heralded for discovering "Langley's Law": that the work required to maintain an airplane wing aloft decreases as its speed increases. Unlike the entrepreneurial Bell and Edison, Langley saw himself as a pure scientist, leaving others to reap the fruit of his labors. Indeed, in his *McClure's* article, he announced his retirement from the field.[4] But the McKinley administration, which had picked up on Langley's work, intuited right away how men in the air could create a whole new method of wartime surveillance. Langley, his imagination stoked, let it be known that if Washington would put up $50,000 for development, he could put a man in the air within two to three years. Warming to the prospect, he put his money where his mouth was and anted up $20,000 from his own pocket.[5]

Langley understood his bargaining power. In France and Germany, countries with imperial ambitions as strong as America's, inventors were making serious progress in aeronautics. Then, in February of 1898, the battleship *Maine* sank in Havana harbor, with massive loss of life. McKinley's administration began plotting retaliation against Spain, which it suspected lay behind the sinking. Langley was confident enough that his government needed him that when he asked an intermediary to intercede for him with President McKinley, he set down autocratic terms: he wanted absolute control of the money and complete secrecy.[6] McKinley, undeterred, continued to show keen interest and asked for photographs of the models flying in air. He then routed Langley to War Department aide George Meiklejohn, who brought in the young assistant naval secretary, brash New Yorker Theodore Roosevelt. The former New York governor would solidify his Rough Rider image in the upcoming conflict, which he would label "a splendid little war." That Langley's good friend Bell served on the board reviewing the proposal insured an inside voice on his behalf. Within a week, the panel met Langley's terms.

A Crash Heard Round the World

The death of Otto Lilienthal on August 10, 1896, made headlines around the world and shook the incipient aviation community to its foundation. If man were to fly, Lilienthal believed, he must first observe the behavior of birds. And so the German aeronaut, a strapping redhead with a full beard, traveled to the Rhinow Mountains outside Berlin, where he completed 2,000 glides in 16 different biplanes and monoplanes, their wings resembling "the outspread pinions of a soaring bird."[7] But unlike those flyers reluctant to risk life and limb, Lilienthal felt it important to conduct manned flights, each carrying the potential for human disaster. Fanning the flames of Lilienthal's passion for aeronautics was Robert Wood, correspondent for the *Boston Transcript*, who traveled with the passionate German and chronicled his exploits. Hardly objective, Wood wrote, "...I have never witnessed anything that strung the nerves to such a pitch of excitement or awakened such a feeling of enthusiasm and admiration as the wild and fearless rush of Otto Lilienthal through the air."[8] But in a trial on August 9, 1896, Lilienthal's glider stalled in the air and plunged 50 feet. He was rushed to a Berlin hospital where he died the next day. His benediction to those who had hurried to rescue him were, "Sacrifices must be made."[9]

The tragic event sobered some scientists and validated others such as Langley, who used unmanned models and believed one never need to place his life on the line in trials. Lilienthal's death caught the attention of many thousands across the world, who had wondered whether it would be Germany's "birdman" who would finally take to the sky. Among them were an Ohio clergyman's two sons, who ran a bicycle repair and rental shop in Dayton, Ohio.[10] Like many Americans, Wilbur Wright and his younger brother Orville had read news stories about Lilienthal since 1890 and a large spread in the popular *McClure's Magazine* in 1894.

Rather than frightening the Wrights, Lilienthal's death reawakened their imaginations. For their analytical minds, it was not enough to mark the man's passing; they needed to know why he had crashed. Wilbur and Orville found it nearly inconceivable that a man who had made 2,000 successful airborne trials could dive to his death in the next one. Would this shake the confidence of those who came after? And how could similar catastrophes be avoided? They turned to a book their frequent use had dog-eared, *Animal Mechanism,* which was long on bird photos and short on how birds' wings actually worked. A busy life at the bicycle shop left little time for inquiry until the spring of 1899, when Wilbur decided to write directly to one of the foremost aeronautical experimenters of the day, Professor Samuel P. Langley of the Smithsonian Institution, and ask for any papers available on the topic of flight. As they knew from reading the newspapers, Langley had launched an unmanned, steam-powered glider, which rose, dipped, and circled for more than a half-mile over water at speeds of 20 to 25 miles per hour, two months before Lilienthal's accident.[11]

Wilbur Wright's missive was among scores of letters raining down on Langley from those newly aspiring to fly, a fraternity that included the misguided, the unbalanced and the opportunistic, all drawn to the prospect by word of Langley's unprecedented $50,000 grant from the U.S. Army Board of Ordnance. The Smithsonian sent the 32-year-old mechanic reprints of articles, Langley's own *The Story of Experiments in Mechanical Flight,* a book by their hero Lilienthal, and a work by Frenchman Louis-Pierre Mouillard, entitled *Empire of the Air.* Smithsonian historian Tom Crouch calls it "the most important exchange of correspondence in the history of the Smithsonian."[12]

Wilbur began to contemplate how buzzards, in the face of wind gusts, could keep their equilibrium by, as Wright called it, "a torsion of the tips of the wings." This led him to build a biplane kite whose wings could be warped at the tips. Whereas some inventors believed the key to flying lay in the kite's basic design, Wilbur thought the craft needed to adapt to changing conditions as birds could do by moving their wings. So he built in a mechanism to manipulate the wings of his kite forward or backward in relation to each other, thus shifting the craft's center of gravity.[13]

By the fall of 1899, Wilbur decided to follow the impossible dream chased by Lilienthal and such trailblazers as Octave Chanute, who was then unknown to Wilbur, but would become a major influence in his work. Though Wilbur had only a high school education, he was not star struck by the reputation of a Samuel Langley, and he read with an objective eye the materials sent to him. When he was finished, he pronounced it as little more than "a hodgepodge of opinion, speculation and guesswork." A year later, Wilbur had built a full-scale biplane glider and transported it 500 miles by rail to a 60-mile long sand dune on North Carolina's outer banks, known as Kitty Hawk. There, Wilbur would begin a three-year series of experimental flights. In 1901 and again in 1902, as Wilbur and Orville came to understand better their avian cousins, they began to see what it would take to put a man aloft in a powered craft. Their 1902 glider was sufficiently sophisticated for an operator to control it up and down, back and forth, and side to side, so the craft could make a left turn, for example, and still maintain its balance.

That history tends to recall the brothers as "Orville and Wilbur" owes more to the fact that Orville survived Wilbur by 36 years than as a reflection of their relative contributions to the mission. Wilbur's seminal letter to the Smithsonian was written in the first person singular, and as late as September 3, 1900, Wilbur wrote his father, Bishop Wright, to let him know he planned to fly his glider at Kitty Hawk. The letter made no mention of Orville being involved. Yet by the end of that year, he had apparently added Orville as a full partner, and from then on, they signed their business checks "The Wright Brothers," with the signer denoting a lower case "ow" or "ww" to indicate his identity.[14]

Those Who Tried and Failed

The fraternity Wilbur Wright joined by writing his fateful letter to Samuel Langley trod the steps that Leonardo da Vinci had walked in the 15th century. Curiously, few had taken Leonardo's work seriously until Britain's Sir George Cayley began to work with gliders in the early 19th century in England. He built a five-foot model with an adjustable cross-shaped tail unit and a sliding weight fitted to the nose, so the operator could shift the craft's center of gravity. But until Cayley learned how to keep his models stable under changing conditions, he realized he couldn't begin to tackle motorized flight.[15]

A generation later, Louis-Charles Letur of France attacked the problem from a different angle; he wedded a parachute with a glider, but was killed in his attempts. His countryman Jean-Marie Le Bris tested gliders shaped like birds in the 1850s and 1860s. Lilienthal realized that his gliders needed to not only look like birds but to act like birds; he catalogued, through his 2,000 test flights, how a glider would respond to changing conditions. Britain's Scot Percy Pilcher emulated Lilienthal's work but followed his idol to his death in 1899 when, during inclement weather, a bamboo rod snapped and caused his craft to lose control and crash.

One of the most remarkable innovators was an American. French-born Octave Chanute didn't take up manned flight until his 60s, when he published a seminal work in the field, entitled *Progress in Flying Machines.* Coming to the field late, Chanute brought the perspective of age and financial security, as one not one seeking personal aggrandizement. This inclined him to foster cooperation and information-sharing among rivals tirelessly, with his only objective being to live to see manned flight. A white tonsure, mustache, and goatee framed Chanute's round face, and his liquid eyes and kindly mien were those of a manic catalyst rather than a prime mover. He followed Lilienthal in building triplane gliders and succeeded in making them more stable. Years later, the Chicago engineer would insure his fame through his correspondence with Wilbur and Orville Wright, totaling hundreds of letters written over many years.[16]

Until the 1880s, manned flight was a metaphor for impossibility. "A man might as well try to fly," one would observe about an obviously impossible prospect. But as man rapidly climbed the learning curve in the 1890s, manned flight was no longer a joke and might, in fact, be lurking just around imagination's corner. By the time that Otto Lilienthal met his death in 1896, the public no longer considered him a fool. Now he was a "martyr to science."[17]

By the 1880s and 1890s, ordinary folk seemed flight-obsessed. Newspaper stories told of experimenters jumping to their deaths from barn roofs, stacked hay bales or hills. But while anyone could craft a crude wooden framework and drape silk across it, powered flight was quite another matter. Cayley had experimented with a helicopter design, building a craft in which twin full-circle rotors flanked a boat-shaped fuselage.

In the late 1800s, tinkerers such as Horatio Phillips came to realize that lift in a properly-shaped wing happens when the pressure beneath it is more than the pressure above it. And F.W. Lanchester demonstrated that what causes the top-wing pressure to be less is that air speeds over it faster than beneath the wing. Now they were getting somewhere and could begin to think of powered flight.

Frenchman Felix du Temple tested a hot-air engine airplane in 1874. A decade later, Russian Nikolai Mozhaiski attached himself to a flying craft and sped down a ski jump, managing to stay aloft for a brief period. But now that aeronauts had discovered how lift worked, some realized that control still eluded them. Alphonse Pénaud managed to design a craft in 1876 that had some built-in internal controls, but he never flew the machine. It would be left to others to try and, when they did, fame and fortune would follow.

A Fortunate Partnership

When the British physicist Sir William Thomson, lately elevated to the title of Lord Kelvin, visited America in 1897, Alexander Graham Bell tried unsuccessfully to engage the pioneer of thermodynamics on the subject of flight. Kelvin revealed his response in a letter he later wrote to Bell's wife, Mabel:

> I was quite sure that your husband would not go on in respect to flying machines otherwise than by careful and trustworthy experiment. Even if the result is to demonstrate to himself that a practical useful solution of the problem is not to be found.... When I spoke to him on the subject at Halifax, I wished to dissuade him from giving his valuable time and resources to attempts which I believed, could only lead to disappointment, if carried on with any expectation of leading to a useful flying machine.[18]

Unfazed by Kelvin's gloomy assessment, Bell pressed on. Yet while Wilbur and Orville Wright would view kite flying as a means to an end, Bell saw it as an end in itself. Although most aeronautical tinkerers used wings to emulate the avian world, Bell found air drag to be so important a factor as to get rid of wings altogether, obtaining lift instead by angling the propellers upward. While this underscored Bell's propensity for original thinking, he soon abandoned this idea altogether.[19]

Biographer Robert V. Bruce contrasts Bell with his contemporary, Thomas Alva Edison. By the 1890s, both had achieved great scientific and commercial success—Bell with his telephone, Edison with his phonograph and electric light. But while both Bell and Edison kept "the fertility of technical imagination" into old age, Edison continued to push his ideas into development and commercial use while Bell "recorded his ideas in his private notebooks and moved on without devoting himself to cultivation and harvest." In short, Bell seems to have fallen victim to the temptation to live off his laurels as a worldwide celebrity.[20]

That Bell was at a loss to explain why he continued to experiment with kites is further proof that his hungry drive had turned to dilettantism.

Alexander Graham Bell, secure monetarily from his invention of the telephone, staked his prestige in backing Secretary Langley financially, technically and personally in his quest to build an aircraft that would be the first to fly. Library of Congress.

National Geographic wrote that kite-flying gave him "moderate exercise in bracing weather amid soul-satisfying scenery. It made sporting demands on his skill and ingenuity. It had the excitement of unpredictability. And because Bell wanted his kites to show up clearly in photographs validating their performance, he covered them in bright red silk. This enhanced the drama of their evolutions, and Bell had an eye for drama."[21]

His reputation already made, Bell didn't need to invent the craft that would propel the first man aloft. He was happy to defer to his close friend Samuel P. Langley, in whom the juices of ambition still flowed. In early May of 1896, at the private preserve of the Mt. Vernon Ducking Club, Bell accompanied Langley on a secret mission to test Langley's model numbers five and six, the results of a decade of effort to develop a practical flying machine. Gracing both machines were two sets of wings, built in tandem with a 14-foot span and powered by lightweight steam engines. When a guy wire snagged on the catapult during the test of Model 6 and plunged it into the Potomac River, they readied Model 5. His team launched the aerodrome, as Langley had decided to call the craft, from atop a houseboat, from which it soared 3,300 feet during the arc of its flight, then doubled back and hit the water. "For the first time," writes historian Thomas Crouch, "a large flying model with a self-contained power plant had remained in the air for a length of time sufficient to demonstrate that it had unquestionably flown."[22]

A Fast-Spinning World

To live in the developed world in 1903 was to be aware of seemingly-endless possibilities for progress, both at home and abroad. Plans were afoot for the Panama Canal, which would cause world trade to mushroom. Teddy Roosevelt started the radio age by sending a direct wire to Britain's King Edward VII from a point near Cape Cod. A contraption some called the buggyaut and others called the automobile had made the first transcontinental auto trip from San Francisco to New York in 70 days. And Boston had beaten Pittsburgh five games to three in the first World Series.[23]

Hitching a steam engine to a craft stable enough to fly more than a half mile had been a huge achievement, but putting a man aboard would be a far greater feat, both practically and symbolically. Langley had pledged to have a man aloft within three years from the time he obtained government financing of his project. Four years and more had elapsed, he had exhausted the initial grant, and a chorus of skeptics sang its derision, but in mid–November of 1902, Langley wrote:

> Everything is ready, and were there still time this season, a flight would be made, but I do not expect one until after the ice has gone; then I, who have never known any great initiatory trial without some mischance, look for what I call our "first smash." When every human care has been taken, there remains the element of the unknown. There may well be something that forethought has not provided for, and I expect it, but excepting for the fact that a human life is now in question, I could make it without fear at all.[24]

When Langley told his wealthy colleague Bell that he was out of money, Bell gave his friend $5,000 to spend on scientific research of his own choosing. Dr. Jerome Kidder left an equal amount in his will. But by 1903, the secretary had torn through both financial transfusions and had withdrawn an additional $13,000 from the Smithsonian's Hodgkins Fund. Trials of the craft in September and October failed dismally, the October test crushing the front wings, rear wings, and rudder. Not to worry, assured Langley, drawing from some deep pool of optimism that managed to elude others. The failure resulted from the way the launch was built, he said, not the machine itself. And correcting that problem now meant the team would have one less worry later.[25]

Assistant Charles Manly, charged with developing the lightest, most powerful motor for the craft, had produced a 22-horsepower engine with a larger displacement than used in earlier models. An August 8, 1903, test of a quarter-scale model assured the team that it could control altitude. A larger challenge was fighting Langley's natural instinct to test some more; after all, his team had been at this for 17 years.

Unlike inventors who traveled huge distances to more favorable, often secret, locations to test their machines, Langley conducted his on the Potomac River, within sight of the crenellated red-brick Smithsonian castle. He and his crew now assured themselves they had thought and re-thought everything that could go wrong. Some mishaps, they realized, had nothing to do with the craft itself, such as the guy wire that snagged on the launch catapult back in 1896. But politically, the time had come when demonstrating progress was far more important than obsessing over pitfalls.

The team scheduled its launch for December 8, on a Potomac River coated with thin ice. In mid-afternoon, two tugboats set off from a wharf at the foot of Eighth Street Southeast, amid strong gusts of wind, towing a flat-bottomed frame houseboat. Langley, at 69 too old to power the craft he had designed, tapped Charles Manly for the task, understanding that should the young Cornell engineer succeed, history would remember Manly, not Langley, as the first man aloft.

More out of caution than pessimism, the Secretary had invited a surgeon to join the select group of witnesses to the event. Northeast weather is subject to constant change, and a propitious day began to sour in late afternoon, when the sky turned dark and gloomy as dusk crept in. In earlier tests, the team might have scrubbed the mission and waited until the next day. But such was Langley's anxiety about money and official patience, that he decided to go for broke. Manly stripped down to his union suit so his heavy clothing would not drag him under should he end up in the drink. Historian Tom Crouch describes how he prepared for what could have been a historic mission:

> The young engineer stepped through the tangle of brace wires and struts into the small fabric-sided cockpit. He seated himself on a board facing the right side of the machine, his hands resting on two small wheels mounted on the right wall of the cockpit. These controlled the up and down motion of the tail and operated the rudder on the underside of the fuselage.... Satisfied with the sound of the engine and the operation of the controls, Manly gave the signal to (R.L.) Reed, who released the catapult at 4:45.[26]

In small boats surrounding the craft, a gaggle of newspapermen, along with friends and invited guests, held their breath.

Hayseeds No More

In his impartial yet encouraging way, Octave Chanute wrote Wilbur Wright in March of 1903 that a prominent French glider experimenter "is much of the opinion that you are ahead of all others" and had asked to take lessons from Wilbur. An informal network of crew members, spies, and saboteurs had emerged in this fledgling world of aeronautics, alternately trading and brokering information in a quest to determine who was likeliest to hit pay dirt. The word circulated by 1903 that Wilbur and Orville, whom more experienced hands had first regarded as hayseeds, had come into their own and were now regarded as legitimate players. Respect brought offers of financial backing, but the Wrights turned away the unsolicited support that other experimenters only dreamed of, wary as they were of outsiders and press attention. For the same reason, Wilbur sidestepped Chanute's offer to steer the distinguished pupil his way.[27]

When regarded as pipsqueaks, the Wrights could be ignored. So one sign that they were now being taken seriously was that Wilbur became the butt of critics, who believed he was out for himself, ignoring his duty to science to advance the common good. Realizing the need to at least keep lines of communication open in the field, Wilbur did a bit of speaking and writing, but only a bit. One could see him wince at a press query about the kite experiments of Alexander Graham Bell: "It is very bad policy to ask one flying machine man about the experiments of another, because every flying machine man thinks that his method is the only correct one."[28] In June, he rebuffed Chanute's suggestion that he send an advance copy of a report on his experiments to Professor Langley, stating that his former mentor, now his rival, could get the information when everyone else did.[29] Wilbur was not being uncooperative, for under the laws of Germany and France, a patent could be held to be invalid if the matter claimed had already been in public print.[30]

By the summer of 1903, tension was in the air, as both the Langley and Wright camps realized that winter would mark the end of the season and a chance for each team to regroup and perhaps develop a leading edge that it could exploit in 1904. So, as fall set in, each test became more important and the need to accomplish its goal this season more urgent. Wilbur had revealed some grudging sympathy for his competitor when he wrote Chanute in July: "Professor Langley seems to be having rather more than his fair share of trouble just now with pestiferous reporters and windstorms. But as the mosquitoes are reported to be very bad along the banks where the reporters are encamped he has some consolation." Wilbur noted his frustration that the specifications of Langley's machine, as they appeared in the public press, made it impossible for him to gauge whether it could succeed. "It is a sure thing," Wilbur stated flatly, "that the speed will not be from 60 to 90 miles an hour with an expenditure of 25 horsepower as the papers have reported its prospective flight."

"I presume you are to be one of the guests of honor at the launching festivities," Wilbur wrote Chanute. Then, tongue in cheek, he observed, "Our invitation has not yet arrived."[31] Chanute, well aware of Wilbur's suspicion that Chanute's associates might include spies for the other side, assured Wilbur that he had received no invitation either. Yet it couldn't have warmed Wilbur to read Chanute's sympathetic sentiment written on Sept. 12: "I am really sorry for Langley. He has had more than his share of mishaps and the pesky reporters are giving him the reputation as a bungler."[32]

Historian Fred Howard says the Wrights and Langley weren't really in competition with each other, but this misses the tension that crackles off the pages of the Wrights' personal papers. On October 16, after expressing regret that Chanute would be unable to visit their Kitty Hawk camp during what Wilbur hoped would be its fateful season, Wilbur wrote, "I see that Langley has had his fling and failed," showing that even in the North Carolina sand dunes, Wilbur had learned, apparently by telegraph, that Langley's first trial of the fall had come a cropper. "It seems to be our turn to throw now, and I wonder what our luck will be."[33]

Time permitted, however, Langley to try again before winter ended the season, so for the Wrights, the clock was ticking. The Wrights were waking up to ice-covered puddles when, on December 2, a shaft on their aircraft twisted off in the middle. Lacking equipment to repair it at Kill Devil Hills, Orville had no choice but to take the train home 500 miles to Dayton to make a new one. Would there be time when he returned to launch a successful trial this season? Might Langley win the grand prize in the meantime? And more dominating than these questions was the imperative that in Bishop Milton Wright's Dayton home, the family would eat Christmas dinner together. During Wilbur's lonely, nail biting wait for Orville to return, he killed time by writing to George Spratt, a former colleague who now wanted to work at the Smithsonian. "I doubt whether your friendship with us would be a recommendation in the eyes of the Secretary (Langley), but if you decide to make application and wish anything from us, we will be glad to respond." Thinking aloud, Wilbur observed that "The fact that you are acquainted with some of our ideas need not stand in the way so far as I can see, for it is now too late for Langley to begin over...."

On December 8, 1903, Orville Wright hopped the train in Dayton for his return trip together with his newly-crafted propeller shafts. As he picked up the daily newspaper, an article jumped out at him. He could not have read the dispatch without a giant surge of emotion coursing through him.[34]

The Primal Urge

"…we shall be able to transport ourselves and families, and their goods and chattels, more securely by air than by water, and with a velocity of from 20 to 100 miles per hour."— Sir George Cayley, Britain, 1809

No one knows how birds, as they swoop, rise, and dip through the air, regard the large species below them that has four limbs and walks upright. We are far more certain of the fascination that homo sapiens, the collective neck craned towards the sky, has with its avian cousins. We stand, with our vastly superior brains, and watch as the winged ones slip the bonds of earth so naturally and soar toward heaven. "Bird-brain," the putdown we use to denote stupidity, suddenly has a hollow ring.

Auceps, who wrote *The Compleat Angler* in 1653, may have captured this anomaly best, watching in awe the falcon, who "makes her high way over the steepest mountains and deepest rivers, and in her glorious carere [*sic*] looks with contempt upon those high steeples and magnificent palaces which we adore and wonder at."

It is the blessing or curse of our species to be unable to accept our grounded state, resigned that if we were meant to fly, we'd have wings. In Greek mythology, when Minos forbade Daedalus to leave Crete, Daedalus could not abide his fate. Soon, he and son Icarus were crafting wings of wax and feathers. And when Icarus crashed to his death because his wings melted from flying too close to the sun, were the heavens sending the bold adventurers a warning? Even those who stayed behind weren't safe, as Apollo's son Phaethon learned when he lost control of his father's sun chariot and alternately froze and scorched the earth.

Ignoring the admonitions of mythology, flesh-and-blood humans sought to disprove the warnings. In 863 B.C., Bladud, the king of Britain, armed himself with wings of feathers and leapt in vain from London's Temple of Apollo. Not to be deterred, the Saracen of Constantinople gathered a great crowd around a tower to witness first flight, as spectators whispered behind their hands their certitude that the gods were punishing him for trying to rise above his natural state.

Yet not all accounts discouraged those who would fly. How inspiring to picture Elijah, in the first biblical account of flight, soaring into heaven on a chariot of fire! And Mercury successfully completed his journeys to earth as a winged messenger of the Roman gods.[1]

The Spiritual Dimension

Early writers lent a spiritual dimension to birds. Phaedrus observed "The natural function of the wing is to soar upwards and carry that which is heavy up to the place where dwells the race of the gods." Indeed, in so doing, birds could escape earthly temptation uniquely. Origen painted colorfully an invidious contrast between men and birds: "If we look on a woman to lust after her, we have become a venomous reptile; but if we have a sense of restraint, even when an Egyptian casts her eyes upon us we shall become a bird, leaving between her hands our Egyptian clothing and flying from her infamous snares."

In the Christian era, Saint John Chrystostom (c. A.D. 345–407) carried the analogy further: "...wings are given to birds; that they may avoid snares. For this reason, men have the power of thinking; that they may avoid sin." Furthering the theological analysis, Iamblichus (c. A.D. 300) said one only need watch birds fly to divine the will of the Gods: "...birds frequently precipitate themselves to the earth and destroy themselves, which is not natural for any thing to do, but this is something supernatural, so that it is some other thing which produces these effects through birds."[2]

It's in the Air

Early observers recognized that one could not understand flight completely by simply watching birds. One must also plumb the nature of the medium in which they flew — that is, the air. When birds flew through this substance, were they slicing a hole in it? Or did the air consist of flexible particles that a bird's wings could compress as it passed through them? Early commentators, trying to explain flight yet uninformed by modern technology, targeted such mechanisms as air resistance, the inherent lightness of air, the forces of action and reaction, buoyancy, interaction of the birds' muscles, and the bird's ability to sense and harness the physical forces through which it flies.

Great debates ensued among Grecian intellectuals. Hero of Alexandria argued, for example, that air is compressible, while Aristotle contended it is a continuous substance. "When any force is applied to it," argued Hero, "the air is compressed, and, contrary to its nature, falls into the vacant spaces from the pressure exerted on its particles; but when the force is withdrawn, the air returns again to its former position from the elasticity of its particles...." The warring theories long survived their proponents, co-existing into the 18th century, when technology begin to supply the answer.

Greek philosopher Plutarch saw air as a fragile, rendable substance and helped empirical evidence evolve from a sporting event to a serious issue: "For while an audience was loudly acclaiming, ravens which chanced to be flying overhead fell down into the stadium. The cause of this was the rupture of the air; for when the voice is borne aloft loud and strong, the air is rent asunder by it and will not support flying creatures, but lets them fall, as if they were over a vacuum, unless, indeed, they are transfixed by a sort of blow, as of a weapon, and fall down dead."

Over time, philosophers as well as scientists came to look at air and water as one continuum, suggesting air becomes denser the nearer it is to the earth. St. Augustine wrote that no birds exist in the upper atmosphere but only in the lower, thicker air, which he considered "very fine water." And since birds and fish can both swim, they deduced presciently that both have their origins in water.[3]

The Enlightenment

Until the Renaissance, deductive reasoning would play second fiddle to superstition and guesswork. It would fall to Leonardo da Vinci to replace sentiment with reason, when in 1505 he wrote his "Treatise Upon the Flight of Birds." Forget the silly notions that birds are ethereal messengers from God or beyond our understanding, he said. "A bird is an instrument working according to mechanical law, which instrument is within the capacity of man to reproduce in all its movements." And so he aped the avian world by rigging a rope and pulley system whose operator would flap its wings by moving his arms and feet. Its failure taught Leonardo a highly-important principle — that the strength and endurance of human muscles were no match for their winged brethren.

Interspersed with formulae and with sketches drawn in the margins, Leonardo's treatise was a compendium of such physical principles as, "The descent of the bird will always be by that extremity which shall be the nearest to its centre of gravity."[4]

Leonardo enunciated three basic principles of flight:

1) That a region of air compressed beneath the wings and between them and the body is what sustains a bird in flight. Leonardo reasoned that if a region of high pressure is thus created, a corresponding area of relatively low pressure must be found above the wing: "...that the air is compressed beneath that which strikes it and it becomes rarefied above in order to fill up the void left by that which has struck it."[5] Explaining the act of flight, Leonardo continued, "When the bird desires to rise by beating its wings, it raises its shoulders and beats the tips of the wings towards itself, and comes to condense the air which is interposed between the points of the wings and the breast of the bird, and the pressure from this air raises up the bird."[6] Borrowed from Hero of Alexandria, the notion that air is elastic and compressible won new credibility through Leonardo's pen, and his influence made sure this theory would play a major part in 17th and 18th century analysis of flight.[7]

2) A bird, by continuous cyclic changes of the angle at which its wings attack the air, can extract energy from a steady horizontal wind and so stay airborne with very little effort. A bird holds its wings above the wind while it glides upwind. At the end of the turn to a downwind direction, it lowers its leading edge so the wings angle downwards relative to the horizontal. "This causes the wind, now blowing from behind the bird, to continue pressing on the lower surfaces of the wings and hence to continue causing the bird to rise." Later, Leonardo came to realize that gravity and horizontal propulsion of the wind are the only forces involved.[8]

3) A bird can vary its effective weight by altering the shape of its body in flight. By combining the forces of the wind and the bird's flapping, the creature can fly by expending less energy than seems likely, which led Leonardo to conclude that human flight would become possible.[9]

Leonardo da Vinci envisioned flying machines eerily similar to the Wright Flyer, in which brothers Orville and Wilbur would make their triumphal flight four centuries later. "Leonardo was almost the only thinker before the Wrights," says historian Clive Hart, "to see that success would depend on a thorough prior analysis of methods of control" by the pilot. "The man in the flying machine," Leonardo said, would be free from the waist up "that he may be able to keep himself in equilibrium as he does in a boat, so that the centre of his gravity and that of the instrument may set itself in equilibrium and change when necessity requires it to the changing of the centre of its resistance."[10]

Leonardo never built the flying machines he sketched, and although his aeronautical progeny seeking manned flight wouldn't for several centuries either, they learned another important principle — that there is more than one way to skin a cat.

"Ethereal Air"

If wing-flapping alone couldn't yet lift man aloft, experimenters might reach the same goal by filling a hollow globe with "ethereal air or liquid fire," in the concept of Roger Bacon in 1250. In 1709, Brazilian priest Bartolomeu de Gusmao showed off a hot air balloon to the court of King John V of Portugal.[11] Yet not until 1753 did Bacon's "ethereal air" materialize as hydrogen, which French brothers Joseph and Etienne Montgolfier harnessed by filling a linen-lined paper bag 35 feet in diameter with hot air, causing it to rise to 6,000 feet. So inspired was onlooker Benjamin Franklin that he called it a "discovery of great importance ... which may possibly give a new turn to human affairs." Too shrewd to risk their own necks, the brothers Montgolfier sent up a sheep, rooster and duck, all of which survived the pioneering venture. Their countryman Henri Giffard demonstrated that a man could both navigate and control the balloon's direction in flight, as he used a 100-pound, one-cylinder steam engine, which drove a three-bladed propeller.[12]

Military strategists took more than passing notice in balloon technology, but in the pre-electronic age, it was clearly crucial that the carriers be manned, if they were to be used for surveillance. The French, who would be leaders in aeronautics into the 20th century, accepted the challenge. In 1783, Francois Pilatre de Rozier and a passenger made the first free flight, traversing more than five miles in 25 minutes. In 1875, Gaston Tissandier took two hapless passengers more than five miles aloft, but despite carrying primitive breathing equipment, they died from lack of oxygen. And German Count Ferdinand von Zeppelin opened a new aeronautical chapter in 1900 when his massive hydrogen-filled airship took its maiden voyage.[13]

Napoleon quickly seized upon the development and became the first to use balloons for military surveillance in 1794. Balloon surveillance helped the Union army in the Civil War battles of Bull Run and Richmond, by mapping out and telegraphing the enemy's position. When the Confederates saw balloons of the enemy gliding overhead, scoping out their positions, they quickly commandeered the silk from ladies' dresses, to make their own balloons. "The great patchwork ship rose in the air only to be captured by the Northerners." President Lincoln's early commitment to balloon technology to spy on the enemy presaged what would become a major national effort a generation later.[14]

A Band of Brothers

Having established that manned balloons could rise and travel under an operator's control was still not enough to slake the primal urge to imitate winged soaring. In the 19th century, birds continued to awe the curious and ambitious, no less than they had before the birth of Christ, in the field of literature as much as that of engineering. Britain's Alfred Tennyson foresaw "Airy navies grappling the central blue," staking out a whole new plane of existence. Historian Samuel Eliot Morison viewed the new pioneers as "a band of brothers, unmoved by gain, unterrified by popular skepticism and the belief that 'God never meant man to fly.'"[15]

Lying on his back aboard *The Beagle* as it circumnavigated the globe, Charles Darwin watched birds soaring above, wondering, "How do they do that?" Their extended wings seemed "to form the fulcrum on which the movements of the neck, body and tail acted. If the bird wished to descend," Darwin ruminated, "the wings were for a moment collapsed; and when again expanded with an altered inclination, the momentum gained by the rapid descent seemed to urge the bird upwards with the even and steady movement of a paper kite. In the case of any bird *soaring*, its motion must be sufficiently rapid, so that the action of the inclined surface of its body on the atmosphere may counterbalance its gravity." Most fascinating was the ease with which a body placed in motion continues its path: "The force to keep up the momentum of a body moving in a horizontal plane in the air (in which there is little friction) cannot be great, *and this force is all that is wanted.*"[16]

To apply the lessons of this developing science, men turned to gliders. The advent of steam engines led to visions of powered flight, but Britain's George Cayley, born in 1773, realized that man first had to learn to stabilize and control a craft before worrying about motors. Starting with five-foot model gliders, he gradually advanced to a triplane glider in 1849, flying a boy a few yards in 1849, and four years later transporting his reluctant coachman across a small valley.[17] No sooner had his frightened employee alighted from the craft than he tendered his resignation, complaining to Cayley that he was "hired to drive and not to fly."[18]

Cayley analyzed birds' flight in depth, recognizing that air pressure twists a bird's "flight feathers" at the tips of its wings into propeller-like blades that produce lift.[19] Hundreds of observations showed him the importance of a wing's concave underside, in generating the resistance that helps generate lift.[20] Yet this British pioneer had learned wisely that man would never fly by simply imitating birds: "...the pectoral muscles of a bird occupy more than two-thirds of its whole muscular strength, whereas in man the muscles, that could operate upon wings thus attached, would probably not exceed one-tenth of his whole mass." This realization led him to seek lightweight, streamlined materials for his aircraft and to understand that a power generator, which he called a "first mover," was absolutely essential to his goal. He talked about "a gas-light apparatus," borrowed from contemporary French experimentation, that would generate power "by firing the inflammable air generated, with a due portion of common air, under a piston," foreshadowing the internal combustion engine to be invented later in the century.[21]

Cayley's Legacy

To Cayley, we owe the configuration that a basic flying craft would take: fixed wings, arched shapes, positive dihedral (see below), fixed horizontal and vertical stabilizers, and movable surfaces, such as rudders and elevators, to control the craft.[22] Cayley used a complex of rotors and rudder to lift his heavier-than-air flying machine, designed in 1842. Two rotors on each side of the craft revolved in opposite directions, while a horizontal rudder behind the fuselage helped raise or lower the plane and a small vertical rudder controlled lateral movement.[23] A key Cayley contribution was his discovery of dihedral, the upward or downward inclination of an aircraft wing from true horizontal. He found that an aircraft with positive dihedral, in which its wings slant up from the point at which they attach to the aircraft, will fly stably until an outside force disrupts it. A craft with wings slanting down, on the other hand, has negative dihedral and is likely to crash unless a pilot constantly keeps it level.[24]

Unlike those who saw aeronautics as pure science or as simply finding a way to keep one man aloft, Cayley foresaw with excitement the commercial implications of flight: "...we shall be able to transport ourselves and families, and their goods and chattels, more securely by air than by water, and with a velocity of from 20 to 100 miles per hour," he wrote in 1809. And while a God-given limit exists to how strong a pilot can be, no theoretical limit exists for the size of an engine that could be built. "...by increasing the magnitude of the engine," he wrote, "10, 50 or 500 men may equally well be conveyed." Cayley's contemporary William S. Henson, designer of a monoplane with a 150-foot wingspread, sketched out a business plan for the "Aerial Transit Company," proposing a regular schedule to major countries and as early as 1842 designed an airport to service it. He was, to put it mildly, a bit ahead of himself.

Cayley suggested the role that nationalism would play in the quest for manned flight; he hoped that "England may not be backward in rivaling the continent in a more worthy contest than that of arms."[25]

Germany's Otto Lilienthal built on Cayley's work by creating ornithopters, gliders in which men ride, flapping manmade wings. His 18 varieties of gliders took off first from the roof of a hangar and finally from atop a 50-foot manmade pile of dirt, allowing the pilot to catch the wind as it presented itself. As with contemporary hang gliders, he used the pilot's body, shifting its center of gravity, to control the craft. Unlike other experimenters, the burly redhead believed in piloting his own crafts, a principle the flying world began to question when one day in 1896, Lilienthal crashed to his death when a strong gust of wind destabilized a wing and caused the craft to plummet to the ground. A wise man, it is said, learns from the experiences of others. But Britain's Scot Percy Pilcher, a student of Lilienthal's work, chose to continue to fly his own crafts, and in 1899 met the same fate as his mentor after a bamboo rod snapped during bad weather, throwing his plane out of control and hurtling Pilcher and his craft to earth.[26]

One of the most interesting, creative, and generous figures in early aviation was Octave Chanute, an American engineer, born in France, who didn't come to flying until in his 60s, after had finished a distinguished and profitable career as a bridge builder. With his white goatee, easy smile, and open manner, Chanute was as important as a mentor, writer, and broker of interests as he was as an experimenter. His seminal 1894 work, *Progress in Flying Machines,* became an instant classic in the field, as a burgeoning number of both scientific and lay readers now searched out eagerly each new report on ongoing experiments. Chanute focused on increasing the stability of Lilienthal's gliders in 1898 by introducing truss construction, a principle borrowed from his days as a bridge engineer. His crafts soared as much as 350 feet along the southern shore of Lake Michigan.[27]

Is Equilibrium the Key?

From Chanute's perspective, the challenges to manned flight lay in achieving equilibrium, complete control and sustained flight. Applying these principles meant increasing the wing surface, warping the wingtips to achieve greater lift, and adding movable planes or rudders, to let the pilot control the craft laterally.[28]

But history remembers Octave Chanute primarily as the mentor of two Ohio bicycle mechanics, Orville and Wilbur Wright, who adopted Chanute's biplane wings in their early crafts.[29] Yet the Wrights also learned negative lessons from Chanute. Their mentor believed that gliders must be built to be inherently stable in the air and thus able to withstand wind currents and gusts. The Wrights couldn't have disagreed more. They felt that flight conditions are so changeable that the pilot must be able to control his craft at all times during flight and that it is this control, not inherent stability, that allows a plane to remain aloft.[30]

Aviation is a classic example of the industrial principle that progress is incremental and not always technological. For all Chanute's focused experimentation, his glider trials contributed far less to the goal of manned flight than his mentoring, particu-

Britain's Percy Pilcher was a disciple of Germany's Otto Lilienthal. Both pioneered successful flights of non-motorized gliders, and both met their deaths from crashes only a year apart just before the turn of the 20th century. National Air and Space Museum, Smithsonian Institution (SI Neg. No. 2002-16640).

larly to the brothers Wright. Retired Boston shoe manufacturer James Means founded the Boston Aeronautical Society in 1895 and its *Aeronautical Annual* and created a clearing house for information so crucial that, as Orville Wright wrote to Means in 1908, "The old Annuals were largely responsible for the active interest which led us [him and his brother Wilbur] to begin experiments in aeronautics." And one of the Wrights' greatest strengths, in turn, was their ability to synthesize the unconnected results of others' experimentation and to establish that three challenges lay in the path of human ability to fly: designing wings properly, balancing and controlling the craft once aloft, and introducing motorized power.[31]

Horatio Phillips is generally considered a relatively minor figure in the airplane's development, yet his experiments with varied thicknesses and arched surfaces for airplane wings helped demonstrate vividly that keeping the air pressure low on the upper surface of wings contributes greatly to their lift. Phillips's countryman, the beefy

F.W. Lanchester, took this a step further when he showed that the faster air travels across the wing's upper surface relative to its under surface, the greater the wing lift. Germany's Ludwig Prandtl translated the concept into mathematical language for the benefit of engineers.[32]

Collectively, hundreds of experimenters, institutional scientists and garage tinkerers alike — some pooling their knowledge for the common weal, others squirreling their findings away for personal gain — had moved the science of aeronautics toward critical mass. For most of history, those who maintained that man would fly one day were dismissed as unbalanced at best. As the 1890s dawned, the most noticeable sign of progress was that no one was laughing anymore.

3

Not So Funny Anymore

"We were lucky enough to grow up in an environment where there was always much encouragement to children to pursue intellectual interests; to investigate whatever aroused curiosity. In a different kind of environment, our curiosity might have been nipped long before it could have borne fruit."—Orville Wright

JUST DECADES AWAY FROM AN agrarian life that stretched back to time immemorial, the industrial revolution had not only transformed entire economies but had knit the human family together, for better or for worse. At every steamship landing in the early 1890s, among the most coveted imports were the wildly popular "ten-center" magazines that broadcasting the latest trends in fashion, business, and entertainment. Seven new transatlantic cables allowed an instantaneous telegraphic link between the continents. The cultural cross-fertilization spurred waves of immigrants to flood American shores as well, with Ireland and England contributing mightily but Germany far in the lead. As if an exclamation point were needed to the proposition that the world was shrinking, the *New York World's* Nellie Bly circumnavigated the entire world in 72 days.[1]

Not only was the very nature of printing changing, as color, photographs, and graphics were fed into supercharged printing presses that reduced newsstand prices, but the very nature of the subject matter had changed as well. During the century's early decades, writers had romanticized rail travel, and the invention of the internal combustion engine suggested people could soon venture at will over hill and dale. Ever restless, Americans now sought a new dimension by looking to the skies. Technology now let them read, soon after the event, the exploits of such pioneers as Germany's Otto Lilienthal. Robert Wood, reporter for *The Boston Transcript,* covered one of the engineer's flights in a glider and became hooked. Having been transported to an alien environment, he sought to take his readers there as well. Wood asked his readers to envision "the spectacle of a man supported on huge white wings, moving high above you at race horse speed, combined with the weird hum of the wind through the cords of the machine...." The sight, Wood enthused, "produces an impression never to be forgotten."[2]

Crude attempts at flight had for centuries given satirists grist for their mills. So in the 1880s, when a friend asked Octave Chanute at a Kansas City dinner party what he did in his spare time, Chanute implored the host to wait until the children went to bed, "for they would laugh at me." Even in the 1890s, a new popular poem, "Darius Green and his Flying Machine," lampooned an inventor who leaped from a barn loft, only to plummet into the barnyard below. Yet the undeniable truth was that people had, in fact, managed to launch themselves and remain aloft for more than a moment, from the dunes of Lake Michigan to the mountains outside Berlin, Germany.[3]

Yet while the public by the 1890s no longer ridiculed those who jumped off haystacks and rooftops, no major investors had emerged to back these exploits commercially, so most experimenters had to wedge their creative time into evenings and weekends. Otto Lilienthal by day, for example, was a respected engineer who owned a company manufacturing boilers, engines, and mining equipment. But each Sunday, the sturdy adventurer, his barrel chest jutting ahead of his broad shoulders, headed for the Rhinow Mountains, a short trip from his home in Berlin.[4]

Lilienthal's weekday lab work enhanced his avocation, because there, in spare moments, he searched for solutions to such crucial issues as how to harness air resistance and what should be the proper camber, or arch, of a wing. He had settled on the arc of a circle with a camber of one in 12. "That is," Lilienthal explained for the uninitiated, "the chord, a straight line drawn from the leading to the trailing edge of the wing, should be twelve times as long as the distance from the chord to the bottom of the wing at the midpoint, where the arch was highest."

Imagine, if you will, a curly red-haired athlete built like a fireplug, straining uphill to the point of launch, trying to tame a huge, white cloth-covered craft, its edges whipping in the wind. Crawling under the wooden structure, Lilienthal would slip his arms into cuffs that helped him control it, take hold with two callused hands of a bar near the wings' forward edge and stand, in the words of historian Tom Crouch, "like an athlete waiting for the starting pistol." Taking three deliberate loping steps down the hill, he would suddenly feel the wind beneath his wings hoist him into the sky, rising eventually to a height of 50 feet. To stabilize the craft, Lilienthal would shift his body's weight ever so carefully, informed by the hundreds of times he had felt the nuanced pressures of pitch, roll and yaw, making it obvious why Lilienthal felt he had to take the obvious risk of flying each trial himself. Later, successful flyers would feel indebted to the intrepid German for teaching them what not to do.

Building a giant database from which he could refine the emerging science of aeronautics, Lilienthal would make 2,000 flights over the next five years in 16 distinct models of gliders. Enthralled by birds as were most early experimenters, he used flexible, or warped, wingtips in his machines. He designed his crafts to glide eight feet forward for every foot of vertical fall.

Soon it was not enough for Lilienthal to be written about. Publications such as the popular *McClure's* magazine, which was in blistering competition with *Cosmopolitan* and on the lookout for cutting edge stories, commissioned Lilienthal to write about his own flights, earning him the popular sobriquets "The Winged Prussian" and "The Flying Man."

With such a small cadre of serious experimenters, it was perhaps inevitable that their work should draw them together. Octave Chanute, for example, first wrote to Lilienthal in 1893, and Prof. Langley traveled to Berlin to meet him two years later, but neither spoke the other's language, retarding the free flow of ideas. Nevertheless, Langley proclaimed Lilienthal "one of the most interesting men I ever met."

An indication of how gliders had caught the public imagination was the purchase of an original Lilienthal machine by self-promoting publisher William Randolph Hearst, to help publicize his *New York Journal.* Augustus Herring, Langley's assistant, boasted to Chanute that he had built a glider to Lilienthal's specifications and flown it 45 feet. But Chanute saw a darker side. Akin to the guilt Alfred Nobel had felt for having left dynamite as his legacy to a troubled world, Chanute couldn't help wondering whether his writings and speeches touting glider flight weren't inspiring would-be but unprepared aviators to place themselves in harm's way.[5]

Only a Matter of Time

For the young and ambitious, transportation's march of progress was so near but yet so far, as the last decade of the 19th century dawned. It was all very good to concede that a better understanding of birds made scientists believe that manned flight was inevitable. But that assertion, by itself, didn't lift a machine made of wood and cloth into the air or let its pilot feel the exhilaration of soaring with the birds.

To those more grounded, it was only a matter of time before someone would harness an internal combustion engine to a bicycle frame and create a new mode of motorized land transport. The gasoline engine, used widely on Midwestern farms to power farm implements, had existed since 1859. Men with such names as Benz, Peugeot, and Daimler were perfecting machines they variously called buggyauts or autocars, but it would still be nearly a decade before American workshop tinkerers reached the point at which they could offer automobiles for commercial sale.[6]

So for those who insisted on instant gratification, the product that transformed the dream into reality was the bicycle. Used primitively since the 1500s in Europe, it took modern form in Britain in the last half of the 19th century. The high-wheeled velocipede, a skeletal-looking contraption with a front wheel as high as five feet and the rear wheel scarcely larger than a basketball, created a national craze in the 1870s when it reach American shores. But lacking a chain drive, the high-wheeler took great strength to ride and tipped easily, often throwing riders over the handlebars. "Get a bicycle," Mark Twain exhorted his readers after trying one out. "You won't regret it — if you live!"[7]

The "safety bicycle," with equal-sized wheels and a name intended to contrast with the dangerous high-wheeler, emerged in the mid-1880s. With chains and gearing, it looks remarkably like the bicycles of the 21st century. Col. Albert Pope shrewdly expanded his scope by franchising his sales operations to already-established department stores or other retail outlets and soon had thousands of showrooms, from St. Petersburg, Florida, to St. Petersburg, Russia, hawking his Columbia bicycles.[8]

With first tens of thousands and then hundreds of thousands of bicycles being sold, young, ambitious people with mechanical bents and questioning minds quickly established their own retail outlets and repair facilities, which let them keep bread on the table while they worked nights and weekends in their garages to perfect their own notions of motorized land vehicles or aircraft. In 1890, two such individuals were 23-year-old Wilbur Wright and his 19-year-old brother Orville.

At Home with the Wrights

The son of an itinerant preacher in Ohio, Wilbur Wright had been bound for Yale until a serious head wound sustained while ice skating knocked out most of his upper and some of his lower teeth and caused a heart disorder, derailing his academic plans. In high school, Orville decided he would become a printer and, after graduation, formed a small business with his older brother under the auspicious name the Wright Brothers.[9]

Though a bishop in his Protestant splinter sect, Milton Wright's salary didn't reach $1,000 a year until he became an editor of religious publications as well. Though money was tight, Wright doted on his boys while their mother, Susan Koerner Wright, infused them with her passion for things mechanical. One would expect Milton to be religious in a doctrinal sense, but he also had inherited a moralistic streak from his father. That Dan Wright had been a teetotaler was unpopular enough, but he also was an outspoken abolitionist, a trait that biographer Tom Crouch says "was enough to get a man strung up in some parts of Southern Indiana," where the bishop's young family spent its early years.[10]

Though Wilbur and Orville Wright are their parents' most well-known children, there were three others, including older brothers Reuchlin and Lorin and younger sister Katharine. If not rich in worldly goods, the Wrights encouraged in their children a questing spirit, a willingness to try something new. Orville, writing after he was internationally famous, recalled, "We were lucky enough to grow up in an environment where there was always much encouragement to children to pursue intellectual interests; to investigate whatever aroused curiosity. In a different kind of environment, our curiosity might have been nipped long before it could have borne fruit."[11]

In a much told and embellished tale, the bishop once bought his two younger sons a toy helicopter, built of bamboo, paper and cork and activated by a rubber band. For boys with mechanical minds, learning that adjusting the wingtips and tail could

The comfortable Victorian home of Bishop Milton Wright at 7 Hawthorn St., Dayton, Ohio, featured a wraparound front porch. Any minute, one of the brothers could emerge from lunch and hop on the waiting bicycle to return to the Wright Cycle Shop. The house would be home to Wilbur and Orville into their 40s. Special Collections and Archives, Wright State University Libraries.

alter the craft's stability was an early lesson that stayed with them. As they became adults, knowing that renowned French aeronautical pioneer Alphonse Pénaud had designed their little toy helicopter resonated with them and they were then starting to etch their own names into aeronautical posterity. The boys went on to build several copies of the toy but noted that "…when we undertook to build the toy on a much larger scale it failed to work so well."[12]

The Wright family, which had moved from place to place following its circuit-riding breadwinner, gained a measure of stability in 1884, when it moved to Dayton, Ohio. Wilbur's heart ailment prevented him from following his two older brothers to college. Orville eschewed college as well, probably because of his closeness to Wilbur, but no grass grew under his feet. He took up printing with entrepreneurial intensity, mastering typesetting and publishing his own weekly newspaper, the *West Side News*, which survived a year before succumbing to competition from larger daily newspapers.[13]

The four-year age gap between Wilbur and Orville had sent them in different directions earlier, but narrowed in significance as they became adults. By 1892, at ages 25 and 21, they sought a business to pursue together, and the new safety-bicycle fad caught their interest. Later generations would obsess about hula hoops and skateboards, but the Wrights' contemporaries across America were agog about the bicycle. Little capital was required to enter the business, so Wilbur and Orville set up the only bicycle shop on the west side of Dayton's Miami River in 1892. They entrusted their printing business to a family friend, as they would their bicycle business a decade later. A year later, tens of thousands of people would come away enthused from the Chicago Columbian Exposition bicycle exhibits, delivering to shops like the Wrights' a ready market. Forswearing tobacco and alcohol, the slim, wiry brothers threw themselves into their new enterprise with gusto. This, not printing, they soon decided, would become their life's work.[14]

Although they were on the same wavelength in business, the brothers' appearances were a study in contrasts. Wilbur, several inches taller than Orville, was gangly and balding, with prominent ears, a thin, tapered face ending at a cleft chin, and a perpetually dour expression. A schoolmate described the taciturn Wilbur as "a man who lives largely in a world of his own." The more compact Orville sported curly, dark brown locks, had a more expansive personality, and dressed for attention. In build and hirsute adornment, he was nearer to their father, Bishop Milton Wright, whose full head of brown hair would become Santa Claus-white in his old age.[15]

No one would call the Wrights' sprawling home on Hawthorn Street opulent, but it displayed a late Victorian comfort, with two libraries, floor-length lace curtains, potted palms, and a gas-burning fireplace. Linked to downtown by a street railway, the West Side neighborhood had become a streetcar suburb. As in many American cities of the day, horse-drawn, and by the 1890s, electrified, trolleys stretched the radius of feasible commutes to downtown factories and offices. After years of moving from place to place as children of an itinerant minister, Wilbur and Orville may have warmed to the notion of a stable home, since they continued to live there into their 40s.

The bishop's full beard and kindly visage contrasted sharply with his wife's square-jawed determination, her dark hair parted severely in the middle and drawn back sharply at the sides. The Wrights' talented but painfully shy mother died of tuberculosis when they were barely out of childhood. Trying to fill the void, their schoolmarmish sister Katharine — now the only female in the family — would come to be as much a nurturing mother as a sister to them, even though she was the family's youngest child. Unlike her brothers, however, she attended college, graduating from Oberlin and later serving on its board of trustees.[16]

In Search of a Common Goal

Clearly Great Britain and the rest of Europe were as strongly preoccupied with aviation as were the United States and Germany. Budding scientists needed to look only as far as the writings of fellow experimenters George Cayley, William Henson, John Stringfellow, Louis Pierre Mouillard, F.H. Wenham, and Alphonse Pénaud, whose toy helicopter had enthralled the Wright brothers, to discover ample knowledge and inspiration for their endeavors.[17] Mouillard had written his classic, *L'Empire de L'air*, a decade earlier. Phillips's claim to fame was constructing a wind tunnel for experiments with model aerofoils in 1885.

Another pioneer experimenting in the fertile 1890s was London engineer F.W. Lanchester, whose day job was devoted to fostering another mode of transportation, as the manufacturer of the motor car carrying his name. But while the Langleys of the world had an institutional base and a subsidized operation, Lanchester's experiments were performed alone and with his own money.

Although agreeing that one should study birds if one hoped to fly, Lanchester became frustrated when he studied the way ornithologists wrote about the object of their affection: "...the typical ornithologist seems to combine in one personality a power of observation equal to that of an immature child with a varied capacity of expression worthy of a professional journalist."

In 1892, Lanchester widened his search for inspiration to America, steaming across the Atlantic to find Professor Samuel Pierpont Langley, by then an international authority on aeronautics. Langley had only a few minutes to spare for him. Nevertheless, Lanchester took away strong memories of Langley's museum of bird life at the Smithsonian.

Applying himself assiduously with one hand to aeronautics and the other to building motorcars with the other, the mesomorphic Lanchester unveiled in 1894 his "vortex theory," his own explanation of how lift propels a fixed-wing aircraft. His paper "The Soaring of Birds and the Possibilities of Mechanical Flight," delivered at the tender age of 25, not only dealt with aerodynamics but foreshadowed aerodromics (power-driven flight) and studied the alternative sources of motive power available. Alas, his paper ultimately was rejected.

Discouraged, he relegated flight to the back burner and went back to making cars, for which he knew he had a market. Years later, he reflected his bitterness at the snub, suggesting that taking out patents had yielded him "the only cheap form of publicity that exists." Moreover, he said, there are no "damfool" readers to satisfy. His 1897 patent, to which he referred in a letter to the secretary of the Royal Aeronautical Society in 1931, mentioned wing warping and looked as if it might set off a patent war between Lanchester and the Wright Brothers, who had claimed wing warping in one of their patents. The patent authorities decided, however, that the reference wasn't precise enough to defeat the Wrights' claim.

A Lanchester biographer describes his subject as follows:

> In the first place, he was certainly not an academic type. Heavily and strongly built, with a large head, yet he was quick of movement and also had something of boyish ungainliness in his appearance. There was a boyish freshness and vigour in his attitude to everything in his own particular field of interest. He thought clearly and

incisively and, when he felt that he was understood, he used a humourous manner of speech, often accompanied by paradoxical remarks and flashes of wit."[18]

What Is "Flight," Anyway?

As steady progress made people of the era realize that manned flight would take place within their lifetime, attention turned to just what "flight" is. Fame and fortune awaited the first person to fly, so it became highly important to define the term. Is it enough for a person to attach himself to a craft and let the wind carry him aloft? Or does the pilot have to be able to shift his center of gravity to steer the machine? Does the plane have to incorporate internal controls, such as rudders, that a pilot can adjust to changing conditions? If so, do the pilot's levers have to regulate side to side movements as well as up and down and backward and forward?

Without a governing authority, "flight" was an arbitrary concept and the subject of heated controversy. Because no one could agree on a common definition, "first flight" would be ultimately agreed upon in retrospect, as one of those truths that are best understood in the fullness of time. Years after the fact, the cognoscenti would gather and decide that, yes, a certain experiment some years ago really represented first flight. Remarkably, then, contestants in the race to the sky rushed toward their goal without really understanding the rules of the game.

Some asserted that "first flight" ruled out any supportive devices on board; others, that an arbitrary distance must be covered while aloft. And what, they wondered, if the distance covered was a loop rather than a point to point voyage. Did that count?

As time went on, a certain consensus developed. It would not be enough for a pilot to launch a plane into the wind from a rooftop or hillock and have it remain aloft for a period of time. No, the craft needed to take off from level ground, be able to climb, and then settle down to earth.

And so, against these developing parameters, legions of experimenters vied for the title of first flyer. Each would need witnesses to prove the fact, but too many witnesses would be embarrassing if the flight was a flop. France's Clement Ader brought legally-sanctioned witnesses, called *huissiers*, with him in 1890 when he sought to fly his monoplane *Eole*, and directed them to record written testimony. Equipped with a steam engine driving a tractor propeller and a severely arched 49-foot wingspan, the *Eole* lifted itself, unassisted, from the ground. Test one passed. But the craft could not sustain flight or allow the pilot to control its flight path.[19]

Vying for fame and fortune alongside Ader was one already used to it. Hiram Stevens Maxim, an American, had abandoned his family in Brooklyn, New York, and migrated to Britain, where Queen Victoria beknighted him following his invention of the machine gun. The weapon was seen as so horrible in its potential carnage that even pacifists hailed its advent, sensing that its very threat would spell the end to all war.

Sir Hiram eschewed the scattershot methods of garage inventors, choosing instead to record his experimental findings methodically and build on them to advance his knowledge. Perhaps sobered by the number of aeronauts losing their lives in experiments, he used a craft held by a tether to avoid using a pilot. Maxim set the airplane on rails, above which was positioned another track on a series of cantilevered supporting arms. The plane was designed to lift itself from the lower rails and engage with the upper rails, allowing its lift to be measured.[20] In 1890, he built his first machine, but its trial ended in despair when a structural failure caused it to crash.

Bell's New Adventure

Amid the tumult surrounding the telephone's invention in 1876, Alexander Graham Bell informed his aide-de-camp Thomas Watson that for their next project they would tackle a flying machine. By 1891, in fact, Bell began to test model helicopters first and then kites. An accomplished self-promoter, Bell had learned marketing from inventing the telephone 15 years earlier, so to attract attention to his next venture, he built his kites from bright red cloth and flew them in the fields near his beloved summer home, Beinn Bhreagh, in Nova Scotia. The native folk had a feast for the eyes watching horses gallop across the open plain, towing vermillion kites which they helped lift into the deep blue skies. At night, they saw a new show, as lanterns placed in the kites' cradles lit up the sky with a deep red glow.

After centuries of ridiculing those who would fly, much of the scientific community, led by such iconic figures as Graham Bell, now began to accept that manned flight under power was imminent. Perhaps even more convincing was the flat assertion of Samuel Pierpont Langley, America's foremost astronomer in his 1891 *Experiments in Aerodynamics,* that "Flight is possible with the engines we now possess." The statement was a corrective to those who believed that a successful flight would have to wait for adequate motors to be developed. Yet the fact remains that Langley's experiments failed miserably. Between 1887 and 1891, he and his staff built more than a hundred models in various wing and propeller configurations, yet "trial after trial ended with the craft falling into the water off the end of the launch rail."[21]

World's fairs and expositions, wildly popular since the Industrial Revolution, have had a way of nudging progress. Colonel Albert Pope saw his first high-wheeled bicycle at the 1876 Philadelphia Exposition, celebrating the nation's centennial, and in 1893, Wilbur and Orville Wright attended Chicago's Columbian Exposition, which featured an International Conference on Aerial Navigation. Octave Chanute, who would become the Wrights' chief source of moral support, had organized the conference, and newspaper coverage called it an "overwhelming success … the public was enthusiastic."[22]

Lessons from a Bicycle

Life experience informs all we do, so it is not unusual that the Wrights' lessons learned as bicycle mechanics would play a profound role in their aeronautical quest. The most fundamental lesson was that a pilot must have the tools at hand to control his craft in each axis of movement. This is far more important, they believed, than trying to make a machine structurally stable by strategic placement of wings, struts, and guy wires. Their writings are a window on how they came to this view:

> The bicycle differs from all other surface vehicles in that it is inherently unstable in both yaw and roll. The cyclist must steer with the handlebars while at the same time maintaining lateral balance through subtle shifts in body position that will keep the machine upright.[23]

At a time when Orville Wright was still in high school and his older brother Wilbur was still recovering from a traumatic injury, the "unofficial chief scientist of the United States" was already immersed in the study of aeronautics. Samuel Pierpont Langley had already amassed honorary degrees from four Ivy League universities as well as Oxford and Cambridge when he attended a lecture in 1886 on aeronautics at a conference sponsored by the American Association for Advancement of Science. The possibilities that emerged from that experience transfixed him. When the Smithsonian Institution in 1887 offered him the prestigious position of secretary, he disclosed his now passionate interest in aeronautics. But he made it clear that his goal wasn't to build an aircraft himself, but only to help find how one might be built.

And so began the Smithsonian's frenetic efforts over the next decade, during which stuffed avian wings affixed to huge spinning wheels helped unlock secrets that birds knew at birth. By 1891, Langley was far enough along to let his fellow scientists glimpse his thought processes in a work, published by the Smithsonian, entitled *Experiments in Aerodynamics.* His proclamation therein that "Flight is possible with the engines we now possess" lent a tone of urgency to the venture, but Langley kept an open mind on the type of engine — steam, electric or internal-combustion — that might be most effective. Internal combustion engines proliferated across the land, particularly on farms, but they were heavy, clunky things. No one understood this better than their builders, who realized that reducing engine weight would increase potential speed and widen their use. Storage batteries weighed even more, ruling out electric motors, so steam appeared the most likely mode.

The nation's capital, then and now, is a magnet for the great and near great, so it is hardly surprising that the nation's greatest scientist began to appear on the guest lists of the city's most prominent hostesses. In an era of gender-segregated gentlemen's clubs, Langley took to attending on Wednesday evenings a conclave of those interested in advancement of science, hosted by none other than one of the foremost practitioners of its practical application, Alexander Graham Bell, whose invention of the telephone a decade earlier had made him not only financially secure but gave him the prestige and leisure time to advance other ideas. Predictably, given his bent for putting scientific knowledge to commercial gain, Bell turned his thoughts toward how his concepts could catch commercial fire and, in fact, he had already used black-powder rockets to fire model aircraft of his own designs.[24]

Bell's Wednesday evening salons during the 1890s, which included some of the brightest and most fertile minds living in greater Washington, were exciting incursions into theory. But by then, Bell's bosom friend Langley was itching to leave his laboratory and to expose his scientific theories to the rigors of nature. He began to build models, the first one 10 feet in diameter and five feet long. Being a realist, the secretary realized that the handmaiden of experiment is failure, so that he'd need a crash-proof surface to offer cushion for crash landings. Later experimenters would use sand dunes, but none such were available in the nation's capital. However, water was in abundance, since the meandering Potomac River ran right by the Smithsonian. In the fall of 1892, Langley bought a flat-bottomed houseboat, measuring 12 by 30 feet. For the next several years it would be a fixture on the river, as curious schoolchildren and journalists alike peered out from the banks.

Two assistants who would become key to Langley's efforts soon signed on. Octave Chanute, doing what he did best, put Langley in touch with one Edward Chalmers Huffaker, a young engineer of informal appearance, given to wearing shirtsleeves and expectorating into a tin spittoon nailed to the wall, contrasting with the formal appearance of Secretary Langley, who often showed up for work in a full-dress morning coat. Also joining the team was Augustus Moore Herring, a well-born Georgia lad whom Chanute had hired to build gliders. The mercurial young man would loom large in not only Langley's future but that of Chanute and the Wright brothers.[25]

"One of the Most Interesting Men I Ever Met"

While American aeronauts were competing feverishly to be first in flight, things were just as intense in Germany, where engineer Otto Lilienthal built industrial equipment during the week and headed to the Rhinow Mountains on weekends to perfect his glider flights using a simple cambered wing. They would work on parallel paths for the next decade, but Lilienthal and Langley had little in common besides starting their names with the same letter. Langley spoke no German and Lilienthal no French or English when the two men met in 1895, yet Langley later called Lilienthal "one of the most interesting men I ever met." Langley was grounded in theory; indeed, every experiment started from the premises developed there. Lilienthal, according to air historian Tom Crouch, had little theoretical interest and focused simply on solving the immediate engineering problem in front of him.

Unlike Langley, Lilienthal was swashbuckling, and the public responded to him in much the same way later generations would admire John Wayne or Evel Knievel. While some scientists shook their heads at Lilienthal's willingness to risk his neck in flying his gliders himself, readers of articles about "The Winged Prussian" in such popular magazines as *McClure's* saw Lilienthal's insistence on flying his own crafts himself as bravery against the odds.[26]

During the first half of the 1890s, white wings soared, dipped, and circled over the Potomac as Langley made some 2,000 flights using a variety of gliders. Designed to fly eight feet forward for every foot the craft fell, the gliders were pleasant to watch when they gently eased down to the shimmering surface of the river. Noticing from his experiments that the tips of birds' wings tended to flap to alter their direction, Langley adopted this technique for his gliders, making the wingtips flexible.[27]

What perhaps impressed Orville and Wilbur Wright most about the Pénaud toy helicopter their father bought for them was how adjusting its wings and its tail changed the way it flew. But Pénaud's theories were far more than child's play and contributed to the ongoing search for stability. Pénaud had created what he considered to be automatic stability by 1871. Using a model with a four-bladed tail, his craft featured two vertical vanes on the tail's top and bottom, designed to keep the craft pointed toward the wind and thus keeping it vertically stable. By keeping the tail slightly below level, he found he could keep the plane horizontally stable. To keep it from rolling from side to side with the wind, he angled the wingtips up from the craft's midpoint, giving it what engineers call dihedral.[28] The nature of experimentation is such that what we reject is sometimes as important to our learning as what we accept. Ironically, though Pénaud was their first aeronautical influence, as adults, Wilbur and Orville would come to reject the Pénaud theory almost entirely.

4

A Critical Mass

*"…I do not think it right to dissect living men even for the advancement of science.
So far as I am concerned, I prefer a post mortem examination to vivisection without
anaesthetics."*— Alexander Graham Bell

THE LINK BETWEEN ALEXANDER GRAHAM BELL and Samuel Pierpont Langley, which had
started out as a professional relationship, deepened into a personal friendship as the
years passed. For years now, the applied scientist had corresponded with the pure scientist about such diverse subjects as theories of gravitation and the use of compressed
air to treat deafness.

It helped, of course, that Samuel Langley and Graham Bell both lived in the
nation's capital, but part of the attraction was that one supplied unmet needs of the
other. Langley, a lifelong bachelor, felt drawn to the warm family life of the Bells.
Mabel Hubbard Bell was as compelling a conversationalist as she was warm hostess.
Her father, Gardiner Greene Hubbard, had helped create the telephone industry and
was the first president of the National Geographic Society, in the process setting up
a handsome trust fund which paid for the family needs. Their daughters Elsie and
Daisy evidently fawned on Professor Langley during his visits, and he regularly sent
them "my love" in his frequent letters to the Bells, even while using more formal salu-
tations—"My dear Mrs. Bell"—when addressing their parents. Langley must have
been a good houseguest as well, for he frequently had dinner at the comfortable Bell
townhouse on Connecticut Avenue. In the summertime, the Bells looked forward to
his visits to Beinn Bhreagh (pronounced Ben Vree'-aah), their beloved vacation home
near Baddeck on Cape Breton, Nova Scotia, the estate's name harkening back to Bell's
roots in Edinburgh, Scotland.[1]

Bell had, by 1895, largely narrowed his attention from other scientific endeavors to the pursuit of aviation. Although he would not begin his own aeronautical

experiments for another decade, the ongoing race to the sky in America and Europe piqued his interest. Proximity and reputation had drawn him to Samuel Pierpont Langley, and Bell's national stature was his own calling card. Just as renowned as Bell, Thomas Alva Edison had tinkered with the idea of motored flight as early as 1880, using fan blades mounted on a vertical shaft to generate lift. A Bell biographer, comparing his subject with Edison, says they both "retained the fertility of technical imagination well into later life. But unlike Edison, Bell did not show it to the public. He recorded his ideas in his private notebooks and moved on without devoting himself to cultivation and harvest, whereas Edison never ceased to push his technical ideas through development and patenting to commercial use."[2]

And so Bell felt compelled to admonish one Martha D. Lincoln, who claimed falsely in a book proposal on "central figures in American science" that she had his "consent and approval" to include a Bell profile.

> I do not recognize the right of the public to break in the front door of a man's private life in order to satisfy the gaze of the curious.... I do not think it right to dissect living men even for the advancement of science. So far as I am concerned, I prefer a post mortem examination to vivisection without anaesthetics.[3]

It seemed natural, then, for Langley to invite Bell on a top-secret mission in 1896, the culmination of nearly a decade of work in his Smithsonian lab. To say Langley's effort to achieve manned, powered flight was all-consuming is an understatement. He even went so far as to hire a philologist to help name the new technology which he was midwifing. Drawing on classical languages, his expert advanced three suggestions: aerobater, meaning "one who walks through air;" anemodromic, meaning "wind-drawn," or aerodromoi, meaning "air-runner." Air historian Tom Crouch notes that Langley's chosen term of aerodrome, in translation means not a flying machine itself but a place where machines fly.[4]

Since 1887, Langley had been working, like most early experimenters, on the challenging problem of stability: structuring the craft so that it could withstand unpredictable wind patterns, believing that the human body could not react fast enough to offset sudden changes. In 1891, the professor mastered stability to the extent that he could add the next layer of complexity — a motor. Considering and rejecting internal combustion, electric, and compressed air engines, he finally settled on a one horsepower, four-pound steam engine for his first model. Feeling the machine should have a larger surface fore than aft, Langley shaped his plane's hull "like a mackeral," to most effectively deal with air resistance. A dismal failure, his first model didn't even make it to a test flight.[5]

Only a fool would contemplate testing these fragile contraptions over anything other than a forgiving surface. So while the Wrights used sand dunes for their cushion, Langley decided early to employ water, not only because it was in abundance in Washington, but because it maximized the opportunity for testing. To make the wind skim across the top and bottom of the wings to generate lift, he would obviously have to launch the craft into the wind. But wind can come from the east, south, north, or west. A fixed track on the ground could accept wind from only one direction, but a houseboat could, at a moment's notice, be turned into the wind.[6]

In the fall of 1892, the professor bought a houseboat measuring 30 feet by 12 feet and towed it down the Potomac River some 30 miles to Chapawomsic Island, near Quantico, Virginia, for testing. He would erect a catapult atop the houseboat and launch his models from it. The drawback was that the skeletal, 30-pound aerodrome, perched atop the houseboat, would be so sensitive to the wind that Langley couldn't launch it effectively in a breeze of more than three to four miles per hour. By the end of 1892, the secretary and his crew had made nine trips to Quantico. They were working on their fourth model, but they hadn't yet launched even one.[7] The foremost dream of the nation's foremost scientist was, at this point, going nowhere.

Enter Octave Chanute, the great facilitator. Langley had become convinced that he needed to develop a more efficient wing design, and Chanute referred him Edward Chalmers Huffaker, a young man he thought could fill that bill. Huffaker and Langley could hardly have been more different, at least in appearance. The highly formal secretary conducted daily inspection rounds, imposing in his morning coat and striped pants. Langley's approach might cause another staff member to snap to attention, but Huffaker would lean back in his chair, coatless, feet perched on his desk, as he spit into a crude spittoon nailed into the wall. In earlier days, Langley, who was used to treating subordinates with aloofness, if not disdain, nevertheless saw Huffaker as a man who might help rescue his foundering project. He commented to a friend that he had little choice but to accept Huffaker "as God made him."[8]

But Chanute didn't stop there. Augustus Moore Herring, son of a wealthy Georgia family, had worked on Chanute's gliders since 1894. Unlike Huffaker, who rose from humble origins, Herring and Langley were both cut from the upper crust. And when Langley began insisting "on absolute obedience" in an "impatient, demanding" way, it was clear the two strong-willed men were on a collision course. Herring was not to remain long in Langley's employ, complaining at one point, somewhat delicately, that his boss had difficulty distinguishing "between ideas of other people and his own." This was a serious charge against a man with such a reputation for rectitude as Langley had, and Herring tempered his suggestion of plagiarism by noting, "Whether this is intentional or not, I cannot say," but underlined his resentment once again by asserting that "the effect is the same."

By the time of Langley's 1895 flight tests, the aerodrome's configuration had changed, with front and rear wings now the same size. The team added a cruciform on a spring, to help maintain balance during a gust of wind.[9]

The Age of Invention

In a year of political turmoil, when William Jennings Bryan's "Cross of Gold" speech galvanized the Democratic challenge to William McKinley and Boss Mark

Hanna's Republican machine, the only constant was change. For 1896 was the year when Americans rode the nation's first subway in Boston, watched the first motion pictures, shown in vaudeville houses; and listened to the first disk phonograph record. Even such an ivory-tower pure scientist as Langley couldn't help be caught up in the celebrity that attended the great inventions of the era and their creators, men such as Thomas Edison and Langley's bosom friend Graham Bell.[10]

The secretary professed no desire to create an actual flying machine; that was for others to do, presumably using his plans as a blueprint. But Langley had spent nearly a decade in the laboratory, building and discarding four models and finally constructing one he deemed airworthy. So even though he had reached retirement age, the professor couldn't yet lay his burden down without trying once again to launch a model successfully. Given his deep friendship with Graham Bell, it was natural he'd want this dear companion by his side to savor the moment. Whether Langley really doubted his chances in May of 1896 or whether he didn't want to court bad luck through overconfidence, Langley telegrammed Bell on May 4, that "I expect to take the 4:25 P.M. train (Sixth Street Station) tomorrow for Quantico, and to spend the night there, hoping to make the trial in the morning. I am bound to say in advance that the prospects are not good for success, but if you will take the chance of a fruitless journey, I shall be delighted to have you come. May I expect you at the station?"[11]

The Potomac River weaves like an inebriate through southern Maryland, the District of Columbia, and into Virginia, snaking by the elegant brick townhouses of Alexandria before the homes become more scattered and then yield to open fields. Traveling by steam train on a day in May, before Virginia weather turns from balmy to stifling, Bell and Langley sat together in a railcar, watching the lush countryside through the open window until they disembarked at Quantico, Virginia. From this shabby shantytown, they hoped to row across the Potomac to Scott's Island, the preserve of an elite group of hunters from Washington, known as the Mount Vernon Ducking Club. By pre-arrangement, four workers awaited them in a nearby marsh, aboard a flat-bottomed boat, cradling a wooden deckhouse with three windows on each side. On closer examination, the 20-foot rail atop the roof, jutting aft, told bystanders this was no ordinary houseboat.

Langley's minions escorted the secretary and his guest into the deckhouse, where they displayed for them the components of Models 5 and 6, successors to the four failed models. With any luck, these would not languish in a laboratory — and Langley had yet to learn just how important luck would be in his career. The models, each measuring more than 10 feet from bowsprit to tail, used two sets of 14-foot tandem wings and small steam engines for power. The ever-demanding Langley peppered the workmen with questions, to make sure nothing had been left to chance in preparing for the next day's trials.[12]

Taking the models out of turn, Langley scheduled Aerodrome 6 to fly in the early afternoon of May 6. At the appointed time, his trusted carpentry superintendent from the Smithsonian pulled a lever that, in turn, released a streetcar spring. This was designed to propel the aerodrome along the rail and off the rear of the boat into the air. But lurking in the bushes was Murphy's Law, intent on an ambush. As guy wires strained to hold the wings in place one of them snapped, letting the left forward wing bend up. The craft plunged into the river, demolishing the wing and both propellers and damaging the engine.[13]

Since failure had become a handmaiden to the crew by now, Langley and company stoically readied Model 5 and by 3 P.M., it was ready to go. A special urgency pervaded the moment, this being the last model on hand. If this craft were to fail as well, it would have to be towed up the Potomac to Washington, and two disheartened scientists would have to climb back onto a northbound train.

With 150 pounds of steam pressure, No. 5 launched from the rooftop rail 20 feet above the Potomac cove. The flight that followed was one the Langley team had long anticipated but which, after their dispiriting experience to date, they could scarcely believe. The aerodrome "moved northward against the gentle wind, falling slightly (3 or 4 feet) at first, then moving ... forward and slightly upward with an inclination of the midrod to the horizon of about 10 degrees, which remained remarkably constant throughout flight." Model 5 had remained gloriously aloft for 80 seconds at a height ranging from 70 to 100 feet, covering a total of nearly 2/3 of a mile as it circled the houseboat twice.[14]

The scientist in Langley knew that not only the scientific community but the public at large would clamor to hear this epochal event recounted. Was this flight just a fluke? the skeptical might ask. So Langley knew right away that once would not be enough. Fighting the temptation to pop the champagne corks, he ordered Model 5, which had come through the test unscathed, to fly again. And in a trial at 5:05 P.M., the aerodrome soared to 60 feet and traveled 2,300 feet. No one had to tell Langley what these two flights meant. No one knew better than the secretary that people were saying his dream had grown beyond experimentation into obsession. How well he knew that the Smithsonian's board couldn't risk its prestige to coddle what some thought was its director's compulsive behavior. And for Langley's crew, the joy of triumph aside, these successful tests—these triumphant tests—meant they still would draw a paycheck.[15] If anyone needed any further proof that the mission had succeeded, he needed go no further than the white-bearded Graham Bell, who in a rowboat not far from the houseboat had taken the only known photograph of the flight.[16]

Twenty years earlier, Bell had listened to his words—"Mr. Watson, come here, I need you"—reverberate around the world and make everyone understand a new day was at hand. Wishing the same kind of encouragement for his friend, he now urged Langley to publicize the monumental flights. But the proper Langley, with his love of solitude, demurred. Taking the bit in his teeth, Bell wrote an account of his watching the momentous flight and persuaded Langley to let him release it to the press.[17]

In the 1890s, a letter to a scientific magazine over the signature of Alexander Graham Bell called for immediate attention. Writing to the editor of "*Science,*" Bell spun out his eye-witness account: "Last Wednesday, May 6th, I witnessed a very remarkable experiment with Professor Langley's aerodrome on the Potomac River;

indeed, it seemed to me that the experiment was of such historical importance that it should be made public."

The secretary had become so well-known that the use of his last name alone was sufficient to introduce him. Whether under Langley's own strictures or in trying to tease the editor by advancing just enough information to intrigue him, it is difficult to say, but Bell next wrote,

> I am not at liberty to give an account of all the details, but the main facts I have Professor Langley's consent for giving you, and they are as follows:
>
> The aerodrome or "flying machine" in question was of steel, driven by a steam engine. It resembled an enormous bird, soaring in the air with extreme regularity in large curves, sweeping steadily upward in a spiral path, the spirals with a diameter of perhaps 100 yards, until it reached a height of about 100 feet in the air at the end of a course of about half a mile, when the steam gave out, the propellers which had moved it stopped, and then, to my further surprise, the whole, instead of tumbling down, settled as slowly and gracefully as it is possible for any bird to do, touched the water without any damage, and was immediately picked out and ready to be tried again.

"No one could have witnessed these experiments," Bell wrote to the editor, "without being convinced that the practicability of mechanical flight had been demonstrated."[18]

Ten days later, *Science* carried Bell's letter, along with a preface from Professor Langley, in which he felt compelled to say that Graham Bell had twisted his arm to release the account of a flight that he still considered a work-in-process.[19]

A German John Wayne

The pulse of the aeronautical community — small but now growing larger — quickened at the word of Langley's triumph and heightened anticipation of the swashbuckling Otto Lilienthal's next adventure. With the *Boston Transcript*'s Robert Wood still in thrall, Lilienthal headed once again for the Rhinow Mountains on August 2, 1896, for one of his weekend jaunts. In the past five years, Lilienthal, working only on a weekend basis, had logged an astonishing 2,000 glides. Lilienthal in flight looked very similar to a contemporary hang-glider, in that the pilot rested his arms on the frame, while standing upright between the wings. Control came only from the pilot shifting his weight.

After watching and reporting nearly a dozen flights, reporter Wood or his editors might have felt public interest waning, so he persuaded Lilienthal to let him pilot the craft himself so he could write a first-person account. If Wood had harbored any doubts about how difficult it was to operate a hang-glider, his flight dispelled them. Just standing on the ground and trying to balance the craft itself caused "utter helplessness," Wood wrote:

As you stand in the frame, your elbows at your side, the forearms are horizontal, and your hands grasp one of the horizontal cross-braces. The weight of the machine rests in the angle of the elbow joints. In the air, when you are supported by the wings, your weight is carried on the vertical upper arms and by pads which come under the shoulders, with the legs and lower part of the body swinging free below.[20]

Wood's readers by now had bonded with the daring young German, as had the young reporter himself. So it may have been just as well that Wood departed for America before his idol's flight on August 9. While flying a monoplane glider at 50 feet, Lilienthal's craft stalled, hurtling the burly, red-headed daredevil to the ground. Rushed to a Berlin hospital, Lilienthal died the next day. If the world was saddened by the event, the aeronautical community was both crestfallen and sobered.[21]

Troubled Days for the Bicycle

By 1897, one might think that Bell and his friend Langley would have been the toast of the scientific town. But skepticism persisted, even at the highest levels. Sir William Thomson, who had become Lord Kelvin, was a prime example. Bell had tried to interest him in aeronautics, but Kelvin would have none of it. Later, he wrote Mabel Bell that he had sought to dissuade her husband from taking on such a foolish venture.

Kelvin's warning evidently had no effect. With a Spanish-American conflict in prospect over Caribbean issues, Bell's fertile mind began to envision the use of aerial reconnaissance and even bombardment in wartime. "I am not ambitious to be known as the inventor of a weapon of destruction," he said, "but I must say that the problem — simply as a problem — fascinates me, and I find my thoughts taking on more and more a practical form."[22]

As with the sewing machine craze before it in the 1870s, the bicycle by the mid–1890s had become a victim of its own success. With the safety bicycle now a decade old, most folks who wanted one already had bought one, and by 1896, industry sales plummeted.[23] The sales and repair business that Wilbur Wright and his younger brother had built up over the past half-dozen years was clearly in danger. A watershed moment was at hand in Orville and Wilbur's lives, causing them to reconsider the future that had once seemed so clear. Perhaps a limitless future in the bicycle business was not what they were intended for, the brothers thought. But if not bicycles, then what?[24]

The Age of Magazines

Erase from your mind any notion of television, radio, VCRs, motion pictures, and the Internet, and print magazines suddenly loom larger as a source of information and entertainment. No wonder Victorian-era Americans waited on their front porches each weekend for the arrival of the *Saturday Evening Post*. Steamship delivery, color printing, photographs and graphics, and the rapid cable transmission of information from Europe enhanced the finished product. Young men seeking to make a splash and line their pockets at the same time turned to magazine publishing, as a century later a new generation would sprout dot.com companies. And just as most dot.coms of the 1990s failed, so did most magazines of the 1890s.

Sam McClure was such a pioneer of his age. By 1895, his *McClure's Magazine's* circulation had broken 100,000. But general interest magazines were so popular that they invited cutthroat competition. West Point-trained John Brisben Walker, for instance, was boosting circulation of his new publication, attractively named *Cosmopolitan*. Now the aggressive marketer set his sights on eliminating *McClure's* by slashing his newsstand price to a dime. Sam McClure, who charged 15 cents, needed every bit of that income to hire such notables as O. Henry, Thomas Hardy, and Rudyard Kipling to fill his pages with fiction and narrative. In desperation, he turned to the man who had hired him fresh out of college to edit his own magazine.[25]

Colonel Albert Pope, known worldwide as the "father of the American bicycle," had founded the national Good Roads Movement to lobby for paving roads coast to coast. Nearly alone among manufacturers, he envisioned that speeding travel would build a market for his bicycles and later, his automobiles. McClure had learned at his mentor's elbow just how important mobility was to a growing society.

So it's not surprising that the energetic young editor would choose a piece entitled "The Flying Machine" to be the lead story in his June, 1897, issue of *McClure's Magazine*. Its author, an ivory-towered professor named S. P. Langley, had elbowed out such literary heavyweights as Robert Louis Stevenson and Arthur Conan Doyle for top billing. Sam McClure, a pioneer of investigative journalism, was about to turn the sensational exposé into an art form. Soon he would hire Ida Tarbell to scathingly assault John D. Rockefeller's Standard Oil, Lincoln Steffens to root out municipal corruption in cities across the country, and Ray Stannard Baker to eviscerate coal-mining companies and the rapacious railroads. McClure knew a good story when he saw one, and he sensed Langley's account of his experiments with air travel, culminating in his successful flight over the Potomac a year earlier, would have readers on the edge of their seats. For as quaint as the topic may appear to readers today, to the public in 1897, it would have been as fresh as a trip to Mars.[26]

Langley was used to writing for an academic and scientific audience and could have been forgiven if his prose were leaden and turgid. At the outset, he climbed down from his pedestal and self-consciously announced that what followed would be a "popular account" of his doings. He took a conversational tone, without patronizing his reader, that struck the mood of a dinner table chat. He frankly admitted his many failures and guided the reader through his thoughts as he tried to correct them. At the outset, he gave a respectful nod to his avian brothers: "Nature has made her flying-machine in the bird, which is nearly a thousand times as heavy as the air its bulk. displaces, and only those who have tried to rival it know how inimitable her work is...."[27]

The secretary proceeded to walk his reader through mad scientist images of tying bird wings to whirling laboratory arms, slogging through swamps to reach his houseboat floating on the Potomac, and accounts of both his failed and successful attempts to fly his aerodromes. Interspersing the narrative were photographs taken by none other than the famed "Alexander Graham Bell, Esq."

But Langley had saved the best, or at least the most intriguing, for last. After 14 pages, he confessed he had run out of space to expound on larger machines that "may be built to remain for days in the air" or to examine air travel's commercial possibilities.

But, he forecast boldly, the flying machine "may be such as to change the whole conditions of warfare, when each of two opposing hosts will have its every movement known to the other, when no lines of fortifications will keep out the foe, and when the difficulties of defending a country against an attacking enemy in the air will be such that we may hope that this will hasten rather than retard the coming of the day when war shall cease."[28]

Langley's exposition may have revealed as much about him as about aeronautics, for he proved to be an uncanny visionary. At a time when no American company yet sold motor vehicles, let alone airline tickets, Langley sketched out a wholly new dimension, not only of travel but of looking at the world. He suggested his readers look upward, to "the great universal highway overhead." In a valedictory, he observed:

> I have brought to a close the portion of the work which seemed to be specifically mine — the demonstration of the practicability of mechanical flight — and for the next stage, which is the commercial and practical development of the idea, it is probable that the world may look to others.[29]

Given the tenor of the bellicose times in which Langley wrote the piece, it would be naïve to conclude that he had simply tossed off his military observations as an after-thought. In an imperial age, with Britain, Germany, Spain, and Japan among others straining to lengthen their reach, warfare was an ever-present reality. Given his prominence, how could Langley not have suspected that he was setting the bait that, within months, his nation's leaders, including the president of the United States, would bite? In that reckoning, however, what would have been sadly beyond his ken was that the course he had set out, carried to its conclusion, would ultimately hold for Langley the most dire consequences.

5

A National Mission

"...his indomitable will, which balked at no obstacle, however great it might seem, prevailed against the advice of his close friends and associates, and even that of his physician, who had counseled him that a resumption of concentrated thought and vigorous endeavor would materially shorten his life, which had already passed three score years." — Charles Manly on his boss, Samuel P. Langley

FOR 48-YEAR-OLD CHARLES D. WALCOTT, the lavish Wednesday evening dinners at 1331 Connecticut Avenue were heady stuff. Invitations to the home of Alexander Graham Bell were cause for discreet bragging rights around town — discreet because Bell guarded his privacy jealously and felt that the public had no right to trample his tulips or finger his draperies as if his house were a museum piece. No gossip about the number of servants or the volumes in Bell's bookcases would find its way back to Walcott's offices downtown at the Smithsonian Institution. But neither would the weighty topics under discussion at these weekly salons, because what was at stake on this evening in the early spring of 1898 was nothing less than the nation's security.

The District of Columbia was, in 1898, a mere embryo of the leviathan it was to become. Still two decades away from the Great War that would propel the nation into international leadership, Washington was a town of trolley cars and carriages with horses clip-clopping on earthen streets, with sprinkler wagons on wheels making the rounds behind them, keeping down the dust, particularly during the city's stifling summers. Paved roads, such as the white asphalt laid not long before on Pennsylvania Avenue, and a handful of primitive gasoline-powered roadsters were clearly exceptions to the rule.[1]

A geologist by nature since he began collecting natural history specimens at age 13 in upstate New York, Walcott was largely self-taught, like his mentor and boss, Professor Samuel P. Langley. Not that this was rare for the age; President McKinley himself had attended only one term of college. Walcott had married early and was only 26 when Lura Ann Walcott died. Charles threw himself into his work, joining the U.S. Geological Survey, where he would rise steadily through the ranks for many years, and becoming its director in 1894.[2]

As a geologist, Walcott was happiest out in the field, studying Cambrian and Permian fossils in such diverse locales as the Wasatch Mountains, the Grand Canyon and the Adirondacks. In 1888, Helena Breese Stevens enticed him out of a 12-year bachelorhood and within a decade, Walcott found himself a father of four, prominent in his field and, at 48, president of the Cosmos Club, one of Washington's most prominent gentleman's clubs. With a long, tapered nose, a whiskbroom mustache and expressive eyes, the ambitious bureaucrat radiated efficiency and inspired confidence among his peers.[3]

Charles D. Walcott, head of the U.S. Geological Survey, is credited with persuading President William McKinley to put his prestige and government money behind a drive to make America first in flight. National Air and Space Museum, Smithsonian Institution (SI Neg. No. 2002-16643).

Holding His Own with the Best

Not yet at the acme of his career, Walcott nonetheless could hold his own with the illustrious assemblage gathered at Bell's home this evening: his boss, 64-year-old Professor Langley; his host, 51-year-old Graham Bell, who had built model aircraft powered by black-powdered rockets; Simon Newcomb, 63, an astronomer who had edited The Nautical Almanac; and two 30-ish wunderkinds, Catholic University's Alfred F. Zahm, now working on a 40-foot wind tunnel capable of 25-mile-per-hour speeds, and the botanist and explorer David Fairchild.[4]

Rounding out the circle was the redoubtable Octave Chanute, catalyst to so many airborne endeavors and mentor to so many aeronauts. Chanute had encouraged these conclaves at Bell's home after Langley dropped a bomb in his lap in 1897. Two months after he had written in McClure's Magazine that the 1896 trials had been his aeronautical swan song, he wrote to Chanute, saying that he could have a manned aircraft flying within two to three years if he could get his hands on $50,000. Why the change of heart? Did he regret bringing down the curtain on a proud career before he had won the prize that had eluded him for so long? His pronouncement was akin to an acclaimed sports superstar deciding to come out of retirement for one more season. And Chanute was not about to let this new opportunity slip through his fingers.[5]

The only guest who might have seemed out of place at the table was Edward Everett Hale, noted reformer, author and soon to be U.S. Senate chaplain. But even he had a link to the sky, having written a fictional account of a manned orbiting satellite.[6] Whether a greater accumulation of aeronautical knowledge and experience could have been gathered in one place anywhere in the world is doubtful.

Now, as the last plates were cleared and the guests retired for brandy and cigars, Walcott found himself a notch below the rest in prestige, perhaps, but on a par with them in power. About to be named Langley's number two man at the Smithsonian, Walcott had learned from his days at the U.S. Geological Survey the ins and outs of the appropriations process and had mastered, at a fairly young age, the art of political massage. "Uncle Joe" Cannon, after whom a current House office building is named, was speaker of the House at the time. After an arduous session on the floor, he often could be found stretching his legs along Pennsylvania Avenue. "Walcott, as if by chance," his biographer recalls, "would draw up beside the curb with a fast-stepping bay and a light buggy and suggest (to Cannon) a drive in Rock Creek Park, but during those rides he never mentioned business. On one occasion "Uncle Joe" paused, his foot on the step and said: 'Walcott, you may have a building for the Survey or one for the National Museum, but you can't have both.'"[7]

Walcott surveyed the assemblage as the evening waned and saw older men, who traded on relationships and reputations built up over a generation or two. But Walcott may have had even more contacts who knew the buttons to push to get things done, men yearning to make a difference and to claw their way up the career ladder while doing it, men like 40-year-old Theodore Roosevelt, assistant secretary of the U.S. Navy. Recently returned to Washington after making headlines as New York City's reform-minded police commissioner, he was still obscure enough that Walcott could misspell his name "Rosevelt" in his diary.

Langley's announcement to Chanute that, at age 64, he was willing to pick up the quest for manned flight had the grapevine working overtime. But even with the commitment of Langley's prestige, the $50,000 he sought was a huge hurdle. If manned flight was no longer the subject of ridicule it had been for centuries, it was also true that no financial backers had yet stepped forward to open their wallets. As the secretary of the Smithsonian, Langley could draw on unrestricted reserves within the institution's coffers, but that, by itself, clearly wouldn't be enough.

As the evening wore on, the brain trust came to realize that only government funding could bring Langley's vision to fruition. A century later, jokes are made about the foolish ideas that governments finance. But 15 years before the federal income tax made big spending possible, public funding for a new idea was nearly unheard of. Yet Walcott realized that one compelling factor increased the odds.

A month earlier, the U.S. battleship *Maine* had sunk in Havana harbor, and fingers pointed nearly unanimously at Spain, whose relationship with the United States was rocky at best. For years, Cuban insurgents had demanded independence from Spain, a rallying cry that had won great support in America. Voices in Congress now called for an early declaration of war.

Germany, among other continental nations, coaxed Spain to avoid war, pressuring Madrid to grant Cuban independence if that would head off armed conflict. Even the pope agreed to mediate between Spain and the insurgents. William Jennings Bryan, who had lost the presidency 18 months before to McKinley, now called for Cuban independence. But Congress and public opinion seemed foursquare in favor of going to war. McKinley, quite against his will, was on the verge of giving Spain a three-day ultimatum to withdraw and calling for 125,000 volunteer soldiers.[8]

Among Walcott's contemporaries, Roosevelt was known to be spoiling for war in the wake of the ship bombing, pledging to avenge this "act of dirty treachery."[9] While McKinley's advisors cautioned him not to react reflexively, advising that troop buildups take time, his blunt-speaking underling with flashing white teeth told friends privately that McKinley had no more backbone than a chocolate éclair. Roosevelt aligned himself with those in Congress who saw an opportunity, in vengeance, to enhance America's colonial reach.

There was abroad in the land what McKinley biographer Margaret Leech calls a "war feeling, the feeling that war was coming, the feeling that makes wars come."[10] And while McKinley hoped to avoid armed conflict, feeling the nation was unprepared for it, he sensed he was about to be swept up by the tide.

President McKinley had proposed an armistice with Spain in March, hoping to buy some time, but pressure from expansionists in and out of Congress had convinced him that war was inevitable. "Remember the Maine" had become a national battle cry, shouted from podiums and pulpits alike. The strain had taken its toll on the president's very appearance. "His face had grown seamed and haggard, with sunken, darkly-circled eyes," recorded his biographer. "He jumped at every sound."[11]

What if the embattled president could be sold on the idea that the first nation with manned, powered aircraft could then conduct aerial surveillance behind enemy lines, giving it the biggest strategic boost since the invention of the machine gun? As unusual as was government support for such a venture, it was not unprecedented. Six years earlier, the French government agreed to subsidize inventor Clement Ader in building a steam-powered, batwing craft that failed in two 1897 trials.[12] If other nations poured money into such ventures, could America afford to be left behind? The Bell assemblage agreed; an approach would be made directly to President McKinley.

Approaching McKinley

A measure of Walcott's respect among Bell's guests is that they deputized him to call upon the president. His task was unenviable, for Langley had set parameters on his involvement that invited a quick rejection. Although no one had forced the secretary to make his bold commitment, at age 64 he knew the project would likely be his last hurrah. He would be sacrificing the contemplation and ease of retirement and perhaps shortening his life as well from the stress of the mission. If he were to take this on, with all due respect to President McKinley, it would have to be on his terms.

Langley had given Bell a memo, explaining how the craft could be used in warfare, both at sea and on land. In it, he posited several non-negotiable demands. First, Langley said, he would have complete control of the money the government allocated to the project. Next, absolute secrecy must prevail. And forget government interference, even the usual audits: he'd have none of that. Only if his government accepted these conditions would Langley agree to participate. It might take a master diplomat to secure these conditions without offending the president.[13]

Yet Walcott *was* a seasoned diplomat and McKinley a nearly-desperate man. Diary notes of Walcott's March 24 meeting with the president are cryptic: "Called on President McKinley at noon and talked with him about Prof. Langley's flying machine."[14] Without further contemplation, the president put his imprimatur on the idea, and right after leaving the White House, Walcott called on Langley to tell him the news. McKinley, newly convinced of the inevitability of war, was evidently eager enough to enhance his military resources that he was willing to grasp at straws.

McKinley had asked to see photographs of Langley's models in flight, such as those that accompanied the *McClure's* article and suggested that Walcott approach George Meiklejohn, top aide to War Secretary Russell A. Alger. The next day, with the president's encouragement in his pocket, Walcott called upon Asst. Naval Secretary Roosevelt and Meiklejohn, later meeting with Prof. Langley to report his findings.[15] Roosevelt agreed wholeheartedly. This was the kind of cutting edge adventure that stirred his juices.[16] And Walcott knew of Roosevelt's capacity to instill passion into whatever crossed his path. Not long before, Walcott had heard Theodore (he was not yet "Teddy") speak to the Biological Society of Washington on a big game hunter's perspective on the classification of mammals. "It was a silly, but rousing, performance." A man with such elan could be of use.[17]

In less than two weeks, a panel was set up to study the matter. Langley could relax, knowing that both Walcott and Bell were chosen to sit on it. Walcott's diary reflects he put away his study of Cambrian brachiopods nearly entirely for the next month, engaged instead with negotiating with government and military officials on how to build a flying machine. Biographer Yochelson credits Walcott for selling the project to the military: "Langley on his own would never have brought his machine to the attention of the military, and even if he had, without Walcott's push and know-how of federal corridors, the military would not have responded."[18]

As spring turned into summer, Langley's civilian committee bit its nails while awaiting word from the Army's Board of Ordnance. On June 18, Langley wrote Bell from Boston's posh St. Botolph Club that, even though the Military and Naval Board had reported favorably on the aerodrome proposal, the Ordnance Board had postponed its meeting. This led Langley to confide to Bell that "the prospect of aid from them is not very encouraging."[19] It was a double regret for Langley, who had turned down Bell's invitation to visit with him and Mabel amid "the blessed breezes of Cape Breton ... instead of melting here in Washington."[20]

Hastened by the fact that America had declared war on Spain on April 24, the Board of Ordnance and Fortification called Langley before it to outline his project. He couldn't have been heartened, in light of his demands for secrecy, to read in *The Washington Post* two days later of the administration's involvement in the project. The board, keeping Langley on a somewhat shorter tether than he desired, approved $25,000 for the project, holding a like sum in reserve.[21] It did let the secretary retain all rights to the final product, which the board dictated would have four wings and a cruciform tail. By December of 1898, approval was complete.[22]

By that time, Walcott had resigned as acting assistant secretary of the Smithsonian. Walcott had pre-arranged a short tenure upon his appointment the previous spring, well-acquainted as he was with how tough Langley was on subordinates. Yet Walcott understood Langley's many strengths as well. He valued their friendship and wished it to continue; that would be possible only if he were out from under Langley's thumb.[23]

Building an Engine

Since a light, efficient engine was central to the mission, Langley's first move upon receiving approval from the Board of Ordnance was to hire New York engine maker Stephen M. Balzer, who had experience manufacturing automobiles. He charged Balzer with building a 12-horsepower engine, weighing no more than 100 pounds, and supports for his propellers, transmission gears, and drive shafts. But success in building car engines somehow didn't translate into airplane motors, and Balzer proved to be an immediate disappointment. Langley left it to Charles Manly, a Cornell engineer he had hired to shepherd the project day by day, to fire Balzer and reconstruct the engine himself.[24] From that point on, Manly was, next to Langley, the most important man on the mission.[25]

As will become evident to the reader later, much of the most important written material on Langley's flights was written after Langley's active life, much of it after his death. In 1911, the Smithsonian Institution published what is still a classic in its field, the *Langley Memoir on Mechanical Flight*. Part 1, written by the secretary, concerns his experiments from 1887 through 1896. Part II, written by Manly, whose title was assistant in charge of experiments, details the experimentation from 1897 through 1903. In Manly's introduction to Part II, Langley's aide-de-camp helps the reader understand why Langley was so demanding and uncompromising in his request that government give him complete control of the project:

> Ten years of almost disheartening difficulties ... had already been spent in demonstrating that mechanical flight was practicable, and Mr. Langley thoroughly realized that the construction of a large aerodrome would involve as great, if not greater difficulties. Nevertheless, his indomitable will, which balked at no obstacle, however great it might seem, prevailed against the advice of his close friends and asso-

Professor Langley, in straw boater at right, places affection-
ate hand on the shoulder of his protégé Charles Manly, who
designed the internal combustion engine for the *Aerodrome*
after no automobile engine builder was willing to build it.
National Air and Space Museum, Smithsonian Institution
(SI Neg. No. 2002-16636).

ciates, and even that of his physician, who had coun-seled him that a resumption of concentrated thought and vigorous endeavor would materially shorten his life, which had already passed three score years.[26]

Langley, convinced that launching from atop a houseboat was still the way to go, set about to procure one measuring 40 by 60 feet, somewhat larger than his earlier boat. As the fall of 1899 approached, he requested the reserved $25,000. Ordnance Board members asked to inspect his work first and visited his "float-ing machine shop," at the Eighth Street wharf on the Potomac, not far from Langley's Smithsonian offices.[27]

As much as Professor Langley had tried to keep his project quiet, he learned quickly how leak-prone the nation's capital

is. And, spurred by his widely-read *McClure's* article, the Smithsonian secretary was becoming an aeronautical icon. It is unsurprising that he would draw abundant cor-respondence from those interested in finding out more about the subject. But Lan-gley was on a deadline; he could scarcely stop to answer correspondence from the curious. That task fell to his assistant, Richard Rathbun.

One letter in June of 1899 came from a small businessman in the Midwest, who wrote to inquire about the best books available relating to flight. "I have been inter-ested in the problem of mechanical and human flight ever since as a boy I constructed a number of bats of various sizes after the style of Cayley's and Pénaud's machines," he wrote. For one who sought the most basic information, the writer had no short-age of confidence: "My observations since have only convinced me more firmly that human flight is possible and practicable." It comes down, he said, only to "a question of knowledge and skill." Rathbun took little note of the letter; hundreds like it came across his desk every month. Dashing off a quick reply, he directed it to a clerk, asking him to gather some recent materials and send them off to this fellow, Wilbur Wright.[28]

6

The Chanute Factor

"He is so sensitive, and has so many illusions as to the value of the device, that the praise which you unduly bestow upon me, and the hint that he might be left out, might cause him to boil over."— Octave Chanute, commenting on talented employee Augustus Herring

IN THE GENERATION BEFORE RADIO, and later television, changed American life, a cornucopia of reading choices greeted the consumer, one not matched before or since. Cities with one or two newspapers today a century earlier had eight or ten, bleating their competing ideologies like an opinionated Tower of Babel. Photographs, color, and graphics dolled up popular magazines, all competing for public attention in ways that soon would instruct those who sold cereal, long johns, or motorcars.

And in 1896, even a casual reader could tell that a breakthrough in aeronautics lay on the horizon. On May 6, Samuel Langley had flown his Model 5 more than a half-mile and, thanks to his eager publicist Graham Bell, the world knew this now. Reporters dogged the daring Otto Lilienthal as he trekked obsessively to the Rhinow Mountains each weekend. Each flight seemed longer than the last one, each alteration to the flying machine seemed more sophisticated. These talented and driven men wouldn't continue to persevere unless they saw gold at the end of the rainbow, would they? In June, engineer Octave Chanute began his long-planned glider tests over Lake Michigan's sand dunes, a mere 30 miles from Chicago. But readers wouldn't be feasting on every detail of the 2,000 glides his team would make that summer. Not, at least, if Chanute had anything to do about it.

Unforgettable Herring

Aeronautics now held the clear focus of public consciousness, but no one had quite the bird's eye view as did a 31-year-old dreamer with a Georgia accent and a trust fund. Augustus M. Herring, son of a prosperous cotton merchant, had moved north at age 18 and entered New Jersey's Stevens Institute of Technology. Soon he committed himself to the cause of manned flight, never thereafter wavering from his chosen path. Herring left the four-year school a semester short of graduation, and the justification he'd stick by to win sympathy within the aeronautical community was that his professors branded as "too fanciful" his paper on "The Flying Machine as a Mechanical Engineering Problem." The fact that his actual thesis was on the marine steam engine, not a flying machine, casts Herring's story in a different light and was a useful fact to those who would study his remarkable career in the days ahead.[1] Herring soon began experimenting with a bi-plane glider, powered by strands of rubber, making one wonder whether this was the project described in his "fanciful" paper.

Public attention was so hot for aeronautics that even an unknown such as Herring could gain press coverage, and he welcomed as much as he could get. The attention his gliders won led him to Europe, where he worked with Otto Lilienthal for a time. By 1895, Herring was back in America, on the payroll of Octave Chanute. He joined Langley's team at the Smithsonian and was part of the crew that took Model 5 up in May of 1896, leaving in time to rejoin Chanute for his mission over the Indiana dunes.

Herring's resume was unparalleled in his involvement with the leading lights of aeronautical experimentation. Yet the main reason he moved around so much was that he couldn't get along with anyone for long. His deep-set, appraising eyes quickly discarded the idea he considered ill-conceived or irrelevant, and his fiercely independent manner often rankled with his employers. Collectively, they vacillated between admiration for Herring's industry and brilliant insights and frustration with his egotism and sensitivity to insult. But clearly in 1896, no one had seen quite as much in the burgeoning field of aeronautics as Augustus Herring.

Langley, who felt that Herring insufficiently appreciated his attention, had whispered in Chanute's ear that Herring was unreliable and indiscreet as well. Herring returned Langley's contempt in kind, decrying what he considered the professor's severe control problem and resenting not being given a freer role in developing his own ideas. But Chanute hired Herring anyway and found him to be hard-working, intuitive, and resourceful. After all, Chanute had never actually flown and needed someone with deep flying experience.[2] Though he'd be loath to admit it, Langley actually owed a debt to Herring, who disabused the secretary of the notion that flat wings provide more lift than cambered ones.[3]

Herring was obsessed with becoming the first man aloft. His passion would serve as the wind beneath his own wings for the next several years. And his important years with Orville and Wilbur Wright, an era that would deepen his own legend, still lay ahead.

An Uneasy Alliance

Their ages alone would inevitably give Herring and Chanute different perspectives. Herring had half his life ahead of him, but Chanute, at 64, was entering his twilight years. The idea of taking a glider aloft at his age was prohibitively daunting; he'd leave that to Herring and his other young assistants. But he was up to his elbows in sketches and designs. And few questioned his engineering ability. Although Herring had become committed to aeronautics at an early age, it was a latter-day conversion for Chanute, after a distinguished career as a bridge engineer. To come upon this short, squat, bald man from behind was not to be impressed, but when he turned around, his kind, lively eyes and white Van Dyke beard lent the 64-year-old Chanute a dignified aura. Wilbur Wright later would say he looked like William Shakespeare.[4]

Octave Chanute, though several decades older than Wilbur and Orville Wright, was their closest associate outside the family. He saw the Wrights as the most promising of many potential aviators and nurtured them in numerous ways, engaging in a correspondence totaling hundreds of letters. But their relationship soured, and they hardly spoke in his later years. Octave Chanute Aerospace Museum.

Born in France, his American-born parents separated when Octave was six, and he moved to New Orleans with his father. There he led a sheltered life, with his father having him tutored at home and not allowed to learn English until he was 11. The sheltering may have stunted his emotional growth, leaving a straitlaced and guileless nature that Chanute carried into adulthood.[5]

A self-taught engineer, he moved to Kansas City in 1867 at age 35, to design the Hannibal Bridge, which would span the Missouri River. How odd he must have appeared in the heartland, with his goatee and penchant for formal dress. Some likened the look to the French Emperor Napoleon III, calling it a holdover from Chanute's birth in Paris. The Hannibal Bridge would last a half-century, quite an accomplishment in that early day of bridge building.

Chanute prospered in his engineering practice, mapping out railroad lines into Kansas for the Atchison, Topeka & Santa Fe Railroad. In those days, railroads built towns around station stops for people who would come only later, so that the rail companies could name towns at will. Four towns in the path of the Atchison line ultimately combined and named themselves Chanute, Kansas. At age 43, Chanute was already president of the American Society of Civil Engineers. While in that position, he developed elevated railroads, which formed the basis of New York City's transit system.

But the love of Chanute's life was clearly aeronautics, one he had kept percolating on the back burner since childhood. When a new Chicago venture preserving railroad ties struck it rich in 1890, he could afford to follow his heart. Aeronautics, at first glance, might seem totally unrelated to railroad and bridge engineering, but Chanute had learned much about the effect of wind gusts on bridges and roof structures and saw logical progressions of this study in exploring the problems of flight.[6] Chanute believed the skills needed to put a man in the air were those of an inventor, a mechanical engineer, a mathematician, a practical mechanic, and a capitalist. Believing it unreasonable to think that one man could bring all these talents to the table, he theorized in a *McClure's Magazine* article in 1890 that only a combine of individuals with varied backgrounds would ultimately achieve flight.[7]

In 1893, Chanute attended the Columbian Exposition in Chicago, which by now had become his home town. There he participated reluctantly in the International Conference on Aerial Navigation, a conclave organized by Albert Francis Zahm, a Notre Dame physics professor, who would soon become a fast friend, and featuring Professor Langley, among others. In 1893, aeronautics was still considered a bit outre', and Chanute worried that he might besmirch his hard-won reputation as an engineer. He agreed to attend only if the fair kept publicity to a minimum. Happily for Chanute, he made many contacts at the conference that would serve him well. And he needn't have worried about people thinking him loopy. The *Pittsburgh Dispatch* attended and editorialized that the problem of flight "is no longer to be considered the hobby of mere cranks."[8]

Chanute designed his 1894 book, *Progress in Flying Machines,* to recount the history of flying experiments, examine the current state of the art, and point the way toward the first manned flight. Besides predictable treatment of such pioneers as Leonardo da Vinci, Chanute shone the spotlight, not without humor, on such lesser lights as an obscure French locksmith named Besnier. A visionary in his own mind, he tried to fly in 1678 in a craft comprised largely of poles resting on each of his shoulders, with paddles affixed to either end. Besnier launched his craft by jumping from a high window and beat the air fiercely with his paddles to keep aloft. Chanute summarized Besnier's attempts, tongue-in-cheek, as "short downward flights aided by gravity."[9]

Younger men on the make would see aeronautics as the path to fame and fortune, but Chanute — already secure in both money and accomplishment — wanted only to see someone actually fly before he died. Just who that would be was less important. His historic role in the race to the sky might most accurately be termed The Great Facilitator. As a broker of talent, information, and even financing, the even-handed Chanute had no equal. But he had strongly-held beliefs about *how* to fly, and these led him to schedule 1896 trials of his own machines.

Chanute thought, for instance, that Professor Langley had placed the cart before the horse when he sent up his motorized model the month before. Motors made no sense, Chanute felt, until the wings had been stabilized, to withstand the wildly fickle wind currents prevailing, unseen, above. Forget whether steam or internal combustion or electricity would best propel an aeroplane. First, figure out how to configure its wings properly. Training the pilot to shift his body weight from side to side as conditions changed, in Chanute's view, was no substitute for making the machine itself respond to those conditions.[10]

Building a Team

Naming Herring to quarterback his team, Chanute now added two key members. William Avery, a carpenter and electrician who had worked with Chanute in his Chicago shop, had built Chanute's original multi-winged glider. He needed Avery, for even though Chanute was a skilled engineer, his mechanical skills were nil.[11] The other addition was a former Russian sailor named William Paul Butusov, who claimed to have flown a manned glider, called the *Albatross,* in Kentucky in 1889. Chanute doubted Butusov's story but admired his skills. In return for his help, Chanute agreed to help the Russian eccentric finance the "reconstruction" of his 40-foot, 160-pound *Albatross.*

On the first day of summer, as a steam locomotive belched and wheezed to a stop at Miller Junction, Indiana, the party of four clambered off the train, together with a kite, two gliders and camping gear. Heads turned as they lugged their burden through the one-horse town on the way to Miller Beach, at the southern end of Lake Michigan. This was high excitement for the little burg. The alert stationmaster dialed up *The Chicago Tribune,* to let the news desk know something was afoot, and soon reporters and curiosity seekers descended, unwanted, on Miller Beach.

A steady northerly wind was blowing, so the crew wasted no time beginning its testing. Here, Herring's experience quickly came into play, for they tested first a Lilienthal-designed glider, which Herring had modified in America. After a week of flights, ranging between 70 and 120 feet long, the glider crashed beyond reclamation on June 29. No matter, said Chanute: "It is a gliding but not a soaring machine and little is to be expected from it." He summed up his feeling towards the whole episode: "Glad to be rid of it."[12]

Next, the team turned to the multi-surface glider, which Chanute had designed himself, but it took some getting used to. "All are afraid because of its novelty," Chanute told his diary on June 24. His strictly experimental craft was a veritable Chinese menu of aeronautical options. It sported six removable wing sections that could be reconfigured in numerous ways, to compare and contrast performance. A spring attached to each six-foot wing responded to wind gusts by letting the wing turn slightly, thus introducing flexibility while maintaining stability.[13] Chanute's approach was brilliant, since it let him learn more quickly and inexpensively than designing a series of gliders with different wing patterns and testing them one at a time. In spite of Chanute's best efforts to conceal the team's whereabouts, the press had found them out, and within days, a reporter from *The Chicago Record* was regularly witnessing the trials and telegraphing copy back to his office for the next day's editions.

By June 27, only five days after they had landed in camp, the team was re-configuring the wings again and again, like children with a giant erector set. Chanute grew increasingly excited by the team's progress. One eyewitness described the nor-mally dignified engineer jumping up and down with joy after his glider flew suc-cessfully, shouting, "I've got it!" Because of his extensive experience in flying gliders, Chanute generally chose Herring to fly most trials, with Avery and Butusov going up occasionally.[14]

After days of mixing and matching, Chanute finally settled on a craft with five pairs of wings in front, offering a total surface of 148 square feet, and one behind, with 29 square feet of surface. He nicknamed this machine the *Katydid*. Over the next few days, they made scores of glides with it. In the process, the pilot's upper arms and shoulders grew sore from hanging over a rail beneath the wings to guide the craft, so the team improvised padding from gunny sacks, to ease the discomfort. On the Fourth of July, marking the nation's 120th birthday, Avery logged 78 feet and Her-ring 82 feet, 6 inches, flying into a northerly wind ranging from 6 to 13 miles per hour. Chanute celebrated Independence Day by rejoicing in his diary that "Winged machine is more compact and handy than Lilienthal's and it promises to be safer & steadier."[15] Satisfied, Chanute and crew packed their gear and climbed aboard the 6:41 train for home. The team left behind for its next visit a cot, an axe, a pail, a lantern, a wash basin, three camp stools, a scythe, a dipper, an oil can, and a scoop shovel.[16]

The Genius of a Two-Surface Glider

Sitting around the campfire after the experiments, Chanute and Herring cogi-tated about a two-surface glider with a tail similar to the one Pénaud had designed. This simple design would soon lead to the breakup of the Chanute and Herring rela-tionship and, in later years, would influence the Wright brothers profoundly.

After a month and a half back in Chanute's Chicago lab, digesting what they had learned on the Indiana dunes, the team returned on August 21, joined this time by Dr. James Ricketts, a physician Chanute described wryly as having "a slack prac-tice and a taste for aviation."[17] They decided this time to shake the plethora of reporters that had hung around them like mosquitoes on their last visit, by avoid-ing Miller Beach. Clearly, public interest now was so aroused that editors flogged reporters to dig up stories wherever they could, to sate the appetites of newly-curi-ous readers. Chanute's team loaded its gliders onto a boat and traveled five miles overnight, through marshland to Dune Park, swatting away bugs throughout the summer night as frogs croaked a welcome.

The weather had largely cooperated during their earlier visit. But on the first day of their return trip, a giant storm unleashed its fury on the camp and, in the process, demolished the wings of Herring's machine. Ahead of the team lay a five-week ordeal, during which they would be tested not only by the weather but by the interplay of their own strong personalities. Butusov had been working again on his *Albatross*, and the crew spent much time erecting a trestle designed to launch it. All the launches would fail. Chanute had humored Butusov along, putting up funds to rebuild the *Albatross,* hoping to gain contributions from the diligent Russian. Even that failed to pan out when Butusov had to rush back to Chicago to attend his wife on the birth and subsequent illness of their child.[18]

Avery had contributed the idea of removing the three-wing glider's lower wing, resulting in the two-surface craft that fascinated Herring and Chanute. Starting off from a hill amid the sand dunes, the biplane managed to glide 97 feet while the pilot hung from a frame beneath the lower surface. The *Katydid* tests proved successful as well, flying successively 188 feet, 256 feet, and finally 359 feet. Staying aloft a bit more than 10 seconds, however, they failed to equal the 12 to 15 seconds that Lilienthal had spent in the air. However, Lilienthal had made 2,000 glides, and Chanute was just beginning. By now, the team had attracted an entourage, and reporters from the *Chicago Tribune,* the *Chronicle,* the *Times-Herald,* and even the *Boston Herald* had taken buggy rides from Miller Station to report on the trials.[19]

Victory Has a Thousand Fathers

Many years later, John F. Kennedy would reflect that "Victory has a thousand fathers, but defeat is an orphan." The Chanute/Herring two-surface glider was indeed a winner and would be copied by no less than the Wright brothers several years later. Now that the Dune Park testing showed that it flew far better than the other configurations the team had tried, perhaps it was inevitable that memories would differ on how that particular configuration came to be.

The two-surface craft that had evolved amid blowing sands and summer winds at Dune Park incorporated a Pénaud-type cruciform tail. Herring's "regulator," an elastic hinge which the pilot could manipulate by pulling cords, attached the tail to the main frame. Chanute conceded the tail design owed much to Herring, but he took credit for the overall design of the craft, a premise with which Herring strenuously disagreed.[20]

The success of the two-surface glider experiments had affected both Chanute and Herring profoundly, inspiring Chanute to write more about it and the control problems that remained to be mastered, while he replenished his resources to continue the quest. Herring waved these concerns aside, feeling the glider needed only a propeller and motor to be viable. Keenly aware that others might be gaining on them, Herring argued that more time spent tinkering around would only risk letting someone else become the first in flight and reap the fame and fortune that would ensue.

Accordingly, Herring returned alone to Dune Park in October of 1896, this time reportedly adding a third wing to the two-surface glider. By increasing the glider's lifting area dramatically, Herring said he flew the length of three football fields while all alone. Assuming his account was truthful, he was in the hapless position of the golfer who shoots a hole-in-one while playing by himself. However, Herring's subsequent reputation for dissembling casts doubt on his account.

In 1897, in spite of the friction that had grown between them, Chanute invited Herring to join him for experiments with bird-wing models, but Herring demurred. Yet he invited his former mentor to witness two-surface glider experiments at Dune Park, this time financed by a young Elmira, New York, banker named Mathias Arnot, who kept Herring afloat as he exhausted the last of his inheritance.[21]

Herring felt his biggest obstacle to first flight wasn't technology but money. So he reportedly offered Arnot half the profits from exhibition if he would underwrite a compressed-air motor for the two-surface glider. Had Arnot not come through, which he did, Herring had been prepared to offer William Randolph Hearst of the *New York Journal* exclusive coverage of the experiments in return for his patronage.

While Langley, Chanute, and later the Wrights considered the press akin to the pesky mosquitoes they swatted away on their swampy treks, Herring embraced and cultivated the press. He alerted reporters to his doings and even tried to interest Barnum and Bailey about sponsoring gliding exhibitions, to stay in the public eye.[22]

Chanute, in some measure, overshadowed Herring's tests with a larger version of the two-surface glider Chanute and he had worked with at Dune Park the year before, and some referred to them as the "Chanute trials," a label that would rankle Herring. One visitor to the camp was James Means of Boston, publisher of *The Aeronautical Journal,* who witnessed the experiment and proposed that Chanute build a motorized machine modeled "on Chanute's two-surface and oscillating-wing glider designs." Chanute hastened to point out in a September letter that

> you are mistaken in assuming that I control the whole of the machine which you saw in gliding flight. I originally made the general design, it is true, but Mr. Herring supplied the automatic regulator, and I should not feel justified in using it without his consent.... He is so sensitive, and has so many illusions as to the value of the device, that the praise which you unduly bestow upon me, and the hint that he might be left out, might cause him to boil over."[23]

Driven by his quest to be first, Herring moved to St. Joseph, Michigan, and worked on a bi-plane, to which he had added propellers and a compressed-air motor. At 88 pounds, the engine was much lighter than a gasoline motor, but its air lasted only several minutes. Although he logged two short flights with this craft, Herring's craft burned up in a fire where it was stored and, out of resources, he was forced to suspend his efforts.

The palpable tension in the aeronautical community had seeped into public consciousness. By 1898, strategic war planners had added flight to their panoply of modern weaponry. News stories on the progress of airborne pioneers moved from inside pages to page one. All across America, ambitious young people began to ask whether the field held room for their dreams. And in Dayton, Ohio, in 1899, 31-year-old Wilbur Wright checked the mailbox each day, waiting for a package from the Smithsonian.

The Wright Stuff

"At the time the Wrights arrived in our community, we were set in our ways. We believed in a good God, a bad Devil, and a hot Hell, and more than anything else we believed that the same good God did not intend man should ever fly." — Bill Tate, Kitty Hawk, N.C., postmaster, 1900

RICHARD RATHBUN OWED HIS JOB in the castle to infertility. Not his own but rather that of a man he had never met. And on a day like this one in the spring of 1899, when incoming mail made the piles of paper on his desk seem to grow before his eyes, he may have wished that Henry James Hungerford had sired a son or daughter. It certainly would have lightened his load. This is no fairy tale, and the castle Richard worked in was very much a real one, although not built in a medieval European town but rather on the shores of the Potomac River in Washington, D.C. With gravel footpaths snaking through formal gardens and an imposing red brick tower crowned with battlements, knights in full armor wouldn't have seemed out of place on the grounds of the Smithsonian Institution, which certainly rivaled any other structure in Washington as an architectural statement. And Richard Rathbun, as its assistant secretary, was the second in charge of a rapidly-growing national institution.

The Smithsonian owes its existence to the obscure chemical discovery of a carbonate of zinc, without which British James Smithson, the bastard son of the first Duke of Northumberland, would not have made the fortune he did. Nor would his carbonite discovery have been named Smithsonite, after its discoverer. Fascinated with the spunk American colonists had shown in their revolution against his own people, Smithson became an admirer of Benjamin Franklin and Thomas Paine. The childless Smithson's will favored his only heir, nephew Henry Hungerford, but provided that if Henry died without children, he would endow, in the United States of America, "an establishment for the increase and diffusion of knowledge." When Henry failed to produce an heir, the die was cast.

Congress accepted Smithson's largesse in 1836, and stevedores loaded 11 boxes of gold coins onto steamships at the London docks to back it up. Taking the bequest of a half million dollars quite seriously, Congress named former President John Quincy Adams to organize a committee to found the institution, a task which took until 1846 to accomplish. Prominent American physicist Joseph Henry became the Smithsonian Institution's chief executive officer, who would be called the secretary.

Architect James Renwick, hired to design the Smithsonian, had won recent acclaim for his work on St. Patrick's Cathedral in 1853, a marble cruciform structure on Manhattan's Fifth Avenue, replete with a dozen side chapels. It was and would remain the largest Roman Catholic cathedral in the United States. The structure Renwick designed for the Smithsonian was grand but not huge, yet still large enough on its completion in 1855 to hold both the Institution's original collections and provide living quarters for the Smithsonian's secretary and his family as well.[1]

It would take the Smithsonian until the 1880s to gather and display its first museum collections. In 1886, Samuel P. Langley, America's foremost astronomer, would become the museum's secretary. Rathbun wasn't complaining, but Langley was not an easy man to work for. He was officious, a bit self-important, and driven. And woe betide the assistant who failed to dot all the "i"s and cross the "t"s. Yet to work with Langley was to feel on the cutting edge of change. Even second-tier employees had fascinating histories.

Take for example Major John Wesley Powell, head of the Smithsonian's Bureau of Ethnography. With a full beard and piercing eyes, Powell was a legendary explorer of the American West, who had risked his life to chart the Grand Canyon after leaving his right arm behind at Pittsburg Landing during the Civil War battle of Shiloh. These were the kinds of people one rubbed up against in the Smithsonian's high-ceilinged halls, as sunlight streamed through the tall windows, making patterns on the highly-polished wood floors. No easy task for custodians, keeping these floors shiny in a day before most streets were paved, as visitors too often tromped into the building with caked mud on their boots.[2]

Langley's successful aerodrome flights over the Potomac in 1896, followed by his widely-read exposition in *McClure's*, had enhanced his stature. Now the Smithsonian was flooded with serious requests for information along with those from the star struck, addicted to touching the garment hem of the famous. Langley was understandably pleased by the outpouring, but this he was also happy to have his assistant handle the minutiae of answering requests. So every inquiry that underscored for Secretary Langley the impact he was making on public opinion simply meant more work for Rathbun. In a day before office copying machines, a request for the 1897 *McClure's* article didn't simply involve a clerk running off another copy but seeing that the print shop had enough inventory to anticipate future needs and budgeting for more printing if it didn't.

Professor Langley had hoped that sharing his thoughts, as he so openly did in Sam McClure's popular magazine, would stir the creative juices in people of talent across the land and, in so doing, advance the cause of science. But for every truly

The Smithsonian Institution and its landscaped grounds were the headquarters of America's crusade to become first in flight. Secretary Langley's offices were in the crenellated castle at the rear. National Air and Space Museum, Smithsonian Institution (SI Neg. No. 2002-16633).

promising inquiry received, there were a couple of suspected crackpots. The challenge lay in telling one from the other. And although James Smithson had endowed the institution in which Rathbun was lucky enough to work, it was Congress that Langley and company looked to for continuing support. A report from a congressman or senator that the Smithsonian had treated a constituent with something less than courtesy could have grave repercussions when the institution's annual appropriation came up.

Just More Fan Mail?

The June 2 mail, for instance, brought a one-page inquiry from a Wilbur Wright of Dayton, Ohio, who claimed he had been interested in flight since he was a boy. Now many thousands of American men could claim that. Wright went on to say that he had "constructed a number of bats (model planes in the shape of a flying bat) of various sizes after the style of Cayley's and Pénaud's machines." This suggested more than a casual interest. Rathbun read on, as Wright proclaimed earnestly, "My observations since have only convinced me more firmly that human flight is possible and practicable. It is only a question of knowledge and skill just as in all acrobatic feats." Easy for him to say. Had he plowed the same fields as Professor Langley for the past 13 years, this Wright fellow might not be quite so confident.

The Smithsonian was not simply a source of information for Wilbur Wright. In his methodical way, he had studied the work of the man who would become his rival. Others contended they had made the world's first flight (there being no common understanding of constituted flight), but Wright biographer Fred Howard notes that "Langley's demonstration had (to Wilbur) a convincing character that none of the others possessed." Wilbur years later would reflect generously that "It had a great influence in determining my brother and myself to take up work in this science and without doubt it similarly influenced others."[3]

Wright felt the need, in his letter to the Smithsonian, to drop the names of books he had read on the subject, including a two-volume treatise on applied mathematics by Marey and Jamieson. Whom was the writer hoping to impress? Did he think that Langley himself might read his letter? "I am about to begin a systematic study of the subject in preparation for practical work to which I expect to devote what time I can spare from my regular business," Wright explained. He requested whatever papers might be available in English on the subject. "I am an enthusiast," he wrote, "but not a crank in the sense that I have some pet theories as to the proper construction of a flying machine." Rather, he said, somewhat disingenuously as it turned out, he needed to understand the state of the art and then simply add his contribution to it "to help the future worker who will attain final success."[4]

If Rathbun kept an "urgent reply" pile, he clearly didn't place Wilbur's letter in it. Nearly three weeks after the letter arrived, he sent off to Dayton a number of works he believed would help Wright. Included were Octave Chanute's 1894 work, "*Progress in Flying Machines*," which treated, among other things, the history of flight; Langley's classic *Experiments in Aerodynamics*, written in 1891; and *The Aeronautical Annual*, a digest of articles on aeronautics, edited by James Means of Boston, for the years 1895, 1896, and 1897; as well as four Smithsonian pamphlets, one by Langley and the rest by Edward C. Huffaker, Otto Lilienthal, and Louis-Pierre Mouillard. This formidable collection would be enough to separate the men from the boys. Rathbun invoiced Wright for a dollar, which Wilbur remitted promptly. Neither Rathbun nor Wright, for that matter, could have known the implications of that simple exchange of letters. Years later, Chanute would call it "the most important exchange of correspondence in the history of the Smithsonian."[5]

Twenty-one years later and after Wilbur's death, his brother Orville testified at a deposition in an aeronautical lawsuit that, upon receiving the rather large package from the Smithsonian and dissecting surgically the work of those who had come before them, he and Wilbur zeroed in early on what they believed to be the crucial

Wilbur Wright (right), four years older than brother Orville (left), was 36 at the time he took his historic flight. Quiet and formal, he was a prolific and engaging and humorous writer, illustrated particularly by his long correspondence with Octave Chanute. Orville Wright and his brother wore white shirts, starched collars and ties even during their test flights, although Orville tended to be more outgoing and flamboyant than Wilbur. Both brothers would remain lifelong bachelors. Library of Congress.

common mistake that caused most of them to fail — that they "had attempted to maintain balance merely by the shifting of the weight of their bodies." Hindsight is 20-20, and Orville by then was working assiduously to burnish the Wright legacy. But he recalled a time when, without ever having tested a sophisticated model themselves, he said the brothers perceived the body-shifting concept as wrongheaded, and "we at once set to work to devise more efficient means of maintaining the equilibrium."[6]

Orville Feathers His Nest

Orville, whose brother was not alive in 1920 to contradict him, may have insinuated himself into aeronautics earlier than the record warrants. Wilbur made no mention of Orville in his letter to the Smithsonian. Indeed, as late as September 3, 1900, when Wilbur wrote Bishop Wright to tell him he was bound for Kitty Hawk to test a glider, he said nothing about Orville. The first indication that they were operating as a team seems to be business checks they used under the account name, "the Wright

Brothers," for their aeronautical pursuits, although that may simply have been a carryover from the common account they used for their bicycle shop.

If Rathbun guessed Wright would be impressed by the learned treatises he had sent him in June, he guessed wrong. Wilbur, upon studying and reflecting, regarded them collectively as a hash of speculation and ill-considered opinion and resolved to go his own way. Stripping the problem of flight down to its essentials, he said it depended on three things: wings with enough lift to raise the craft, a system of internal controls, and, of course, a lightweight motor, although this third essential would remain on the back burner until he had refined the first two.[7] Within this framework, Wilbur cherry-picked from the work of others and discarded what didn't suit him. While Lilienthal had prized lift in importance over the other two elements, Langley concentrated on a power plant. Wilbur, by contrast, would always be set apart from the rest by emphasizing control in the three axes of movement: yaw, the ability of a craft's nose to turn left or right; pitch, its movement up or down; and roll, in which one wing moves up or down relative to the other.[8]

Wilbur gleaned his new insights from watching the tips of birds' wings as they fly; how in maneuvering, a bird bends the tip of one wing up while bending the tip of the other wing down, a phenomenon their friend Chanute would call "wing-warping." The principle would become absolutely vital to the way the Wrights approached flight.[9]

Wing-warping introduced an exciting new dimension to flight. A pilot didn't simply glide where the wind took him. Now, by using levers and ropes, he could slant the end of one wing downward, causing it to rise; slant the other one upward, causing it to fall and, in the process, could actually turn the craft. No more a passive participant, the pilot now determined his own fate. This newfound control was akin to the revolution then taking place in ground transportation, in which the invention of the automobile allowed people used to dependence on fixed railroad tracks and schedules to travel instead when and where they wanted.[10]

Within a month after the Smithsonian package arrived at the bishop's home in Dayton, Wilbur (with or without his brother Orville[11]) tested a model successfully, incorporating wing-warping. "It responded promptly to the warping of the surfaces, always lifting the wing that had the larger angle," Wilbur wrote afterwards. He was ready for the next step, testing a man-carrying machine, whose pilot, through the use of cords to warp the wings, could control the plane's side-to-side movement. But adding to the payload required greater lift and, therefore, added wing surface. Relying on tables developed by Otto Lilienthal, Wilbur concluded that in a 16-mile-an-hour wind, a bit more than 150 square feet of wing surface would be enough to support the weight of a man.[12]

But where to test it? Wilbur would need a place with reliable wind velocities of at least 16 miles per hour and, remembering a man would be aboard, a place with a forgiving surface, such as water or sand. Wilbur sent off a letter to the U.S. Weather Bureau and caught up with his bicycle work over the long winter, planning to begin serious testing in the spring of 1900.

Hooked on Aeronautics

Any doubt that Wilbur Wright was hooked on aeronautics in 1899 would be dispelled in reading his first letter to Octave Chanute, the beginning of a long correspondence that both men would find mutually rewarding. Chanute was internationally known by that time, and Wilbur wasn't shy about exploiting the knowledge of anyone from whom he felt he could learn. "For some years I have been afflicted with the belief that flight is possible to man," he wrote the older man. "My disease has increased in severity and I feel that it will soon cost me an increased amount of money if not my life," foreshadowing the wry humor that would punctuate his letters for the rest of his life. Wilbur told Chanute he was trying to order his bicycle business so he could carve out several months later that year to experiment. He wrote the letter nearly a full year after first writing Langley. Yet while Orville's 1920 deposition puts him squarely in the midst of his brother's early experimenting, Wilbur's introductory letter to the man who would become the brothers' mentor mentions Orville not at all.[13]

Wilbur Wright had been haunted by the death three years earlier of Otto Lilienthal, not out of grief for a man he never knew but, rather, puzzled that a man could have completed 2,000 glides successfully, only to be done in by the next one. A typical glide lasted only several seconds, and Wilbur concluded that Lilienthal had spent a total of only about five hours in the air. So while the gross number of glides suggested great experience, Lilienthal at his death was still an inexperienced pilot. As to the German's strategy of shifting his center of gravity to stabilize his glider, Wilbur shook his head. "Birds use more positive and energetic methods of regaining equilibrium than that of shifting the center of gravity."[14] Moreover, even a strong man could have only a limited effect on the craft, and this fact restricted the possible wing span and wing surface.[15]

Wilbur was discovering the basic balancing act between control and stability that would cause engineers to knit their brows in the years ahead. One could fairly easily build a stable structure that could fly point to point reliably but which was almost impossible to steer. Yet building in controls sufficient to move the craft up and down or to the left or right burdened the pilot with manipulating cords and levers continually just to stay on course.[16]

Pitch, roll and yaw all needed to be addressed, but Wilbur believed that roll, the side-to-side movement of the craft, was the key challenge. Here again, birds were his faculty advisers, as they revealed to Wilbur that they adjusted their wing tips up or down to adapt to changing conditions. Relying on materials around him in his Dayton shop, Wilbur used a bicycle inner tube box to illustrate the effect and built a small model.[17]

In recognizing the importance of roll, Wright leapt far ahead of the man who would become his mentor, Octave Chanute. The venerable engineer had proven more than willing to correspond with Wilbur. But Chanute felt Wilbur wasted his time concentrating on roll. What Chanute failed to realize was that roll enabled a craft to turn rather than simply submitting to the will of the wind. Wilbur realized early that if a pilot could position the left wing above the horizontal and the right one below it, the higher wing would rise, causing the craft to bank to the right.[18]

A High-Minded Attitude

Wright initially took a high-minded attitude toward the drive to put a man in the air. "I make no secret," he said, "of my plans for the reason that I believe no financial profit will accrue to the inventor of the first flying machine, and that only those who are willing to give as well as to receive suggestions can hope to link their names with the honor of its discovery."[19] In the letter to Chanute, he then unveiled his plan:

> I shall in a suitable locality erect a light tower of about one hundred fifty feet high. A rope passing over a pulley at the top will serve as a kind of kite string. It will be so counterbalanced that when the rope is drawn out one hundred & fifty feet it will sustain a pull equal to the weight of the operator and apparatus, or nearly so. The wind will blow the machine out from the base of the tower and the weight will be sustained partly by the upward pull of the rope and partly by the lift of the wind....[20]

This method, Wright theorized, would allow the aeroplane to stay in the air "for hours at a time" since the rope was counteracting gravity. This would give him much more experience in responding effectively to changes in wind conditions than would the few seconds of a glider flight. Wilbur made no secret that his day job prevented him from throwing himself headlong into the venture. His window of opportunity lay in the months from September through January, when the bicycle business slowed down.[21]

As much an innovator as Wright would become, he clearly stood on the shoulders of many others in learning how wings harness wind. Indeed, as early as the 18th century, Cayley and others had worked with wind tunnels. Subjecting wing models to varying rates and direction of wind, they learned to predict how a wing would react to changing wind conditions. Formulae developed from these tests could tell Wilbur, at any given wind speed, how much weight his craft could carry and how much surface his wings would require.[22]

Unlike Richard Rathbun, Chanute had wasted no time in responding to Wilbur Wright. He told Wilbur he agreed that profit in such a venture lay far down the line and suggested that Wright consider winter experiments in either San Diego, California, or St. James City, Florida. The drawback of both sites, he said, was the lack of sand dunes and, for that, he steered Wright to coastal Georgia or South Carolina.

From the beginning, the elderly engineer and the bicycle mechanic less than half his age clicked. Wright was taken with Chanute's selflessness in the cause of first flight, and the bishop's son described Chanute's efforts in a return letter as "missionary work."

In an aside that would seem ironic when considered three years hence, Wright offered, "What one man can do himself directly is but little. If however he can stir up ten others to take up the task he has accomplished much."[23]

While still tethered to the bicycle shop during the warm months, by August of 2000, Wilbur was making plans for winter testing. He wrote a Chicago lumber company about the kind of wood to use to build his glider. The Keith Lumber Company advised it should be "sapwood, clear, straight-grained and thorough seasoned." The next month brought the first reference to Orville in the family correspondence, as sister Katharine wrote her father, apparently traveling at the time, that "Will" was about to leave and that Orville would join him "as soon as Will gets the machine ready." Will had settled as a destination on Kitty Hawk, North Carolina, which he described in a letter to his father as "a narrow bar separating the Sound from the Ocean." The U.S. Weather Bureau had told Wilbur that Kitty Hawk had the sixth-highest average wind in America. And the fact that it lacked hills and trees, Wright theorized, "offers a safe place for practice." Ironically, Myrtle Beach, South Carolina, might today herald itself as the birthplace of flight but for the fact that its town fathers failed to reply to the same letter of inquiry that Wilbur sent to Kitty Hawk.[24]

A Distant Outpost

Kitty Hawk was in 1900 best described as a distant outpost, located on a thin, sandy chain of barrier islands, some no wider than a football field, paralleling the swampy mainland. Arriving in North Carolina by train on September 8, Wright wrote that it had taken several days to locate anyone who knew how to get there by boat. Finally, one Israel Perry volunteered to take him there on a flat-bottomed schooner, which Wilbur wrote later needed constant bailing to keep afloat. Wright's first letter home was less than promising: He told the bishop that he was staying with the village postmaster, William J. Tate, in a two-story frame unpainted house with unplaned siding, no plaster on the walls, no carpets and very little furniture, books or pictures. And this house, he observed, was "much above average."[25]

But the Tates made up in hospitality what they lacked in luxury. When Mrs. Tate learned the morning Wilbur arrived that the weary traveler hadn't eaten in 48 hours, she stoked the kitchen fire and laid on a heaping plate of ham and eggs. When she learned that Wilbur needed to assemble his glider and connect white cloth to its wings, she gladly donated her sewing machine to the assembly effort, which he accomplished in the Tates's front yard.[26]

Rather innocently, Wilbur asked the Tates if he could board with them, which set off a brief tense encounter revealing of both guest and hosts. Unknown to Wilbur, the Tates had only two upstairs bedrooms, so accommodating Wilbur would force the four Tate family members into one bedroom. The Tates excused themselves to caucus together. Addie Tate's main concern was whether the remaining bedroom would be up to the standards of Wilbur Wright, who had, after all, arrived at their door after

Kitty Hawk postmaster William Tate and his wife, Addie, sitting, with children Irene, 3, and Pauline, 2, on front porch of post office, which doubled as their family home. Woman standing may be Addie's sister, Maxine Cogswell. Special Collections and Archives, Wright State University Libraries.

his grueling trip, still in a shirt and tie, a nearly unheard-of dress standard in their parts. Overhearing the conversation, Wilbur sought to dispel the family's doubts and announced to the family: "I should not expect you to revolutionize your domestic system to suit me, but I should be considerate enough to subordinate myself to your system so as not to entail any extra hardship on you."

To this simple family's baffled stares, he added an explanatory coda: "I'll be satisfied to live as you live."[27] A friendship had been cemented that would last decades.

Bill Tate, like so many of the folks the Wrights met and got to know at Kitty Hawk, were seafaring men, many with walrus mustaches, skin like leather, and hard eyes that spoke of hardship. Tate once described the locals as follows: "Denied the advantages of good schools, subsisting upon the fruits of a battle with the sea, having little or no transportation, and being out of touch with the outside world, the average man had become immune to the fact that there was anything new."[28]

Only three years after his mother's premature death, when he was still a boy, Tate's father's boat capsized in heavy seas on its way back from the mainland. In spite of lashing himself to the boat, Tate's father froze to death before the boat reached shore. Sent to an orphanage, Bill managed to rise from the ashes, attend college, and become a county commissioner. Wilbur could hardly have found a more respected friend in his new environment. And yet selling Wright's new-fangled idea to the man-on-the-street in Kitty Hawk wouldn't be easy. In Tate's words: "At the time the Wrights arrived in our community, we were set in our ways. We believed in a good God, a bad Devil, and a hot Hell, and more than anything else we believed that the same good God did not intend man should ever fly."[29]

In spite of the desolation of the place, Wilbur would meet many Bankers, the nickname longtime residents of the Outer Banks called themselves. Wright learned from the locals that not only had European explorers discovered the narrow spine of land as early as 1524, but Blackbeard the pirate died in an ocean battle at its southern end in 1718. Some miles to the north, Blackbeard could have located on a map a town labeled as Chickahauk, which over the next century somehow transmogrified into Kitty Hawk. Another notable visitor evidently made less of an impression on the locals than they did on him. Nineteen-year-old Robert Frost, seeking to broaden his New England horizons, fell into a hunting expedition looking for ducks and had a rousing good time in the process: "I went with them, without a gun," Frost recalled. "And I was afraid of my life all the time. They were drinking all the time, you know, and shooting in all directions. Really, really a wild expedition. I didn't think I'd ever see my mother again."[30]

Turning to his forthcoming experiments, Wilbur said his motorless machine was nearly finished, and he would devote his first season's experiments to achieving equilibrium. To do so, he expected his crafts not to lift far off the ground and to always land in the sand. In this way, repairs to the craft could be kept to a minimum and life and limb preserved. Aside from the obvious tragedy inherent in a death such as Lilienthal's, Wilbur also viewed it as a waste to science of accumulated experience. But as much as he shook his head sadly at the Lilienthal experience, Wilbur revered some of the German's basic methods. These and those of Pilcher would supply warm inspiration on cold, blustery Kitty Hawk nights.[31]

Orville Joins the Team

By all accounts, the impetus and execution of the Wrights' early experiments and planning had lain with Wilbur exclusively. But on September 26, 1900, Orville left Dayton to join his brother in the North Carolina dunes, packing tea, coffee, and sugar, since Wilbur had advised him these were in short supply at Kitty Hawk. Waving goodbye to him was his loyal sister Katharine, a bespectacled school teacher, who would do her best to keep the bicycle shop intact during the next few months and who would be the Wrights' chief correspondent during the next three years. Orville had finally cast his lot and would be at his brother's side continuously through their fateful flight three years hence.[32]

Kitty Hawk did not impress Orville, who told his sister on October 14 that "You never saw such poor pitiful-looking creatures as the horses, hogs and cows down here. The only things that thrive and grow fat are the bedbugs, mosquitoes and wood ticks." But through it all, he and Wilbur had taken "the machine" out for several hours a day on three separate days, once in a 36 mile-an-hour wind. The average Kitty Hawker may have greeted the Wrights skeptically, arms folded in front of them, but Postmaster Tate had now become a fast friend, not only housing and feeding the Wrights but speeding through his daily work so he could stroll down to their launch site in his spare hours to witness the trials. After all, diversions were few in Kitty

Katharine Wright, right, younger sister of Orville and Wilbur, laughs with close friend Harriet Silliman. She was the only college graduate among five Wright children. She lived into middle age with Orville and incurred his displeasure when she left him at age 52 to marry for the first time. Library of Congress.

Hawk. One evening, Tate invited the brothers to help carve up a wild goose which one of his neighbors had killed out of season.

After two weeks of straining the already-crowded Tate homestead, Wilbur and Orville moved down the beach and pitched a tent a half-mile away to the south. In setting up camp, the normally-thrifty Wrights had made one fortunate, if lavish, purchase — a German Korona-V camera, which at $85 cost six times more than their first manned glider. How telling that acquisition was. For all of Wilbur's attempts in correspondence to play down his and Orville's role in the race to the sky, this one purchase suggests the brothers knew well that they were deeply involved in a quest to make history. It is no coincidence that the Wrights left for posterity excellent visual documentation of their early exploits.[33]

What clearly impressed Orville the most about the Outer Banks was the omnipresent and all-pervasive sand: "The sand is the greatest thing in Kitty Hawk and soon will be the only thing. The site of our tent was formerly a fertile valley, cultivated by some ancient Kitty Hawker. Now only a few rotten limbs, the topmost branches of trees that then grew in this valley, protrude from the sand."[34]

Whole houses and forests, Orville said, were obviously covered. Wilbur and Orville were not toiling in obscurity; he assured his sister that "We need no introduction in Kitty Hawk" and that they were both addressed respectfully as "Mr. Wright."[35]

The first Wright glider looked anything but graceful. With piggybacked short, wide wings and in the front a stumpy device, called an elevator, to direct the craft up or down, the craft is best described as squat. Wilbur had begun a notebook of formulae, sketches, and notes, memorializing the insights gained from repeated glides. One early observation was that the buzzard, whose wings use the dihedral angle (wings angled upward or downward from its body), seem to maintain equilibrium better than hawks and eagles, which keep their wings level. He peppers the text with other pithy aphorisms: "No bird soars in a calm," he wrote one day. "Birds cannot soar to leeward of a descending slope unless high in the air," on another. In spite of the robust winds they usually encountered, Wilbur wrote that they found even a 20 mile-an-hour wind couldn't lift the machine, forcing them either to alter the wing curvature or increase the wing surface.[36]

The Wrights' letters home reveal the contrast between the brothers' personalities. Wilbur seems, for the most part, serious, contemplative, sometimes almost monastic. Orville lightens the mood, his letters to his sister tending to be long and funny. Not infrequently, he writes about food and, often, the absence of it. "We are living nearly the whole time on reduced rations. Once in a while we get a mess of fish, and if our stuff comes about the same time from Elizabeth City — which stuff consists of canned tomatoes, peaches, condensed milk, flour and bacon & butter — we have a big blowout or, as the Africans would say, 'a big full.'" Orville was taken with the taciturn locals and their wry sense of humor. He wrote Katharine that he asked a fisherman who was the richest man in Kitty Hawk. "Dr. Cogswell," the fisherman replied. "How much does he have?" Orville asked. "Why, his brother owes him fifteen thousand dollars."[37]

The two Northerners may have been in North Carolina but it was, after all, mid–October. In spite of using two blankets each, Orville wrote that we "almost freeze every night." When the wind blew on his head, Orville said, he pulled the blankets up over his head, causing his feet to freeze, at which point he reversed the process. They decided to leave their stove on all night and often spent time awake during heavy blows, anxiously waiting for the tent to be blown away.[38]

"The Perfect Engineer"

Wilbur Wright was a 33-year-old bicycle mechanic and self-trained aeronaut, but his letters to Chanute don't suggest he was at all intimidated by Chanute's lifetime of engineering experience and accomplishment. Chanute, for his part, was clearly impressed by his unschooled correspondent. He called Wilbur "the perfect engineer — isolating a basic problem, defining it in the most precise terms, and identifying the missing bits of information that would enable him to solve it."[39]

Octave Chanute had been helpful to the Wrights and many other aeronauts, and the Wrights clearly wanted to keep him involved as they pursued their experiments. But they felt no pressure to always take his advice. For example, the Wrights' craft had the pilot lying horizontal, face first, a method Chanute had cautioned them would invite injury. But by then, Wilbur had flown enough glides to conclude that position wouldn't be unsafe.[40]

Chanute had advised against the Wrights constructing the lower wing at a dihedral angle, warning that wind gusts could strike the upturned ends of the wings from the sides. He had also cautioned against erecting a 150-foot tower to help keep their craft aloft for long periods. Instead, on October 10, the Wrights built a 30-foot derrick, although they used it for only one test.[41] In a letter to his sister Katharine on October 14, Orville recalled the inauspicious test:

> Well, after erecting a derrick from which to swing our rope with which we fly the machine, we sent it up about 20 feet, at which height we attempt to keep it by the mampulation of the strings to the rudder. The greatest difficulty is in keeping it down. It naturally wants to go higher & higher. When it begins to get too high we give it a pretty strong pull on a ducking string, to which it responds by making a terrific dart for the ground. If nothing is broken we start it up again. This is all practice in the control of the machine.... "After an hour or so of practice in steering, we laid it down on the ground to change some of the adjustments of the ropes, when without a sixteenth of a second's notice, the wind caught under one corner, and quicker than thought, it landed 20 feet away...." We dragged the pieces back to camp and began to consider getting home. The next morning we had "cheered up" some and began to think there was hope of repairing it.[42]

Wilbur had spoken and written to Chanute and to Langley of his commitment to science and the importance of contributing to aeronautics rather than to personal gain. In this spirit, Chanute had asked the Wrights for permission to mention their work in his writings. What a compliment the internationally-known aeronaut had paid two rank amateurs! But in a November 26 letter to Chanute, Wilbur demurred, "...for the present (we) would not wish any publication in detail of the methods of operation or construction of the machine," although he did segregate certain data that Chanute could use. He allowed the machine to be described as of a "double-deck pattern" with 177 square feet of wing surface, including a rudder of 12 square feet, and that the operator lay on the bottom surface, face down and head first. He also revealed the element that set their experiments apart from nearly all the rest — the ability of the pilot, through steering, to alter the inclination of the wings to balance the craft.[43]

In spite of Wilbur's squirrelly reaction, Chanute was thrilled. His protégés seemed to have made great progress. Immediately upon receiving Wilbur's letter, he sent back his praise for "a magnificent showing" but couldn't resist twitting the brothers, adding "provided that you do not plow the ground with your noses."[44] Chanute's inquiries about how the Wrights wanted him to refer to them reveals the team spirit they had built in spite of Wilbur's earlier dominance. Did they want him to call them the

"Wright brothers" or "Wilbur Wright and brother," probably referring to the fact that most of his contacts had been with Wilbur, not with Orville. But Wilbur wrote back, asking they be identified as "Messrs. Wilbur and Orville Wright."[45]

Wilbur knew their machine would eventually have to incorporate a motor, so means of powering the craft were never far from his mind. The good fortune of the Wrights and of aeronauts generally was that experimenters in automotive engineering were by then trying to build an engine that produced the greatest power for the lightest weight, all at a time when the fledgling motorcars weighed only several hundred pounds. Professor Langley long had felt that any such motor needed to build in power over and above what was needed to fly the craft under normal conditions, to deal with unforeseen contingencies. Wilbur Wright, on the other hand, discarded this theory. Overall lightness, he felt, was more important than contingencies, so when he shopped for a motor, he'd be looking for one with only just enough power to be serviceable under normal conditions.[46]

Turning for Home

Katherine Wright, who had gamely agreed to keep the bicycle shop afloat during her brothers' absence, wrote in mid–October that a person hired to run the shop hadn't worked out, and she had dismissed him. The brothers were coming to realize they'd have to leave soon, so they prepared to do some final glides, then depart. On October 19, their last day of testing, they decided to leave Kitty Hawk and trudge four miles south through ankle-deep sand to Kill Devil Hills, whose hills of sand stood much higher than those at Kitty Hawk. Their glides at the new site that day, ranging longer than a football field, proved the most auspicious of their visit. Not coincidentally, they never returned to glide at Kitty Hawk.[47]

In 1900, Wilbur and Orville Wright dipped their toes in the aeronautical waters for the first time, and they found the temperature to their liking. While confining their experiments merely to gliders, they developed in their first season of experimentation a biplane that managed to soar for more than 300 feet. During the winter, they would spend their weekends and evenings applying aerodynamic tables developed by Lilienthal and their American rival, Langley, and in building new wings for a bigger glider.[48]

When Wilbur wrote the Smithsonian in May of 1899, he was mildly intrigued by aeronautics. When he and Orville set off for Kitty Hawk in the fall of 1900, he presented the trip to his father as, in large part, a vacation. By the time the calendar turned to 1901, Wilbur's and Orville's quest would best be described as an obsession.

8

No Simple Matter

"They chewed us clear through our underwear and socks. Lumps began swelling up all over my body like hen's eggs."— Orville Wright in letter to sister Katharine about a plague of mosquitoes

"Huffaker was a mountain man with a first-class education but little sophistication. The Wrights were city boys with modest educations but considerable savvy. The Wrights' do-it-yourself attitude extended to such mundane tasks as preparing meals and doing the dishes, which Huffaker wanted no part of. He was more inclined to give moral lectures to Wilbur and Orville — two men who have gone down in history as models of upright character."— Biographer Stephen Kirk on Wright crew member Edward Huffaker

SOME FORTUNATE RETIREES ENJOY AN autumnal glow in which they revel in passing on the lessons of a career, of a life, to an eager new generation before senescence enfeebles them. So it was with Octave Chanute at the turn of the new century. Now financially independent and the object of respect and admiration from young, talented aeronauts, he was free to aid, in a myriad of ways, those individuals he considered the most promising, without the day-to-day pressure to earn a living. But the role of mentor was a two-edged sword, since not all of his protégés appreciated Chanute's efforts.

One such was Augustus Herring. What a year earlier had been a simple disagreement between them about who deserved credit for developing a flying machine was about to grow into a public, vitriolic spat, which threatened to stain both of them. Since the 1898 trials, Chanute and Herring had had little to do with one another, although they continued to work feverishly on parallel tracks toward their common goal of manned flight. But on Halloween day of 1900, Herring paid a visit to Chanute.

Herring felt he had made progress on his quest to build a lightweight engine and came to engage Chanute, for whom he still had great respect, in his endeavor. By this time, Edward Huffaker and George Spratt had supplanted Herring as Chanute's bright young acolytes, so Chanute no longer cared to link up with the volatile Herring. However, in the course of that conversation, it seems Chanute mentioned a piece he was preparing for the *London Times* supplement of the *Encyclopaedia Britannica* on flying machines. This was a red flag to Herring, who remembered reading four months earlier an article by Chanute in *McClure's Magazine,* in which the editors labeled a photo of the glider developed by Herring and his backer Arnot as a Chanute machine.[1]

Herring managed to hold his tongue but soon thereafter wrote Arnot, then in Venice, who contacted the *Britannica*. He asked its editors to review the Chanute offering, to make sure it gave Herring his due. The object of his subsidies, Arnot said, had "risked his life to attain the first flight known in history." As overblown as Arnot's proclamation seems in retrospect, he had as good a claim as anyone to "first flight" recognition in the days before conventional wisdom defined that term. On becoming aware of Arnot's communication, Chanute wrote directly to Herring on March 24, 1901. Tension crackles from the pages of his surgical rebuttal:

> I have your letter of 17th, and much regret to find that, upon reflecting on the subject, you think that I have not done you sufficient justice in my writings. It is natural for every man to overvalue his own achievements. I do it myself, but the following is my own understanding of the facts:
>
> Ist. While we were still in camp I made and gave you, on cross-section paper, a sketch of the two-surfaced machine with a Pénaud tail to serve in building the 1896 machine. This you assigned as a reason why I should join you in applying for a British patent at the time that I disclaimed any share in the design of the propelling arrangements.[2]

Chanute had only begun. In seven further enumerations, he charged that the carpenter William Avery, not Herring, was responsible for modifying the two-decker's tail successfully; that Herring had no claim to the success of the Chanute machine after having abandoned the project three years earlier; and that he had given Herring more credit in his writings than he ever gave to crew members Avery and Butusov. And in what must have stung Herring the most, he concluded that Herring's total accomplishments didn't rate his mention in the same breath with the world's leading aeronautical pioneers. "Go on and demonstrate some important results," urged Chanute, "and there will be no lack of appreciation in my writing."[3] With that letter, Chanute washed his hands of his ungrateful student. He needed to waste no more time on such types; for two young men in Dayton, Ohio, who showed a good deal more promise than Herring, were eager for his help.

A New Alliance

Five days before Chanute wrote his blistering letter to Herring, he had received one from a more respectful Wilbur Wright. Anticipating the end of the bicycle season in a few months, Wilbur was like a horse, pawing the earth and eager to race. Now planning a second season of experiments at Kitty Hawk, he had written for Chanute's advice in buying an anemometer, with which he could measure wind speed and strength. Chanute, as ever a wealth of information, agreed to lend the Wrights one, created by a Monsieur Richard in Paris.[4]

Halfway preparations were excusable during the Wrights' first few weeks at Kitty Hawk, but if the brothers were to make real progress, they knew they must set up a fully-equipped camp when they returned. Orville and Wilbur would extend their stay to six to eight weeks in July and August this time. What allowed them to take so much time away during the bicycle season was the hiring of cigar-chomping Charlie Taylor, a family friend who agreed to mind the store for $18 per week, a $3 raise from what he had been earning.[5]

The brothers planned to erect a 16 by 25-foot wooden structure, 6.5 feet high, largely to protect the machine being tested from the fierce winds of the Outer Banks, that were both an advantage and a drawback. Each surface of the 75-pound glider would measure 7 by 22 feet, with its forward rudder 4 by 5 feet, bringing the total surface area to approximately 315 feet. They would pitch a peaked sleeping tent just outside the wooden shed, within view of "Big Hill," the 90-foot sand dune from which they planned to fly. The brothers' first-year goal had been to cover the most distance. Their developing sophistication told them now that a truer test was length of time aloft.[6]

After Herring's prickly communication, Chanute must have been warmed to receive an invitation from the Wrights to visit them in Dayton or in camp that fall. It would, Wilbur told his mentor, "give us the greatest pleasure."[7] In a short note a few days later, Wilbur cautioned Chanute about coming before the Fourth of July, since he and his brother would be working 12 to 14 hour days in the bicycle shop. But in mid–June, Wilbur told Chanute that he and Orville had moved up their departure date to July 10, probably because of Charlie Taylor's availability. While adopting Chanute's flood of suggestions selectively and with diplomacy, Wilbur also missed no opportunity to stroke the old man's ego. Upon reading a piece by Chanute in *Cassier's* magazine, Wilbur wrote, "I only regret that so few investigators seem to be actively at work trying to gain the knowledge and skill necessary to manage aeroplanes in the air. There is really no other way of solving the problem. Balloons will not do."[8]

Bishop Wright told his diary on June 26 that his household had been favored with a notable visitor, a "Mr. O. Chanute," who spent several hours with the Wrights. "He is an authority on aerial navigation." With the bishop's wife now deceased, it fell to daughter Katharine Wright to be the hostess for a luncheon she knew meant a great deal to her brothers. Carrie Kaylor Grumbach, who would serve for decades as Orville's housekeeper, assisted in preparing the meal. A half-century later, she recalled that Miss Wright had determined that melons would be served for dessert. Katharine was so eager to please that she told Carrie that if one melon looked better than the other upon cutting, she should serve their guest from the better one. To her horror, the 15-year-old Carrie discovered that one melon was not ripe enough to serve, so she cut up the riper one in five small pieces so everyone could have a taste. Such even-handedness was not what Katharine had intended, with a distinguished guest in attendance, and for some time afterwards, Carrie was in the doghouse.[9]

In a matter of months, Wilbur and Orville Wright had risen to the top of Chanute's list of protégés. He thought their work so promising that he offered to send his two trusted assistants, Edward Huffaker and George Spratt, to the Wrights' camp that summer. Huffaker had designed a glider for Chanute, who was not pleased with its mechanical details. "If you think you can extract instruction from its failure," he told Wilbur, he'd be happy to send them down "to serve under your orders."[10]

Wilbur Wright Joins the Big Leagues

By now, the untutored Wilbur Wright had become a genuine player in the aeronautical game, to the degree that this high-school graduate had two scholarly articles accepted by *The Aeronautical Journal*. The articles were entitled, "Angle of Incidence," a lengthy disquisition on the angle at which an aircraft and the wind actually meet; and "The Horizontal Position During Gliding Flight." Chanute would read the latter with interest, since it was he who had cautioned the Wrights for their own safety not to have the pilot lying prone and facing forward. "The late Herr Lilienthal was convinced that the upright position of the operator constituted the essential factor of safety in flight," Wright wrote, "and Chanute, Pilcher and others have agreed with him."

However, Wilbur continued, what may be gained in safety may be lost in control. A fall, for instance, can be controlled more easily from the prone position than a standing one, he said. "Moreover, the great muscular exertion to which the operator's arms are subjected (while in a standing position) soon brings on a fatigue which seriously depletes his energy."[11]

Wilbur's self-righteous reply to Chanute's offer of the services of two seasoned men was characteristic of his reluctance to be in anyone's debt. "(We) do not feel that we have a right to ask you to bear the expense entailed, unless you feel that you yourself are getting your money's worth," Wilbur wrote Chanute, who promptly assured him concerning Spratt, that "I will be compensated by the pleasure given to him, even if I do not utilize him hereafter."[12]

Chanute's recent bitter experience with Herring may have prompted him to raise the matter of the security of the Wrights' work product. After saying that he considered Huffaker "quite reliable," he felt moved to observe that, "I think he is discreet concerning other people's ideas.... I mention this as you told me you have no patents." Here, Wilbur set Chanute at ease graciously in an Independence Day letter, as they prepared to set off for Kitty Hawk shortly thereafter: "We of course would not wish our ideas and methods appropriated boldly, but if our work suggests ideas to others which they can work out on a different line and reach better results than we do, we will try hard not to feel jealous or that we have been robbed in any way."[13] The anvil of life experience would smash and reshape Wilbur's generous spirit in the years ahead.

The Wrights reached Kitty Hawk on July 10 at the start of a week of torrential rains. Their auspicious test at Kill Devil Hills on the final day of their 1900 stay led them to adopt that hillier terrain, four miles south of Kitty Hawk, as a base camp. It actually consisted of three hills—90 feet, 60 feet, and 30 feet high, their names derived from local folk stories of battles with the devil, whose eventual fate the hills' name suggests. If the village of Kitty Hawk, population 200, seemed a distant outpost, Kill Devil Hills might as well have been the surface of the moon. No settlement to speak of existed there, the place was not part of any incorporated town, and no roads led to the Hill.[14] In a day before four-wheel drive vehicles, the Wrights would have to drag their gear over sand the four miles from Kitty Hawk Landing.

Wilbur later wrote of that experience, "These hills are constantly changing in height and slope, according to the direction and force of the prevailing winds."[15] (Indeed, over the next century, "Big Hill," the largest of the three, would migrate 450 feet to the south while the smallest hill disappeared completely through erosion.)[16]

Huffaker joined the Wrights eight days later. Since Chanute couldn't get away, he had directed his assistant to keep a diary for him, the first entry of which contained Huffaker's description of the Wrights' workshop, about 1,000 feet from the base of the Kill Devil Hill. It had, he said, "a low pitched roof, covered with tar paper. The ends are closed with falling doors, hinged on a level with the eaves, and both can be opened and closed at will. When raised they are supported by props. The building sets north and south, and the south door has a smaller door for entrance when it is closed." In a letter to sister Katharine, Orville called the building "a grand institution with awnings at both ends."[17]

A Mosquito Plague

Chanute's plan was to join them later, and Wilbur wrote his mentor on July 26, with an appeal to bring supplies when he came. He told Chanute they had recently endured "the greatest storm in the history of the place," no small event in a place so exposed to the raw elements. During the howling windstorm, in which sand stung their cheeks like needles, the Wrights' new anemometer read 93 miles an hour. Then came a full week of rain, bringing out more mosquitoes than "the oldest inhabitant (of Kitty Hawk) has ever experienced."[18] Wilbur asked Chanute to bring another tent and eight yards of finely-meshed mosquito netting. Mosquitoes had bred in the marsh-laden dunes since man first stood on Kitty Hawk sand in the 1500s, and now produced what locals called the worst plague on record.

Orville would write that when he and his companions tried to tent netting over their sleeping cots, "the tops of the canopies were covered with mosquitoes until there was hardly standing room for another one; the buzzing was like the buzzing of

Dan Tate, left, and Edward Huffaker help launch the Wright glider from Kill Devil Hill in July, 1901. Wilbur Wright, in shirt and tie, is at the controls. Special Collections and Archives, Wright State University Libraries.

a mighty buzz saw." Spratt had arrived the night before, a week behind Huffaker who, driven to distraction by the mosquitoes, wrote in his journal: "...the mosquitoes are so slender that they slip through the meshes and after making a meal off of us are too large to get out again and so tend to accumulate," he moaned. Even smudge fires, fueled by tree stumps dragged from the surf, failed to dissuade the pests. And if this were not a sufficient distraction, the party lost its drill bit in the sand while drilling for water for a well and thereafter had to drink the water runoff from the shed roof.[19]

The swarming pests hardly improved Huffaker's mercurial temperament. Already well-known in the aeronautical community, he had won the mathematics prize at Emory and Henry College in Tennessee when he graduated in 1888 and had applied himself to flight research since 1891. Fascinated with the flight of soaring birds, he monitored their movements with a stopwatch while jotting his findings in a notebook. If he needed a closer examination, Huffaker would just aim his shotgun and shoot the birds out of the sky.

Edward Huffaker, irascible aeronaut, showed talent and drive in working with Octave Chanute but won the enmity of the Wright brothers in their Kill Devil Hills camp with his self-indulgent ways. National Air and Space Museum, Smithsonian Institution (SI Neg. No. 2002-16642).

Chanute's explicit instructions to Huffaker that he work under the Wrights' direction may have chafed on the proud young aeronaut, who in age was a contemporary of Wilbur's. For he knew that his paper, "On Soaring Flight," was one of the original source materials the Smithsonian sent to the Wrights when they were rank amateurs only two years earlier.[20]

On Chanute's recommendation, no less a figure than Professor Langley hired the young Tennessean for his staff. As Langley watched, Huffaker launched from the roof of the Smithsonian a glider that soared some 600 feet, leading his impressed employer to assign Huffaker to design wings for his aerodrome. Huffaker found Langley's crotchety disposition difficult to take but managed to stay with him long enough to be part of the1896 trials, which soon emerged as one of the signal events in the rapidly advancing field of aeronautics.

Huffaker left the Smithsonian in 1899, and soon thereafter Chanute commissioned him to build a five-winged glider. It was after his Dayton visit in June of 1901 that Chanute stopped off in Chuckey City, Tennessee, to check on Huffaker's project and found it sorely deficient in design. Chanute, who as an engineer would contribute the Pratt truss to airplane design for strength, recognized to his dismay that his protégé's talent as a theoretician far outstripped his skill as a builder. Portions of the glider's frame, for instance, were built of paper tubing. Nevertheless, he decided to put Huffaker and the Wrights together, to see what good might come of it.[21]

A Doomed Relationship

Wright biographer Stephen Kirk sees the Huffaker and Wright relationship doomed from the start:

> Huffaker was a mountain man with a first-class education but little sophistication. The Wrights were city boys with modest educations but considerable savvy. The

Wrights' do-it-yourself attitude extended to such mundane tasks as preparing meals and doing the dishes, which Huffaker wanted no part of. He was more inclined to give moral lectures to Wilbur and Orville — two men who have gone down in history as models of upright character.[22]

Not enough room existed for the Wrights and Huffaker at the same camp, physically or philosophically. With the Wrights' larger 1901 glider completely filling the small shed they had built for it, Huffaker had to store his glider outside, exposed to the extreme Outer Banks elements. A rainstorm ruined the paper tubing that helped hold it together, and the glider was destroyed before ever being tested. The Wrights showed little regret, doubting the frail craft was really airworthy, but felt a bit sad for their friend Chanute, who had financed the venture.[23]

For all his unfortunate personality, Huffaker was bright and intuitive, and lent some valuable insights to the Wrights. As a person, they liked the affable George Spratt a great deal more, though he was a total novice. Spratt graduated from medical school in 1894 only to find himself afflicted with heart disease, in a day when much of a country doctor's day was spent in the grueling work of driving a horse and buggy to make housecalls, often having to dig his wheels out of deep ruts. Spratt clearly was not up to the job, and his brief office practice in Pennsylvania languished when patients turned to doctors willing to make house calls.

Spratt was an assiduous bird-watcher, noticing that sea birds, whose flights are usually point to point, have few tail feathers, while land birds, who must frequently turn, dip, and climb, have extensive tail feathers, which gives them control. His experiments included capturing birds and cutting off their tail feathers to gauge the effect it would have on flight. After the difficult 1901 season, Huffaker would never be invited back to the Wrights' camp; Spratt would be.[24]

Sixteen days after returning to Kitty Hawk, the Wright brothers finished the glider over whose plans they had labored during the cold Ohio winter. Wasting no time, they took it up the next day and made 17 glides on Kill Devil Hills, all with Wilbur at the controls, of what then was the largest glider ever flown. The Wrights' 1901 glider, with more than 300 square feet of surface, dwarfed Pilcher's, at 165 square feet; Lilienthal's, at 151; and Chanute's double-decker, at 134 square feet. They had added to the previous year's model a forward "elevator," whose squarish surface they mounted in front of the main wing. Its job was to stabilize the glider by preventing its nose from dipping toward the ground in flight. An operator still tended to over-control it, they found, so they cut the surface area of the rudder by about half, to 10 square feet, but to no avail.[25]

The elevator wasn't the only thing that didn't work right. Although critical of Lilienthal in some respects, the Wrights had come to rely on his tables, as the work of one who had plowed the field before them. For maximum lift, the German had recommended a wing camber of 1:12, so that at their highest point, the wings would be an inch high for each 12 inches from front to back. Yet when the Wrights used this curvature, the machine gave only one-third of the lift Lilienthal had projected, meaning they'd have much less time in the air than they had hoped. The head resistance turned out to be twice what they had calculated, and unlike the 1900 machine, this year's model didn't tend to speed up in flight. To gain more time in the air, the Wrights arranged for their helpers to tether the craft in flight by holding ropes on the ground, giving the pilot more time to experiment with controls.[26]

The Wrights had internalized one basic fact: an aircraft's center of gravity must align with the center of the wind's pressure. The center of gravity in a Wright plane was fixed, unlike in the Lilienthal crafts, where a pilot could alter it by shifting his weight. Accordingly, the only option open to the Wrights was to alter the center of pressure beneath the wings, largely by manipulating the elevator, or front rudder, to move the craft's nose up or down, as the wind changed. With flat wings at the horizontal, the wind's pressure centered on the leading edge of the wing. Introducing curved wings, however, tended to complicate matters, since the center of pressure tended to race from the leading edge to the rear of the wing. This pressure from the underside on the rear of the wing pushed it upward, causing the craft's nose to dive in high winds. To counteract this effect, Wilbur slid himself toward the rear of the craft, but then he had a hard time reaching the elevator controls[27]

Gliding in Shirt and Tie

Gliding was physically arduous for the team in North Carolina's July heat, as each footstep sank into the sand as they trudged up Kill Devil Hills. Making no concession to the sweltering conditions, Wilbur and Orville dressed each day in white shirt and tie and wore hats, to the amusement of the locals. With Wilbur lying prone on the lower wing, his hands and feet at the controls, his companions to the left and right would grasp the wingtips and sprint forward through sand as fast as they could, then release the craft into the onrushing wind.[28]

Chillingly, the last glide of the first day was eerily like the glide that took the life of their mentor Lilienthal five years earlier. Wilbur was aloft when the nose began to lift, nearly toppling the craft over backwards before the pilot managed to right the plane.[29]

As they ran into one obstacle after another, the Wrights were coming to conclude that, somehow, this year's model, informed by a whole season of testing, was less responsive than the one that came before.[30] Trying to keep their spirits up in the face of continuing and unexpected discouragement, Wilbur catalogued the positive results from the 1901 tests: The machine, larger than the previous year's model, had proved sturdy, the wing-warping concept seemed to work, they had achieved a glide of 19 seconds, and had proved wrong those who said a craft as large as theirs was doomed to disaster. Salve to their wounds, all this, and justifiably so. But it couldn't erase the very real challenge in their path, which Wilbur sketched out in nearly literary terms months later:

Wilbur Wright pilots a glider at Kill Devil Hill in July, 1901. Special Collections and Archives, Wright State University Libraries.

> The balancing of a gliding or flying machine is very simple in theory. It merely consists in causing the center of pressure to coincide with the center of gravity. But in actual practice there seems to be an almost boundless incompatibility of temper which prevents their remaining peaceably together for a single instant, so that the operator, who in this case acts as peacemaker, often suffers injury to himself while attempting to bring them together.[31]

He then summarized the setbacks they had discovered: a lack of lift, control problems with the front rudder, increased resistance, and slow acceleration as the craft glided downhill.[32]

Wilbur Wright's letters and diary entries were typically all business. He made a typical entry on August 5, the day after Chanute had arrived: "...Tests made without operator. Angle of elevation 6 degrees. Velocity 17 mi. per hr. Drift 15 lbs. Weight 100 lbs. Experiments on hill. Angle of incidence 6 degrees. Fall 10 Degrees. Velocity 28 mi. per hr...." Reading through the many hundreds of pages of the Wrights' writings during those fateful years from 1900 to 1903 would be dry stuff indeed without the leavening effect of Orville, particularly when he wrote their sister Katharine, often giving insight into their domestic life as well.

A Role for Orville

On July 28, Orville snatched a moment to give Katharine a window into everyday life at camp, before serenading his companions with his mandolin. Huffaker and

Spratt were washing the white ceramic dishes after a dinner, cooked over a wood fire, which likely included canned tomatoes or asparagus with biscuits, their only fresh produce perhaps an apple. On the morning in question, Orville told his sister that the assemblage hadn't risen until 7:30 A.M. and apparently squeezed in some trials before sitting down for breakfast after 11 A.M. Besides his work on "the machine," he let Katharine know he was responsible for all the cooking. In letters to her, Orville would often intersperse his prose with humorous sketches, illuminating what life was like in camp. One can picture the schoolmarm in her floor-length Victorian skirt, flashing a toothy smile in amusement in her Dayton sitting room as she read her brother's lively missives.[33]

The windswept dunes on which they set up camp had no modern infrastructure, requiring them to use a Webbert pump to drill for water. In wry despair, Orville wrote to Katharine that, "Well (pun), we got no well; the point came loose down in the sand, and we lost it! Oh misery! Most dead for water and none within a mile! Excepting what was coming from the skies." But that was exactly what they'd have to settle for. They carefully positioned a dishpan under the tent roof to catch what they could, though he reported it tasted of soap they had rubbed on the tent canvas to prevent mildewing.[34]

Soon thereafter, mosquitoes arrived "in a mighty cloud," he told Katharine, "almost darkening the sun." Then ensued an experience to which "the agonies of typhoid fever" paled by comparison, he said. "They chewed us clear through our underwear and socks. Lumps began swelling up all over my body like hen's eggs." The assemblage alternated in pulling blankets over them to ward off mosquitoes and sweating through their clothes in the July heat from the blankets themselves.[35]

As the sun sank lower in the western sky, painting patterns in muted gold upon the sands outside their tent, it was time to light the kerosene lamp if the brothers wanted to continue to write. While Orville wrote to Katharine, Wilbur madly scribbled in his journal sketches, charts, and formulae designed to wrest success from disappointment. They knew the clock was ticking toward their approaching departure time and knew they must hastily remodel the craft in hopes of better results. They added and reshaped the spars of the wings to flatten out the curvature of the wings and began launching the craft as a kite, letting it waft up 20 or 30 feet in winds approaching 20 miles an hour, then watching it glide to the ground. At a juncture when time was short, not having to trudge back uphill after each flight to re-launch the kite was a great timesaver. Happily, the shallower camber of the wings paid off, preventing the craft from nosing over.[36]

A Visit from Chanute

Following up on the visit months earlier in which Octave Chanute had charmed the Wright family, the brothers had now invited him to camp. The old man arrived on August 5, watching, suggesting, cajoling, and consoling, as the Wrights sought to

Dr. George Spratt captures life at the Wrights' 1901 camp on the Outer Banks. Shielding themselves from the North Carolina sun are Octave Chanute, Edward Huffaker, and Wilbur and Orville Wright. Special Collections and Archives, Wright State University Libraries.

salvage a troublesome season. Wing-warping, the concept Chanute had named and which the Wrights thought they had mastered in the 1900 season, now seemed to elude them. Wilbur had designed cables to attach to the wingtips for control. When one wing dropped, the pilot would move his hips to the higher side to balance the craft. The plan worked acceptably on the straightaway, but in turning, Wilbur wrote that "things began to fall apart rapidly."[37] Banking into a turn, he had found that the craft would sometimes turn toward the higher wing, rather than away from it.

Huffaker's and Chanute's diaries were more upbeat than that of the Wrights. On August 9: "...A number of excellent glides were made, Mr. Wilbur Wright showing good control of the machine in winds as high as 25 miles an hour. In two instances he made flights curving sharply to the left, still keeping the machine under good control — length of flight in each case 280 ft. Longest flight about 335 ft."

One accident, which marred that hopeful prospect, underscored the basic tradeoff implicit in the Wrights' design. While skimming a foot above the ground on one flight, Wilbur shifted his body to the right after watching the left wing dip but neglected to adjust the fore-and-aft control at the same time and plunged into the ground, breaking some ribs from the rudder and bruising his nose and eye.[38]

Chanute left camp on August 11, stopping on the way to order some groceries to be sent to the Kill Devil Hills camp. Ever-generous, he added to the delivery basket a lantern and some hash, which he said was "to fill up the chinks." Soon afterward, he wrote, suggesting they take "plenty of snapshots." Posterity is grateful to Chanute that they did.[39]

By August 22, some six weeks after arriving in camp, the Wrights departed the marshy Kitty Hawk Landing in Dan Tate's boat, took a launch downstream to Manteo and then the ferry to Elizabeth City, where they boarded a waiting train for Dayton. The brothers were in a funk. The more sophisticated their understanding of flight problems had become, the more hurdles they encountered, like the grapes of Tantalus receding from their grasp. They were so depressed that Wilbur expressed doubt they'd continue with experiments.

The bishop's sons had witnessed the smirks of disbelievers as they told their bicycle shop customers of their new passion. They had seen Kitty Hawkers fold their arms across their chests, witnessing the hubris that led two young men to disregard God's teachings in their quest to fly like birds. Could it be, perhaps, that the extreme disappointment of this summer season was a message from on high? As the steam locomotive snaked through the southern countryside 500 miles north to Dayton on this sultry day, the Wright brothers stared out the open windows of their smoky railcar and brushed flakes of black soot from their clothing.

Thinking back on this moment years later, Wilbur recalled making a prediction to Orville that must have shaken him to his shoes, given the tenacious dedication they had made to their pursuit. Man would eventually fly, he said, but "it would not be within our lifetime." Orville's recollection was even more apocalyptic. Wilbur told him, he said, "Not within a thousand years would man ever fly." It was, beyond a doubt, the Wright brothers' darkest hour.[40]

The Clock Ticks On

"...it is worse than useless to try to get even as much as one-third the ordinary work done if there is the slightest excuse for tightening anchor ropes, watching passing boats, or wasting time on any of the multitudinous small variations from their usual routine of life."— Charles Manly, reflecting on efforts of his crew

Now and again in the life of a nation, an event occurs which sends a shudder through its entire population. It might be a natural tragedy, the outbreak of war, or the death of a beloved figure. The nation seems frozen with preoccupation in the aftermath; then, after a period of mourning, daily life resumes.

On September 6, 1901, some two weeks after the Wrights broke camp at Kitty Hawk, President William McKinley stood in a receiving line at the Pan American Exposition in Buffalo, New York, when 28-year-old Leon F. Czolgosz, an unemployed wire millworker and disciple of the anarchist Emma Goldman, joined the queue. His right hand, wrapped in a large white bandage, concealed a .32 revolver, and as the genial president reached out to greet him, Czolgosz pumped two shots into his body at close range. McKinley died from his wounds eight days later.[1]

Workmen across the country swathed public buildings in black, and newspapers ran screaming headlines usually reserved for war. The Wrights by then were back in Dayton, and their correspondence file contains letters from Wilbur to Octave on September 6, the date of the assassination; Octave to Wilbur on September 8, Wilbur to Octave on September 10, Octave to Wilbur on September 13 and again on September 15 and Wilbur to Octave on September 16, but nowhere is there a mention of the event that had transfixed the nation. The failure to note the loss of not only their president but of a fellow Ohioan underscores the single-mindedness with which the Wrights and their senior adviser pursued their common mission.[2]

A Role for Roosevelt

On the surface, McKinley's assassination would appear to be a setback for the Langley forces, in that it removed the person who had symbolically launched the crusade to make the Smithsonian secretary the father of flight. In reality, however, it brought to the fore one who was even more enthusiastic in Langley's behalf, the fiercely ambitious vice president, Theodore Roosevelt.

Before coming to Washington in 1897, Roosevelt had been the crusading police commissioner of New York City, when he teamed up with the *New York Herald*'s Richard Harding Davis to eradicate crime in Gotham root and branch. They discovered how a politician and a journalist could work together symbiotically to advance both their careers. When he moved to Washington as the new assistant secretary of the Navy, Roosevelt got to know Langley as a member of the fashionable Cosmos Club. Heading the club was Charles D. Walcott, the bureaucrat who would sell McKinley in 1898 on backing Langley's effort and who would become his deputy at the Smithsonian. Langley had a keen eye for up-and-coming talent, so he put Roosevelt on his invitation list for the Potomac River trials of his flying machine.

Roosevelt, in appreciation, decided to bring along a journalist he evidently felt could help Langley. His companion was an Indian-born, 31-year-old British writer of books and magazine articles. He recently had published to great popular acclaim *The Jungle Book,* a volume of children's stories. Rudyard Kipling, who appeared regularly in such magazines as *McClure's,* would write later about the aeronautical experience in his 1937 memoir, *Something of Myself:*

"Through Roosevelt I met Professor Langley of the Smithsonian, an old man who had designed a model aeroplane driven—for petrol not yet arrived—by a miniature flash-boiler engine, a marvel of delicate craftsmanship. It flew on trial over two hundred yards," Kipling remembered, but felt compelled to note that it "drowned itself in the waters of the Potomac, which was the cause of great mirth and humour to the Press of his country." Not to unduly malign the host of this exclusive gathering, Kipling went on to recount Langley's reaction to the trial. He "took it coolly enough, and said to me that, though *he* would never live till then, *I* should see the aeroplane established."[3]

Roosevelt loved to be on the cutting edge and might have used his favorite word of praise, "bully," to describe the trial. In any case, the experience cemented Teddy Roosevelt firmly into Langley's corner. So when Langley, Walcott and the others attending Bell's Wednesday evening salons in 1898 decided that first flight depended upon federal government support, Roosevelt was only too glad to do his part. Not yet 40 and several months away from being tagged with the indelible label "the Rough Rider," Roosevelt's calling card didn't yet have the cachet that opened doors automatically. But what he lacked in stature, he more than made up for in drive.

Langley's newest friend promptly penned a letter of support to his superior, Navy Secretary John Long. He had personally witnessed Professor Langley's "flying machine" soar over the Potomac River, he enthused, and could testify that "The

Crash landings in the Potomac River became commonplace to the Langley team during its many trials. Tugboat in rear and rowboat, left, hold rescuers, poised to retrieve wreckage and pilot. National Air and Space Museum, Smithsonian Institution (SI Neg. No. 2002-16638).

machine has worked." Then, in somewhat tortured prose for so prolific a writer, he made his pitch: " It seems to me worth while for this Government to try whether it will not work on a large enough scale to be of use in the event of war."

Roosevelt asked Long to appoint a board of four officers with scientific backgrounds, to see if these crafts could be built "on a large scale." Long vacillated at first, then agreed to the plan, naming Commander Charles H. Davis the board's chairman. Davis quickly became a Langley disciple and issued a report, calling the potential for air warfare "revolutionary."[4]

Roosevelt easily enlisted General Adolphus Greely, chief of the U.S. Signal Corps, who was a fast friend of Langley and an early advocate of his plan. Thanks to Langley, Walcott, and Roosevelt, the McKinley administration was now seeded in high places with avid aeronautical advocates. But the plan hinged on appropriations, so Roosevelt and Greely together approached Congress. Notably, they corralled Senator John Mitchell of Wisconsin, whose son Billy would become an aeronautical pioneer while an Army general in the 1920s. Greely, a heralded explorer of the Arctic who would win the Congressional Medal of Honor, was already a friend of Mitchell's. So intertwined were their lives that Greely personally took Mitchell's son Billy under his wing when he joined the Army, and Billy returned the favor by writing Greely's biography.[5]

Between Roosevelt's effort in the Navy Department and Greely's in the War Department, they together gathered the votes to build a flying machine. Chairman Davis became sufficiently enthusiastic to predict it would be "revolutionary in questions of strategy and offensive warfare." Soon thereafter, Roosevelt left the planning sessions, beckoned by what he called the "splendid little war" against Spain now raging in Puerto Rico, whose imminence had inspired McKinley to back the Langley project. Roosevelt enlisted his old newspaper friend, Richard Harding Davis, who would ride directly beside Roosevelt on his famous uphill charge at the Battle of Las Guasimas and would impress upon the public mind the dashing image that would become the emblem of his career. *Red Badge of Courage* author Stephen Crane, who had been unlucky enough to incur Roosevelt's disfavor, was banished to the rear of the column and journalistic oblivion.[6]

Roosevelt's departure did nothing to lessen Greely's commitment to the effort. On May 25, he wrote War Secretary Russell A. Alger, stressing "the great importance of such a machine for warfare and the great good that would result to the world at large should the flying machine be made practicable." Mitchell's biographer credits Greely for exerting the muscle to land the $50,000 grant for Langley's experiments.[7]

The Glide Path to the Dream

So as the December, 1898 holidays approached, Samuel Pierpont Langley was already on the glide path to realizing his dream while the brothers Wright hadn't yet discovered theirs. Little did Professor Langley know, as he signed his contract with the War Department's Board of Ordnance and Fortification, that he was already at the acme of his fame and influence. In a letter to the board on December 12, he predicted that the $50,000 earmarked for the project would be more than enough and that he'd need no more than half of it during 1899. Smoothing the feathers of those who feared Langley's aeronautical ventures would detract from his duties as secretary of the Smithsonian, Langley made it clear that "my services are to be given to the Government in such time as may not be occupied by the business of the Institution, and without charge."

Greely had written that Langley had a fear of failure that would have a lasting effect on his reputation. Yet the section of the contract relating to the need for privacy until the venture's successful conclusion was replete with "whens," not "ifs." One may assume this positivism came either from his own need to pump himself up or from a political impulse to lend assurance to his funders.[8]

Langley had been operating a Smithsonian laboratory for his aeronautical experiments for more than a decade. It was an expansive place, with high ceilings, a great wall of windows, and overhead skylights, built to maximize available light in a day before electric lights were in common use. There, workmen with long white butchers' aprons covering their ties and dress shirts labored over Langley's blueprints, altering his models constantly as one or another field test suggested a new strut should be added here or removed there. Langley's chief assistant Charles Manly recalled later that the shops and labs "grew to a size far beyond what seemed even remotely possible at the beginning of the work."[9]

The fact that his glider had stayed aloft for 80 seconds during his 1896 trials told Langley that he had mastered stability. His highest hurdle ahead would be to create a suitable engine for the craft. As Langley and his team grew more frustrated with the lack of progress on this front during the spring and summer of 1899, the Wrights were just cutting their eye teeth on the materials Langley's office had sent to them. Hoping to unlock the secrets of flight as they leafed through the writings of such pioneers as Lilienthal, Chanute and, yes, Langley himself, they became more and more suspicious that the leaders they had hoped to follow were, in fact, chasing each other down the wrong path.

The Mother Lode

Most of what we know about the quotidian struggles in the Langley camp during those trail-blazing years come from a hefty volume the Smithsonian published in 1911, five years after the secretary's death, called the *Langley Memoir on Mechanical Flight*. Nearly a century after its publication, Smithsonian archivists still regard this prodigious work, replete with photographs, charts, sketches, and formulae interspersed throughout its generous narrative, as the mother lode. Langley wrote the first half, covering the years from 1887 through 1896, in the kind of accessible prose laypeople found so enjoyable in his 1897 *McClure's Magazine* piece on the 1896 trials. The second half, written by Charles Manly, covers the years from 1897 through 1903, and is a lifeless, turgid narrative.

That the entire work was published after his mentor's death gave Manly, whom the title page describes as "Assistant in Charge of Experiments," a certain license to burnish his own reputation while preserving the legacy of his employer. In describing the preparation for a field trial that failed, Manly is not shy about observing, in an aside, that he had warned Langley not to do it. In the numerous Potomac River tests that took place during the spring and summer of 1899, each failed test seems to have its own scapegoat, some hapless workman who forgot to do this or did that too clumsily. A typical comment: "…even the best workmen, who have had several years of experience, cannot be relied on in anything which requires that everything be done *exactly right* and not *nearly right*."[10] Remarkably, Manly himself emerges largely without blame.

While the Wrights would show supreme confidence in the ability of people to control an aircraft internally (people named Wilbur and Orville, at least), Manly's skepticism seems to underscore Langley's belief that humans couldn't react quickly enough to changing conditions, so that each craft must build in stable structures that could, themselves, withstand and adapt to those changes.[11]

What Kind of Engine?

Langley had decided already that a steam engine would be too fragile and an electrical motor too heavy for practical use and had settled, by default, on gasoline power. The nascent automobile industry was the one place in America where gasoline motors of any size were being produced, not yet in huge factories but largely in garages and small workshops. However, automobile manufacturers hadn't yet felt the need to produce lightweight engines, and those Langley approached wouldn't guarantee that they could meet his specifications. Accordingly, Manly and company decided to build an aircraft frame that could accommodate a gasoline engine but which could be retooled, if necessary, to accommodate steam. Models 5 and 6, tested in 1896, were steam-powered, and Langley decided to retest them before ordering any changes. But he discovered, in hindsight, that the engines had been so poorly designed that they needed to be rebuilt, which took several months, and delayed retesting until the spring of 1899.[12]

Even though the new aerodrome would be vastly larger than the ones tested in 1896, Langley decided that launching it from atop a houseboat would still be the best plan, so he ordered a larger houseboat built. The dynamic operating during the upcoming trials would differ greatly from what had prevailed in1896, since Congress and the administration were watching closely to make sure Langley didn't fritter away the $50,000 made available to him. For example, one contract required the houseboat manufacturer to complete work by the time the engine was built or pay a heavy penalty. But delays plagued the engine builder, who produced a 100-pound, 12-horsepower motor yet couldn't make it work. This set back progress across the board, since the crew had awaited the engine before finalizing the aerodrome's steel frame, hoping to test it with the motor running. Eager not to waste any more time, Langley decided to build a one-eighth model, which could test the new launching apparatus.[13]

To Langley, the proposed 60-foot by 40-foot houseboat would be multi-purpose and not only would allow the aerodrome to fly off its rooftop but serve as a portable repair shop, a storage barn, and sleeping quarters for the crew. But erecting the boat was no simple task. In its center would be a turntable 48-feet square and weighing 15 tons, resting on a double circular track, which the walls of the boat had to support, to avoid having to put up columns in the middle. Three trussed girders atop the roof supported the superstructure.[14]

Intuitively, increasing the scale of the boat and the aerodrome might call for enlarging the size of all systems proportionally. In 1896, the crew had carried the aerodrome and wings separately up a ladder to the roof. But for an 1899 aerodrome weighing 640 pounds, 350 of that representing steel frame, the team clearly needed more than human power. It decided instead to cut a trap-door in the roof and to haul the craft up through it with ropes and pulleys. To their dismay, they found the craft too large for the trap-door. Back to the drawing boards.

The crew next built a large door at the rear end of the boathouse, through which they could carry the fully-assembled craft and place it on a raft consisting of lattice flooring over pontoons, which they moored at the rear end of the boat. To raise the frame, they used a large mast and boom, built carefully to avoid contact with the craft's wings.[15]

Revisiting Success

A time comes in any long, frustrating course of endeavor when one longs to revisit the scene of earlier success, to recapture the heady feeling of accomplishment. And so it was in the spring of 1899. Determined to make its best use of time while the New York engine builder labored to arrive at the optimal mix of weight and power, Langley's crew took to the Potomac River to retest Aerodromes 5 and 6, whose successful flights three years earlier had bathed the Langley team in public adulation. Not to trivialize the importance of these 1899 tests: They would test much that the team had learned in the intervening three years.

The flights began on June 7 and continued through August 3. The unmanned models would hurtle down the roof track, dip as they left their moorings, catch a gust of wind and rise, circle around, and plunge or float to the river surface, with their structural features alone, not any human input, keeping them aloft. The first trial lasted 57 seconds, about half the duration of the longest 1896 flight. Meanwhile, uninformed by Langley's experiments hundreds of miles away, the brothers Wright were separately coming to the conclusion that aimless soaring and gliding were meaningless without building controls to harness the wind, controls that humans could manipulate.

Manly's frustrations surface in the Langley *Memoirs* not only about human error but about workmen's failure to follow directions: "…the workmen get certain ideas of their own as to how the work should be conducted, and it is almost impossible in assembling the aerodrome to prevent them from making adjustments which are quite different from those which they have been directed to make…"[16]

Langley had purposely chosen a site 40 miles down the Potomac in 1896 to avoid the media and rubber-necking spectators. It had worked well enough then to incline him toward the site again in 1899. Its drawback was being away from their extensive lab equipment and, no less, the challenge of keeping up worker morale so far from home. Langley finally decreed that his team would take a train back to Washington on Saturday afternoons, returning to the trial site on Monday morning. Manly, however, plainly had little regard and no little contempt for the men he supervised, observing that "…it is worse than useless to try to get even as much as one-third the ordinary work done if there is the slightest excuse for tightening anchor ropes, watching passing boats, or wasting time on any of the multitudinous small variations from their usual routine of life."[17]

A July 29 test of Aerodrome No. 5 illustrates the seemingly haphazard course of flight during these summer trials. After 90 seconds required to raise 120 pounds of steam pressure, the craft took off into a three-mile-an-hour southeast wind:

> The launching apparatus, with the disappearing track, worked perfectly, and the aerodrome started straight ahead, dropping slightly at first, but immediately regaining its level and going ahead, gradually raising its bow to an angle of about 8 or 10 degrees, and slightly slacking up its speed by the time it had gone about 300 feet. It then made a circle to the left a radius of about 75 feet and started back. As soon as it had made this turn it regained its level and directly regained its speed. But as soon as it had speeded up again it elevated its bow, which slackened its speed as before. It then again righted itself, still going in the same direction and crossing the sand-bar on the point of the island at a height of about 40 feet.[18]

The narrative continues an equal length before describing the craft touching down, after a flight of about 2,500 feet, making one wonder how the writer could take contemporaneous notes of such detail without missing a beat.[19] Manly considered the trials to have gone well and felt the results could be used to balance the large aerodrome and to build an apparatus from which to launch it.

The crew now busily installed the superstructure, turntable and all, on the houseboat roof, to accommodate the launching track. Yet another winter would be on its way before work began on the launching track and car. In a comedy of interdependencies, the launching car couldn't be completed until the engine was built. During the winter, the only thing launched was a new century. Work proceeded on the full-sized aerodrome frame, which would await delivery of the rotary cylinder engine, so the two could be tested together.[20]

A Sputtering Engine

Upon signing the historic contract with the Board of Ordnance, Langley had retained Stephen M. Balzer, a New York auto builder, to build a 12-horsepower engine along with supports for the gears, shafts, and propellers. But the engine's progress moved in fits and starts, as Belzer felt the need to make a series of changes throughout the next year and a half. The contract delivery date of February, 1899, now stretched into the next century, with no firm date in sight. The problem was that the rotary engine simply didn't generate enough power. In Langley's *Memoirs*, Manly writes of Balzer's travails not without empathy for the engine builder's job but with evident frustration, as the clock ticked away and official Washington drummed its collective knuckles on the tabletop, waiting for the finished product.[21]

By May of 1900, the team knew it that if it couldn't fix the engine's flaws immediately, it would have to locate a new builder or revert to steam power. In an aside, Manly observed, "…even the contemplation of this was appalling."[22]

On May 6, Manly took the bit in his teeth. Traveling to New York to visit Balzer's shop, he immediately started testing to learn the effects of changes Balzer had made. After several weeks of trial and error, the two could develop only four horsepower continuously, a mere third of the required power. With great regret, Manly decided to abandon the engine. Now he and Langley were back to square one.

They knew European builders of internal combustion engines had far outpaced their American counterparts, largely because they had started earlier, so Langley and Manly took a steamship to Europe in June to search for an engine builder. They spent six "very discouraging" weeks knocking on doors and hearing again and again what they most feared: that building a 12-horsepower engine weighing less than 100 pounds was simply impossible. Could it be that the premise underlying powered flight was itself flawed?[23]

Manly didn't think so. While in Europe, an array of engines he saw exhibited at the Paris Exposition convinced him that building a lightweight engine was indeed possible. Although never having built such an engine himself, Manly volunteered to take on the project for the professor. The notion behind Langley's aerodrome project had been to bring together the best and the brightest, with unlimited money, to achieve an historic breakthrough. Now, the only potential creator of what Langley considered the most important element of his aerodrome was a rank amateur. But what other choice did he have?

Ten days in August on board an America-bound ship gave Manly time to think through the challenge he faced. On reaching the New York docks, Manly dropped in on Balzer and gave him the bad news. The hapless engineer had not only exhausted the contract price to build an engine for the manned craft and a smaller one for the one-quarter model but had, in Manly's words, "practically bankrupted himself" in spending $8,000 to $10,000 from his own pocket on the ill-fated project. The latter sums the Smithsonian had advanced to Balzer as loans, so he remained liable for them. In sympathy for Balzer's plight, Manly agreed to forgive the loans, in return for taking various parts of the two engines, feeling they might be of some use to him.[24]

Remarkably, in spite of his lack of experience, Manly almost immediately began to hit pay dirt. By September 18, he had managed to crank out 18.5 horsepower with the engine turning 715 rpms. The engine in operation was a strange sight, its shuddering metal hulk swathed in wet cloths, since Manly hadn't gotten around to building a waterjacket for it.[25]

As promising as was Manly's initial triumph, many months of work lay ahead. Simply building an engine to Langley's specifications would have been relatively easy, but Manly's task was far greater than that. The unpowered aerodrome would require extensive modifications to allow it to accommodate a heavy, shuddering engine. The frame had to be sturdy enough to accept extra weight. Supports had to be able to withstand constant engine vibration. Then the modifications themselves had to be tested. Manly couldn't do the job overnight, yet Washington bureaucrats kept glancing at the calendar as month yielded to month and 1901 yielded to 1902. Professor Langley had not forgotten his promise that, given $50,000, he would have a man in the air in two to three years. Tension in the Langley camp grew as the four-year mark approached.

10

A New Lease on Life

"If I take this piece of paper, and after placing it parallel with the ground, quickly let it fall, it will not settle steadily down as a staid, sensible piece of paper ought to do, but it insists on contravening every recognized rule of decorum, turning over and darting hither and thither in the most erratic manner, much after the style of an untrained horse. Yet this is the style of steed that men must learn to manage before flying can become an everyday sport." — Wilbur Wright, in speech to the Western Society of Engineers, September 18, 1901

WILBUR AND ORVILLE RETURNED TO Dayton in late August of 1901, announced sadly to their family that their obsession of the past 28 months had been a fool's errand, and resumed their bicycle business with renewed vigor, giving up forever their dream of first flight.

That might well have been the script for the remainder of their lives had it not been for one wise old owl, who charged himself with keeping the dream alive. Waiting for the brothers when they walked into the Hawthorn Street homestead, with its welcoming, wraparound porch, was a note from Octave Chanute, designed to bolster their spirits. "I think you have performed quite an achievement," he said, "in sailing with surfaces wider than any which I dared to use." Chanute had once again proved he would give whatever it took to achieve first flight, whether it be technical advice, contacts, financial subsidies, or a well-timed word of encouragement.[1]

Only days later, Chanute wrote again, this time to invite Wilbur to address the Western Society of Engineers in Chicago on September 18 on new gliding experiments. It was a talk that Chanute, as the society's president, was well-positioned to arrange. The taciturn Wilbur was inclined to turn down the invitation, until ever-solicitous sister Katharine "nagged him into going." She wrote her father that "He will get acquainted with some scientific men and it may do him a lot of good."[2] Reluctantly,

Wilbur gave in but cautioned Chanute, "...not to make my address a prominent feature of the programme as you will understand that I make no pretense of being a public speaker."[3]

Wilbur, lost in thought much of the time, gave little attention to his appearance, so Katharine and Orville, the fashion plate of the family, took him in hand. When he arrived in Chicago, bound for Chanute's home, Wilbur wore Orville's overcoat even though he was several inches taller than his brother. Packed in his suitcase were Orville's collars, cuffs, and cuff links, which Wilbur would wear to the big event.[4]

Wilbur on the Stump

The Wrights had declined earlier invitations to speak and publish. Sensitive that their failure to obtain patents on their inventions left them vulnerable to competitors, they were reluctant to expose their trade secrets to the world. Yet, Wilbur's speech to the engineers was quite detailed and candid. His protestations to the contrary, he demonstrated an accessible speaking style, laced with the kind of nuance and humor that had made him good company at Kitty Hawk:

> If I take this piece of paper, and after placing it parallel with the ground, quickly let it fall, it will not settle steadily down as a staid, sensible piece of paper ought to do, but it insists on contravening every recognized rule of decorum, turning over and darting hither and thither in the most erratic manner, much after the style of an untrained horse. Yet this is the style of steed that men must learn to manage before flying can become an everyday sport.[5]

In his talk, illustrated with lantern slides of glides by the Wrights and others, Wilbur offered insight into how important photography was to an aeronautical experimenter's work, not merely to record his accomplishments, but to help analyze his ongoing performance:

> In looking at this picture you will readily understand that the excitement of gliding experiments does not entirely cease with the breaking up of camp. In the photographic darkroom at home we pass moments of as thrilling interest as any in the field, when the image begins to appear on the plate and it is yet an open question whether we have a picture of a flying machine, or merely a patch of open sky.[6]

Just as Graham Bell had been forced to coax Samuel Pierpont Langley into publicizing his accomplishments, so too Octave Chanute promoted the reluctant Wright brothers by reprinting 300 copies of Wilbur's speech, mailing them off to specialists in the aeronautical community and encouraging their reprinting in such prestigious magazines as *Scientific American*.[7]

The Blanket Thief

Before launching into the serious business of correcting the problems that had plagued the team during its summer encampment, Wilbur took a minute to touch base with Dr. George Spratt, who had made up in affability what he may have lacked in technical expertise, getting off a slap at Edward Huffaker in the process, and once again, demonstrating his finely-honed sense of humor:

> When we came to pack up (after the summer encampment), I made the unpleasant discovery that one of my blankets that had lived with me for years on terms of closest intimacy, even sharing my bed, had abandoned me for another, and had even departed without a word of warning or farewell. Although I regretted to part with it, yet I felt happy in the thought that its morals were safe, as it was in the company of one who made "character building" rather than hard labor the great aim in life![8]

From the Wrights' perspective, the best thing about Huffaker was that he was now gone for good. His preachings about morality, while not carrying his own weight in camp duties, had driven the brothers to distraction. Wilbur had already released some of his frustrations about Huffaker in a letter to Chanute, in which he acknowledged his "good judgment in most things" but called him shiftless and bemoaned his habit of "laying stop watches and anemometers uncovered upon the drifting sand, and using a light camera as a stool."[9]

The brothers were keenly aware that they must keep perspective amid the demands of an enveloping avocation that would destroy their livelihood if they let it. Chanute was convinced the Wrights were onto something, yet the goal he shared with them would take longer to attain if they could only work on aeronautics in their spare time. So he relentlessly sought ways to let the brothers devote full time to their efforts. When Chanute offered to subsidize their efforts in late 1901, Wilbur politely demurred, suggesting the temptation of money might cause him and Orville to neglect their bicycle shop. He never seemed to think it possible to make a living in the aeronautical world and accepted that, as likely as not, the brothers' experiments would fail, and they would have to return to selling and repairing bicycles full time. They had better maintain a livelihood, the level-headed older brother concluded, in case fate dashed their dreams.[10]

Not only had Chanute acquired means from his lucrative engineering practice and railroad tie business, but he had wealthy contacts as well, among them steel magnate Andrew Carnegie. As Christmas approached, Chanute wrote Wilbur, trying to entice him with the possibility of a $10,000 a year stipend from his friend. Even such a sum, at the time when a working man earned a dollar a day, couldn't turn Wilbur's head. "I think it possible that Andrew is too hardheaded a Scotchman," he replied, "to become interested in such a visionary pursuit as flying."[11]

Left unsaid in Wilbur's communications to Octave was the obvious fact that accepting financial aid from benefactors would put the brothers in debt to them, something their straight-laced upbringing under the bishop's roof had taught them to avoid. How much better to keep expenses under tight control and own 100 per cent of whatever benefits would accrue to them? Wilbur's meticulous notebooks showed the brothers' entire expenses to date, including the two encampments at Kitty Hawk, had remarkably totaled less than $300.[12]

Striking out on his proposal of direct subsidies, Chanute next tried to interest the brothers in entering a $100,000 aerial competition at the 1904 St. Louis World's Fair.[13] Wilbur again was unimpressed. Only one prize interested him, and that was first flight. Besides, he asked Chanute, what if in laying out his secrets in the winning entry, someone stole them and became the first to fly? Who would have won then? Wilbur's reply to Chanute reveals a mind trained to think surgically: "Mathematically it would be foolish to spend two or three thousand dollars competing for a hundred thousand dollar prize if the chance of winning be only *one* in a hundred."[14] One observation to Chanute suggests that Wilbur may have been wary of the Wrights being lumped in with crackpots who would inevitably apply:

> The newspapers are full of accounts of flying machines which have been building in cellars, garrets, stables and other secret places, each one of which will undoubtedly carry off the hundred thousand dollars at St. Louis. They all have the problem "completely solved," but usually there is some insignificant detail yet to be decided, such as whether to use steam, electricity or a water motor to drive it. Mule power might give greater ascensional force if properly applied, but I fear would be too dangerous unless the mule wore pneumatic shoes. Some of these reports would disgust one, if they were not so irresistibly ludicrous.[15]

A Lavish Present

In late May, in a letter that took the brothers' breath away, Chanute told them he was having built multiple-wing and double-deck machines and giving them to the Wrights as presents. In Wilbur's verbose manner, he wrote, "…it surpassed our capacity for belief that you were intending to exercise the virtue of benevolence on so magnificent a scale as your words seemed to imply."[16]

Chanute was so irrepressibly generous and enthusiastic in his escalating efforts in their behalf that Wilbur had to bite his tongue when the elder man insisted on giving the Wrights' work unwanted publicity. For all Chanute's good intentions, he seemed insufficiently mindful of the fact that premature disclosure of trade secrets, not protected by patents, could have wiped out everything the Wrights had worked for. In fairness to Chanute, he had urged the Wrights repeatedly to apply for patents, but between their bicycle business and their passion for flight, they just hadn't gotten around to it.

One should not conclude from Wilbur's preoccupation with flight that he was a narrow-gauge thinker. In a letter to Chanute, he wondered whether men of wealth could be harnessed to solve "the flying problem" the same way such explorers as Admiral Robert Edwin Peary found backers to enable them to search for the North

Pole.[17] Wilbur spun out his solution: to create the Croesus Fund for the Promotion of Aeronautical Science, which would fund promising aeronautical experiments, all of which would be labeled Croesus Fund projects. That way, he said, benefactors could benefit from their link to successful outcomes without owning them. Alternatively, he suggested, such a fund could award a large cash prize, such as that recently established by the Swede Alfred Nobel, to spend a fortune amassed from his invention of dynamite.[18]

A preoccupied Chanute dashed off a quick note, promising to take Wilbur's thought-provoking letter with him on a trip to the West Coast. Entitled by his age and accomplishment to live the good life, the old man embarked in January for a business and pleasure trip to Pasadena, California, where he would remain for several months.[19]

Unlocking the Secret

While reconnecting with their thriving bicycle business, Orville and Wilbur now spent every spare moment trying to tease out from the mountains of data they had gathered the reasons why their carefully planned glider flights the past summer had failed so dismally. In his meticulous manner, Wilbur analyzed each flight in great detail and plotted the results, recording such factors as wind resistance, speed of flight, lift, and drift.[20]

He and Chanute wrote back and forth constantly, as both men scoured the computations of other experimenters, notably Lilienthal, whose tables showed clearly that the Wrights' craft should have generated more lift than it did at Kill Devil Hills. Reluctant to criticize the findings of such an icon as Lilienthal, Wilbur first eliminated any possibility of error in the calculations he had made. Finding nothing, the inescapable conclusion was that the problem lay with Lilienthal's tables.

It might surprise some that, to test this conclusion, Wilbur turned to the bicycle. Yet time and again, it seemed the brothers' years as bicycle mechanics paid off handsomely in helping them understand motion on an entirely different plane. Most notably, they would borrow the bicycle chain drive to link the propellers and motor when they got around to motorizing their biplane. As to the Lilienthal problem, they mounted a bicycle tire rim perpendicular to the front wheel of a bicycle and attached a tiny wing and flat plate to it. The startling conclusion, after pedaling the strange contraption down a Dayton street, as is further described in the notes, was that the fabled Lilienthal had greatly overestimated the wing's lift.[21]

The ingenious bicycle rim experiment confirmed their hypothesis, but the Wrights needed to replicate it under controlled conditions. They built a wind tunnel six feet long and 16 inches square with a two-bladed fan at one end, sending a stream of air through the wooden box at a constant 27 miles an hour, to see if it would yield the same results as with the bicycle wheel. To use the wind tunnel to the fullest, they tested not only the kind of wing surface Lilienthal had used but also a variety of shapes and configurations, to see which lifting surface would yield the best results. Again borrowing from their bicycle shop, they connected a metal balance, made from bicycle spokes and hacksaw blades, to the floor of the tunnel in such a way that it would move with the wind. A glass window cut into the top of the tunnel allowed the brothers to monitor movement of the balance as it measured lift against drag.[22]

Crossing the Threshold

Somewhere in the midst of their painstaking experiments in the winter of 1902, Orville and Wilbur came to realize that they had crossed a threshold. The assumptions they would make from now on as to such factors as lift and drag would no longer be those of experts who had gone before, such heralded figures as Lilienthal and Langley. They were now among the authorities, and the data on which they — and those who came after them — would base future flights would be their own.[23]

Through the window into their wind tunnel, the Wrights could watch a controlled wind strike the leading edge of a wing and study its effects. Professor Langley had long held that a sharp-edged wing would offer less resistance than a rounded edge, but upon testing, the Wrights debunked that theory. In *Experiments in Aerodynamics,* his seminal 1891 work used as a launching point for legions of aeronauts, Langley described his findings. He talked of hitching a square flat plate to a 30-foot-long whirling arm, which he spun around at high speed, adjusting the plate so it would hit the wind at angles ranging from 0 to 45 degrees. Langley then plotted a curve of the results, which showed a smooth progression until it reached an irregular break at 30 degrees.

Remarkably, the Wrights noted the same break in their testing and raced back to Langley's book to see how he explained it. The data table Langley used to plot a graph carried an asterisk at 30 degrees, leading to a footnote. One can see Wilbur's finger on the page, anticipating Langley's answer to that mystery. But the footnote read "Omit," allowing Langley's curve to continue smoothly. The secretary's apparent inclination to disregard inconvenient facts dropped Langley greatly in the Wrights' esteem.[24]

Strength Through Adversity

While the Wrights greeted the spring of 1902, made stronger by adversity, the Langley team had encountered delay after delay, as crafting an engine for the aerodrome proved more difficult than anyone had anticipated. But at last, the pieces had begun to fit together, and by June, the engine was ready to test. The time had come to convert theory into practice.

In operation, once the engine had reached full speed, the plan was for the launching car to be released. The thrust of the propellers, combined with the pull of coiled launching springs, would shoot the car forward on its track. Just prior to reaching the track's forward end, a cam would cause a clutch to open and release the car. The team made sure to keep the weight of the launch car as low as possible, so it could reach soaring speed within the length of the short track available atop the house-boat. To do this required removing the car's entire floor, making it a simple box frame with cross-braces.[25] Rather than strapping the aviator into his own car, Manly decided to give him maximum freedom of movement, allowing him to stand or sit on a wooden seat, cushioned by sponge blocks, in a three-foot by five-foot interior space. The wisdom of that decision would become evident as the race to the sky played out. Finally, they outfitted the pilot's crude cockpit with a tachometer, to let him monitor engine rpms.[26]

Workmen now installed in the aerodrome the engine only Manly had been able to build and hitched it up to the propellers and the aerodrome frame. On the shop floor the crew installed a short track and mounted the launching car atop it. The team had feared that the combined power of the springs and the engine might cause the engine to break loose from the car during launch. Those fears dissipated as they fired up the new engine and watched its propellers develop an average thrust of 450 pounds, as all connections held fast. The vibrations, Manly said, caused a "rather unpleasant" effect on the joints of the aviator's knees after several minutes. But, in operation, the frame wouldn't rest on a shop floor but would be suspended in the air. So the crew hung it by springs from the shop ceiling, and the harsh tremor gave way to "a slight general and rapid tremor of the whole frame," which was entirely tolerable. Manly likened the two types of vibration to those experienced in a motor vehicle supported on metal tires versus pneumatic tires.[27]

No one factor separated the Langley and Wright teams in philosophy more starkly than the extent to which they believed in the capacity of the pilot. The ability of the pilot to control all movements of his machine was at the heart of the Wrights' experiments. Langley's team saw human error as likely to thwart success and even court danger or death. Relying on the aviator to maintain the machine's equilibrium was risky, they felt, because human reaction time following an unforeseen problem would be too slow to correct it in time. They looked for a way to maintain equilibrium automatically, so the aviator could concentrate on just staying on course.

Given the vagaries of wind patterns, such adjustments would have to be made constantly. Controls to do just that had been built into the Langley team's one-quarter scale models used in the 1896 tests. Its initial plan for the manned machine was to teach the aviator how to work the controls himself. But now, Manly decided simply to keep the same controls in the larger craft that had worked so well in the smaller. All they gave the pilot was the ability to override a control manually, if he felt it necessary.[28]

The Lure of Government Money

Government money, which would become pervasive during the century that lay ahead, was rare in the days before 1913, when Congress introduced the federal income tax. So the fact that Langley had corralled $50,000 raised eyebrows throughout the aeronautical community. Since the secretary of the Smithsonian was a government official, those in need of funding sent a continual flood of requests to his office, seeking government backing to carry on their experiments. This put Langley in the difficult position of being, at once, a leading contender in the race to the sky and the perceived gatekeeper of funding for those who sought the same goal. It was an unfair burden, since Langley had no pot of money for outsiders, although he had managed to tap internal Smithsonian resources for a little here and a little there, as his Board of Ordnance money ran short.

The Wrights, by 1902, had emerged as Langley's chief challenger, but since they turned away any offer of outside funding, they fortunately weren't a problem. Had they chosen to seek a grant from Langley to continue their quest, they would have required the secretary to turn down his chief competitor in attaining a goal that would inevitably bring the winner fame and fortune.

One of those needing money to continue his research was the Wrights' friend, Dr. George Spratt, who had built a device to measure how wind and other forces affect a plane's wing. Octave Chanute, ever seeking to support his friends and bring talented people together, agreed to write Langley in Spratt's behalf, to seek a small grant. The application may have middled Langley, since it was well known that Spratt had been a member of his chief competitor's team. However, he turned it down anyway. Trying to soothe Spratt's feelings, Wilbur suggested to him that the turndown might reflect conflict Langley had experienced with Chanute. Spratt, who had proven himself a boon companion in 1901, agreed to rejoin the Wrights at Kitty Hawk for his second season in 1902.[29]

Putting It All Together

As spring drew on, the Wrights distilled the insights accumulated from the writings of aeronautical pioneers and from their wind tunnel experiments to build a new glider to test in the summer and fall. The purpose of the wind tunnel had been to determine the most efficient wing design, so it wasn't surprising that the new wings would look markedly different from those used in 1900 and 1901. Wing span had lengthened by 10 feet and width had shortened by two feet, giving the new wings a sleeker look. The camber, or curve, was less pronounced, so the wing appeared flatter. And tellingly, the wing surface area increased to 305 square feet.

To help fix control problems the brothers had encountered in 1901, the Wrights installed a double-surface vertical rudder at the rear of the craft, in a fixed position. The crew would be similar to that of the previous year, since Chanute had leaned on the Wrights to take Huffaker back, in spite of his distasteful disposition. Remarkably, the old man's manner was so ingratiating, Wilbur would have been hard put to say no, but he put the burden back on Chanute to keep his protégé in line. And for the first time this year, their older brother Lorin would come to visit and begin to carve out a niche for himself in the race to the sky.[30]

The Wrights' expanded kitchen in their 1902 camp included a variety of canned goods, including tomatoes, asparagus, peaches, and Chase and Sanborn coffee. Orville did most of the cooking. Special Collections and Archives, Wright State University Libraries.

As the summer flew by, Orville and Wilbur appropriated the Wright family home as their workshop. As Katharine wrote her traveling father, "Will spins the (sewing) machine around by the hour while Orv squats around marking the places to sew. There is no place in the house to live, but I'll be lonesome enough by this time next week and wish that I could have some of the racket around."[31]

When the brothers arrived back at Kill Devil Hills in late August, sand had drifted so high as to cover their shed. Orville and Wilbur shoveled for hours to uncover their camp and spent their first 11 days laying stronger foundation posts, digging a deeper well, and enlarging their facilities. Their plans to create a more substantial camp matched the high hopes they had for their test flights in 1902. They added a kitchen and a living room, if a stark, clapboard-floored space with a woodstove in the middle can be called a living room. They made a loft of the roof peak, constructing six beds atop the rafters.[32] By early September, the brothers were ready to assemble the new machine, eager to subject their lab findings to a field test. On September 21, Wilbur wrote Chanute that they had already made 50 glides with the new machine. Wilbur had done most of the piloting the year before, but Orville was now learning to fly and would be at the controls of many of this year's glides.

By early October, the brothers were getting off an average of 25 glides a day,

Augustus Herring piloting the Chanute/Herring oscillating wing glider on October 13, 1902, at Kill Devil Hills. Assisting are probably Wilbur Wright, left, and Dan Tate. Special Collections and Archives, Wright State University Libraries.

weather permitting, flying distances up to 500 feet or more. At night, in front of the stove, with Orville strumming his mandolin in the firelight, they shared the satisfaction of having puzzled out a complicated formula, as they had done during the winter, and crafted a solution. The one drawback seemed to be their decision to keep the rudder in a fixed position, which Orville believed helped cause a crash when he was at the controls. They decided to hinge the rudder, letting the pilot adjust its surface when the low wing encountered increased drag.[33]

At Chanute's prompting, the Wrights had agreed to test other craft during their fall season. One was a multi-wing glider designed by Augustus Herring, who would accompany Chanute to camp in October. That Chanute could even endure his company in the face of Herring's proven disloyalty and mendacity is remarkable in itself. Yet the old man's dedication to the cause of first flight made him pursue any avenue that had a chance of leading there. Chanute also persuaded the Wrights to test an "oscillating wing machine" designed by a Californian experimenter named Charles Lamson. The Wrights plainly considered this an imposition on their already-scarce time, but it was becoming increasingly difficult to turn down their generous benefactor. The crew gave up on the poorly-designed Lamson craft in only two days. And the test of Herring's machine ended dismally, his longest flight falling short of 50 feet.

Huffaker could be forgiven for being in foul temper. When the Wrights were raw greenhorns, they had studied his work. But the failure of his own machine in tests frustrated the irascible aeronaut, as it became more and more apparent that time and the Wrights had passed him.[34]

The breakup of camp in mid–October was in stark contrast to that of the year before, when Wilbur felt moved to say that a millennium would pass before man could fly. The brothers realized now that their 1901 mistakes resulted largely from relying on the work of others. Together, they had puzzled out those errors, corrected them, reconfigured their craft, and had flown it successfully. Pledging from the beginning not even to consider a motorized craft until they had mastered the problems of control, the Wrights were now confident enough to take the next big step.

The Invitation

"Mr. Chanute has interested me in your experiments. Is there time to see them? Kindly write me."—Samuel P. Langley to Wilbur and Orville Wright, 1902

"It is characteristic of all our family to be able to see the weak points of anything, but this is not always a desirable quality as it makes us too conservative for successful business men, and limits our friendships to a very limited circle."—Wilbur Wright to Dr. George Spratt, 1902

IF TED WILLIAMS HAD INVITED a sandlot team to his home to give him tips on hitting, the baseball world would have been aghast. An unexpected invitation delivered to Wilbur and Orville Wright on an autumn day in 1902 was no less stunning. Samuel Pierpont Langley, arguably America's greatest aeronaut and the man President McKinley had chosen to usher America into a new age, was inviting two small-city bicycle mechanics to Washington, to show him how people could fly.

How much had changed since Wilbur Wright told his father only two years earlier that he and Orville were going to North Carolina for a vacation. Not only had the notion of first flight obsessed both brothers since, but the aeronautical community had sat up and taken notice of their efforts as well. Not that the Wrights encouraged the attention. They would have much preferred to toil in obscurity until they perfected the craft which, they hoped, would change the world.

Against this backdrop, the efforts Octave Chanute devoted tirelessly in the brothers' behalf had proved a mixed blessing. The Wrights had forged a personal bond with him during weeks of battering winds, stinging sand, and tenacious mosquitoes, but they'd delude themselves if they thought Chanute's first loyalty ran to anything other than the idea of lifting a human aloft, whoever that might be. So it surprised no one that when the Wright party broke camp for its third year on October 14, Octave Chanute and Augustus Herring took a detour to Washington, determined to look up Professor Langley and fill him in on the work the Wrights had accomplished.

Chanute and Herring would make their approaches separately, for while both were accomplished in the field, they knew that the secretary held one in much higher esteem than the other. Not surprisingly, the secretary's schedule just couldn't seem to fit Herring in, but he welcomed Chanute with open arms. During that audience, Chanute gushed about the advances he had seen with his own eyes and implored the secretary to go to Kill Devil Hills to see the Wrights' accomplishments for himself.[1]

With what mixed emotions Langley must have received the news of the brothers' triumphs. These were the total neophytes who a scant three years ago wrote to him as the world-famous aeronaut who had already been chasing first flight for more than a decade.

Following Facts Where They Lead

But a good scientist follows the facts dispassionately wherever they lead. "After seeing you, I almost decided to go, or send someone," Langley wrote Chanute the next day, "to see the remarkable experiments...." In short order, Langley wired the Wrights at Kitty Hawk: "Mr. Chanute has interested me in your experiments. Is there time to see them? Kindly write me." What must have been their reaction to a cable from this heraldic figure? Professor Langley, asking to visit their camp? Wanting to learn how he could make the breakthrough they all sought?

Langley may have been an icon to many Americans and some scientists. But seeing him up close through his writings and experimental findings had, to the Wright brothers, exposed this god's clay feet. Their discovery the previous winter that when Langley ran into an experimental finding he couldn't explain, he had just ignored it, had peeled the scales from their eyes. They were in awe of him no longer. So Wilbur told Chanute of his answer to Langley, in ho-hum fashion: "We replied that it (a visit) would be scarcely possible as we were intending to break camp in a few days. He made no mention of his experiments on the Potomac."[2]

Not being able to gain a meeting with the secretary, Herring wrote Langley instead. Always the loose cannon on the deck, he now displayed his untrustworthiness as well. He made Langley a veiled offer to turn on the Wrights by sending him his thoughts on the arrangement, form and curvature of airplane wings, fresh from studying the subject in depth, under the Wrights' direction, at Kill Devil Hills. The secretary may not have been as formidable a scientist as Washington's political leaders perceived him to be, but if anything, he was an honorable man. Reading through the lines, he sensed Herring was offering to spill the Wrights' trade secrets for a price and would have none of it. Langley had endured his fill of Herring as an employee in earlier days, and Chanute had warned him in recent days of his fear "that he is a bungler."[3]

The Deadline Passes

Even after the Wrights brushed him off in October, Langley continued to show intense interest in their operations. The secretary had exceeded his self-imposed deadline to achieve first flight. He had used up the $50,000 appropriation from the Army Board of Ordnance more than a year earlier. To soak up Langley's growing deficit, his friend Graham Bell had contributed $5,000, and Langley had siphoned off a $5,000 unrestricted bequest to the Smithsonian from Dr. Jerome Kidder, a New York physician and manufacturer of x-ray machines. Now that success still eluded his grasp, could it be that Langley pressed his competitors so hard because he had begun to doubt his own methods?[4]

Secretary Langley had helped evolve the conventional wisdom that supplying a pilot with control devices was unimportant if you built stability into your aerodrome. Now, as the 1902 holiday season approached, he contacted Chanute again, trying to understand the workings of the Wrights' control system, the very element he had earlier dismissed as largely irrelevant. And how like Langley to appear imperious while begging! He offered to pay the way of one of the Wrights to come to Washington but made it clear he expected the brothers to share their hard-won trade secrets with him. Chanute, plainly embarrassed at the secretary's "cheeky" tone, asked the Wrights how he should answer such a bold request. Just say that neither of the brothers have the time right now to go to Washington, answered Wilbur dismissively.[5]

Langley just wouldn't let things lie. Trying mightily to keep the correspondence alive, he sent Wilbur a pamphlet from the Smithsonian entitled, *The World's Greatest Flying Creature,* referring to the pterodactyl, which he took great pains to compare with his 1896 steam-powered airplane. If he felt such a portrayal would impress the Wrights and perhaps entice them to meet with him, he was wrong. Tongue in cheek, Wilbur wrote Chanute, "Perhaps you have noted the mention contained therein of the Maxim and Lilienthal machines." Wilbur's irony, that by not even identifying two pioneers who laid the foundation for his own experiments Langley could elevate himself above them, was too nuanced for Chanute's literal engineering mind. In a return letter, Chanute confessed that he had again perused the Langley pamphlet closely but couldn't find mention of either Maxim or Lilienthal.[6]

Basking in Triumph

After Dan Tate had ferried Chanute and Herring downstream to Manteo to make connections home, Wilbur, Orville, and George Spratt were left to bask in the glow of a triumphal season, one as upbeat as the end of the 1901 encampment had been depressing. The record is silent on whether, in spite of their nose-to-the-grindstone discipline, they took an evening to relax at sunset, as Orville strummed his mandolin, giving each other the 1902 equivalent of a high-five.

From Kill Devil Hills, Orville wrote enthusiastically to sister Katharine: "...we now hold all the records! The largest machine ... the longest time in the air, the smallest angle of descent, and the highest wind!!!" In the two days following Chanute's and Herring's departure, the remaining members of the team made 250 glides, stretching their distance record to 622.5 feet and time aloft to 26 seconds.[7] These

Orville Wright prepares to pour coffee, a favorite Wright beverage, in the ramshackle Kill Devil Hills sleeping quarters. Steamer trunk used to transport clothes and supplies between Dayton and the Outer Banks is in foreground. Special Collections and Archives, Wright State University Libraries.

records still lagged behind those of Langley's 1896 trials, but the Wrights' flights were both *manned* and *controlled*. They also had built the first wind tunnel to pre-test wing configurations, charted wind resistance for the first time, and invented numerous aircraft improvements.[8]

But Wilbur's and Orville's natures did not suggest they rest on their laurels. On Halloween, Bishop Wright met his boys at the Dayton station on the 3:15 P.M. train, to celebrate their homecoming. They looked in on their bicycle operation to make sure it was still healthy, then turned quickly to the challenge of motorizing their craft: to build an engine strong enough to lift the machine but light enough to keep it aloft. The brothers had been so focused on control that they now realized they knew practically nothing about engines or "screws" (propellers). Reflexively, they put an S.O.S. out to their friend Chanute. Regrettably, he told them he was packing to leave for four months in Egypt but invited them to write him at a forwarding address.[9]

By early December, Wright Cycle Co. letterheads fell like snowflakes onto the desks of dozens of automobile manufacturers, as the brothers sought an engine weighing 180 pounds or less, generating at least eight horsepower, and free of vibration. Among more than a dozen replies were those from such auto pioneers as Daimler Manufacturing Co. of New York and Winton Motor Carriage Co. of Cleveland. Unhappily, no company said it could meet the Wrights' specifications. Having plowed the same ground as Langley and Manly had a couple of years earlier, with the same results, they now adopted the same solution Manly had used — to do it themselves.[10]

Charlie to the Rescue

The Wrights' unexpected resource turned out to be a mechanically-savvy high-school dropout they had hired to mind their bicycle shop while they were away. Charlie Taylor, whose coarseness clashed markedly with the Wrights' gentility, smoked 20 cigars a day and worked for 30 cents an hour.

Taylor, who had never built an engine before, wrote later about the experience:

> The first thing we did as an experiment was to construct a sort of skeleton model in order that we might watch the functioning of the various vital parts before venturing with anything more substantial. Orv and Wil were pretty thorough that way. They could not take anything for granted but worked everything out to a practical solution without too much haste. I think this had a lot to do with their success. When we had the skeleton motor set up we hooked it up to our shop power, smeared the cylinder with a paintbrush dipped in oil, and watched the various parts in action. It looked good, so we went ahead immediately with the construction of a four-cylinder engine.[11]

Building an engine from scratch called for Taylor to be as much a sculptor as an engineer. He began with a hundred-pound block of steel and cut from it a 19-pound crankshaft. Using only a lathe and a drill press, he fashioned four water-cooled, horizontal cylinders, which ultimately developed 8.25 horsepower or 12 horsepower if they revved it up. Yet this crude engine, which lacked a carburetor and fuel pump, weighed a scant 140 pounds.[12]

With no spark plugs, the brothers used what Taylor called "the old make and break system of ignition." They created a spark by opening and closing two contact points inside the combustion chamber. The engine could generate 12 horsepower, but the Wrights had to incorporate the fact that the drive shaft, sprocket, and chain system alone would absorb 2.5 horsepower, leaving only 9.5 horsepower to lift the machine and its operator, together weighing a hefty 700 pounds.[13]

Charlie Taylor's recollection of the engine's fuel system suggests how primitive it was:

> A one-gallon fuel tank was suspended from a wing strut, and the gasoline fed by gravity down a tube to the engine. The fuel valve was an ordinary gasoline petcock. There was no carburetor as we know it today. The fuel was fed into a shallow chamber in the manifold. Raw gas blended with air in this chamber, which was next to the cylinders and heated up rather quickly, thus helping to vaporize the mixture. The engine was started by priming each cylinder with a few drops of raw gas.[14]

To keep weight at an absolute minimum in the very short flights they anticipated, the gas tank held only four tenths of a gallon. Given that the crude engine would run only at full-throttle also suggested its flights would be brief.[15]

Since Taylor's initial job was to mind the bicycle shop while the Wrights were away, he didn't see much of them at first. But building an engine during the winter season put him cheek by jowl with two of America's foremost inventors and gave him an unparalleled chance to see them in action. "Both the boys had tempers," Taylor recalled, "but no matter how angry they ever got, I never heard them use a profane word. The boys were working out a lot of theory in those days and occasionally they would get into terrific arguments. They'd shout at each other something terrible. I don't think they really got mad, but they sure got awfully hot."[16]

Just as the Wrights had turned to the nascent automobile industry in their quest to build internal combustion engines, so they sought to learn the ins-and-outs of propeller design from the boating industry. They found, to their surprise, that no one had done much theoretical work on predicting the thrust a boat screw would furnish. The logistics needed to propel a boat through the water were evidently less sophisticated than those required to launch a flying machine into the air, maintain her aloft, and land gently.

To those more easily daunted, the lack of any empirical testing on airplane propellers would have brought the project to a dead halt. For what the Wrights would have to do was to build a multitude of propeller designs and try them out sequentially, to see which operated the most efficiently. But the Wrights simply had no time for this. They knew, from Chanute and others, that Langley was under great pressure to complete his work and reach the goal he had promised to achieve for so long. And the Wrights had come too far to simply give up.

A High-Stakes Gamble

As they forged ahead in the spring of 1903, Wilbur and Orville made a high-stakes gamble: that they could design and build, *on their very first try*, a propeller powerful enough to lift and propel the aircraft. Biographer Harry Combs, a pilot and aviation expert, explains what this approach meant in the world of aircraft technology: "There is no way that one can overdramatize what the Wrights accomplished in their propeller design. The idea of developing a formula to incorporate all the information they needed into an analytical form was something that would challenge a modern computer programmer."[17]

Starting from scratch, Wilbur and Orville soon found that a propeller is remarkably similar to an airplane wing, in that the propeller moves forward because the pressure on the back of its blade is greater than on the front, just as the greater pressure beneath an airplane wing than above it causes the wing to lift. Their final product was twin propellers, measuring 8.25 feet in diameter, constructed of three laminated layers of spruce glued together, then shaped. Covering the propeller tips was light duck canvas glued on tightly. The brothers mounted them at the rear of the machine, not the front, so the air stirred up by the whirring blades wouldn't interfere with the wings' lifting surfaces.[18]

For three seasons and hundreds of glides, the Wrights had worked with anonymous gliders, shaping and reshaping these impersonal hulks of wood, wire, and canvas. What better indication that the Wrights knew that 1903 was to be a fateful year than their decision to attach a name to their craft? From now on, the *Flyer* would be a member of the team, as fully as if it occupied a seat at the dinner table. But while their 1902 model was sleek in appearance, with longer, slimmer wings than previous models, the *Flyer* would revert to the squat, boxy style they had used in earlier years. Less attractive to look at, it would be immeasurably sturdier, to withstand the vibrations and pressures exerted by a gasoline engine and dual propellers.

"Good Enough" Won't Do

To strengthen the craft, the brothers attached stay wires between the front and rear uprights, except for the ends of the wings, which needed to remain flexible. They stabilized the center of the glider and the leading edges of both wings. The pilot could still flex the wings' rear outer edges, which would function like ailerons of a later age. The waste-not, want-not philosophy under which the Wrights had been raised had led them to use bicycle spoke wire to build trusses, to support the wings. Building the *Flyer* with spare parts and items found around the house would make a good story, but it wouldn't be true. For the Wrights knew during 1902 that they had come too far now to settle for good enough.

In Brooklyn, contractor Washington Roebling won world acclaim notice 20 years earlier for building the Brooklyn Bridge, one of the strongest in the world. The Wrights now adopted Roebling's own multi-strand wire to make trusses for the *Flyer*. They left nothing to chance, as they tinkered with each member, reinforced the muslin covering the wings, and lightened the craft wherever possible.[19]

The Wrights had prided themselves at keeping their hobby in perspective, but by early 1903 the *Flyer* was an octopus, spreading its tentacles everywhere. Katharine had already described to her father how flight preparations had transformed the family home. The *Flyer*, substantially larger than the 1902 glider and boasting a 40-foot wingspan, was too big to be assembled in the store's workroom. A customer entering the bicycle shop would see only wings, struts, and skids, and hope an alert clerk would see him, exit a side door, and walk around to the front of the store to serve him.

Earlier Wright crafts showed harmony in symmetry, with each side being a mirror image of the other. The motor would change all that. It was now located on the right-hand side of the wing and weighed some 50 pounds more than the pilot, who lay to the left of the motor. The right wings had to be four inches longer than the left, to give the engine additional lift.[20]

Seeking a Patent at Last

Chanute had repeatedly urged the brothers to apply for a patent on their ideas and had even sent them a copy of a patent he had helped obtain for Louis-Pierre Mouillard of France in 1896.[21] The press of their quest led them to put it off again and again, but with the growing sense that 1903 could well be the breakthrough year, the Wrights sent in their application in March. As men who had puzzled out answers to amazingly-complicated scientific problems, the Wrights may have felt they didn't need a patent attorney. Or perhaps it was the same thrift that had held the entire spending on their venture to $300.

Crackpots had deluged the U.S. Patent Office with applications for a variety of supposedly airworthy vehicles, so clerks looked upon one more application with a gimlet eye. The patent examiner told the Wrights that six other patent applicants had made claims similar to theirs and disallowed their application, also stating their product was clearly "incapable of performing its intended function."[22] His strongest advice was that the brothers engage competent counsel. Yet the looming task of planning for the epochal 1903 season would prevent the brothers applying again until 1904.[23]

In early April, Chanute sent the brothers peremptory instructions to have their pictures taken right away: "You are therefore upon the receipt of this to go to the photographer and be 'took'." Send me the prints in Chicago, he directed them, along with extra copies to distribute throughout the aeronautical world. Their self-appointed publicist explained that the Wrights' experiments were attracting great attention in Paris, where people called their trials "toboggan rides on the air." The magazine L'Aerophile wanted Chanute to write an article about the Wrights, illustrated with their photographs. Since Chanute's consent to write the article was payback to the editor for an unrelated favor, Chanute leaned heavily on the Wrights to meet his request.[24]

Weeks later, Chanute received word from Wilbur that the publicity-shy brothers hadn't yet screwed up their courage to face the camera. Only half-humorously, Chanute wrote back: "I am ashamed that men whom I have praised so highly in Europe should have so little courage to face a camera; Go and do so right away," Chanute commanded.[25]

Challenging Assumptions

As scientists, the Wrights had been willing to challenge assumptions, such as the monumental error Lilienthal had made in calculating lift of a plane's wings. This led Orville, in a letter to George Spratt, to observe, "...if we all worked on the assumption that what is accepted as true is really true, there would be little hope of advance."[26] In the same spirit, Wilbur wrote revealingly to Spratt, admonishing him for giving in too quickly in an argument they were having on a technical point. "It is characteristic of all our family," Wilbur told the doctor, "to be able to see the weak points of anything, but this is not always a desirable quality as it makes us too conservative for successful business men, and limits our friendships to a very limited circle."[27]

Wilbur and Orville constantly argued. Those who didn't know them might have thought they disliked one another. But this interplay, especially on scientific matters, worked to bring them nearer the truth. Not infrequently, the brothers would start on opposite sides of an argument. They each would be so persuasive that they'd convince the other and end up arguing a point of view opposite from their original. Wilbur explained his philosophy of truth in a letter to George Spratt:

> No truth is without some mixture of error, and no error so false but that it possesses some elements of truth. If a man is in too big a hurry to give up an error he is liable to give up some truth with it, and in accepting the arguments of the other man he is sure to get some error with it. Honest argument is merely a process of mutually picking the beams and motes out of each other's eyes so both can see clearly.[28]

A Fourth Pioneer

When aeronautical literature of the day spoke of the leading contemporary pioneers, they universally included the late lamented Otto Lilienthal, Samuel Pierpont Langley, and, increasingly, Wilbur and Orville Wright. Most accounts added a fourth name, that of Sir Hiram Stevens Maxim, as well. Though an American, Maxim had never met the Wrights, since he migrated to Great Britain after abandoning his family in Brooklyn, New York. A brilliant but mercurial inventor, Maxim didn't restrict himself to one field of endeavor as did Langley and the Wrights. He invented the hair curling iron at age 26 and followed up with a mousetrap, an automatic sprinkling system, steam-powered water pumps, and engine governors.[29]

A cruel streak marred the considerable talents of the man whom Queen Victoria would dub a knight in the early 1880s. Disdainful of household help, all of whom he labeled "stupid," he experimented on them for his own entertainment, if not edification. Hiram had read, for example, that the sensations of extreme cold and extreme heat are the same. One day, in view of a kitchen maid, he heated a poker red hot and cooled another to below zero. As soon as her back was turned, Maxim "slapped the cold poker on the back of her neck while talking about the intense heat of the cold poker." The young girl shrieked as Maxim "dissolved in laughter," then gave her notice in "a fit of frenzy."[30]

Maxim lived in a family of inventors. His brother, Hudson Maxim, gained patents in the field of munitions; and his son, Hiram Percy Maxim, graduated from the Massachusetts Institute of Technology at age 17, became one of the nation's earliest manufacturers of gasoline and electric-powered automobiles, and in the early years of the 20th century invented the Maxim Silencer, which would become the technological basis for the automobile muffler.

Maxim pere had found fame and fortune in Britain and the Continent. While there, he invented the machine gun, which by itself would cement his reputation in history. Not only did the bellicose welcome the machine gun. Even pacifists heralded it as an advance for humankind, since the carnage it would wreak was obviously so horrible as to stop war altogether.[31]

Since the Wrights cared little for travel, it is not unusual that they and Maxim had never met, in spite of their common interest. But during the winter of 1903, Chanute learned that Maxim was coming to America and volunteered to make an introduction to the Wrights. Maxim had experimented with manned flight, developing his own version of screws (propellers) and engines, and Chanute sent the brothers material describing Maxim's endeavors.

The Wrights evidently devoured them with interest, although they apparently didn't think it worth their while to make Maxim's acquaintance. After all, aeronautical proof was in the pudding, and Maxim had never achieved any more success than legions of aeronauts before him. His work is notable in that, while the Wrights were struggling to keep the weight of their craft below 700 pounds, Maxim had built a monumental airplane weighing four tons in 1893, with two huge steam engines and a wingspread stretching more than 100 feet. Maxim was nothing if not self-confident, and he boasted to the media that "Propulsion and lifting are solved problems. The rest is a mere matter of time."[32] One can imagine the argument he and the Wrights could have had over that statement. Maxim's moment of truth came in July, 1894, when his massive craft surged down an 1,800-foot track on cast-iron wheels in its long-awaited quest to rewrite the history books. Its entire flight lasted two feet before it collided with two wooden restraining rails and crashed.

The Wrights had refined their calculations to such a degree that, having in hand the specifications for Maxim's motored craft, they deduced that in one of his trials, his craft must have traveled 37 miles per hour. They knitted their brows when they came upon a report that the actual speed had been 42 miles per hour, only to learn shortly thereafter that the report, not their calculation, had been in error. The actual speed was indeed precisely 37 miles per hour.[33]

Wilbur Omits a Detail

On June 24, 1903, Wilbur returned to the Western Society of Engineers, to which he had spoken nearly two years earlier, again at Chanute's invitation. He and Orville had now made more than 1,000 glides, and he regaled the audience with the technological progress that this accomplishment represented. He mentioned that he and his brother would be returning again to Kitty Hawk within weeks. But, to avoid premature publicity, he left out one salient detail that would have transfixed the audience: the machine they would test this year would be under power.[34]

As summer arrived and the imminence of a fourth season on the Outer Banks sharpened the brothers' planning, Chanute asked the Wrights whether he could send

Professor Langley an advance copy of his forthcoming article in *The Aerophile* that dealt with the Wrights' experiments. It should have been obvious to Chanute by this point that any insight Langley gained thereby to propel him to a successful first flight could potentially wipe out everything his young friends had worked for over the past four years. As ever, the brothers were courteous to their insensitive mentor and advised him simply to let Langley learn of their advances "through the regular channel."[35]

To add to their anxiety, Chanute wrote on July 17 to ask whether the brothers had heard that Langley was about to test his man-carrying machine. Wilbur wrote back several days later, observing that "Prof. Langley seems to be having rather more than his fair share of trouble just now with pestiferous reporters and windstorms," calamities of which the brothers Wright were well aware. Showing obvious interest in the state of Langley's experiments, he went on: "It would be interesting to attempt a computation of the possible performance of his machine in advance of its trial, but the data of the machine as given in the newspapers are so evidently erroneous that it seems hopeless to attempt it."[36]

Testing their mentor, Wilbur ventured, "I presume that you are to be one of the guests of honor at the launching festivities." Tongue in cheek, he added, "Our invitation has not yet arrived." In reply, Chanute assured Wilbur, "I have no invitation from Langley either." Given the close association he had enjoyed with the secretary over the years, Chanute's omission from the invitation list is striking until one realizes the secretary knew well that Chanute had close ties to the Wrights and was eager not to give them any information they might not already have.[37]

By September 9, Wilbur and Orville had started shipping equipment and supplies to Kill Devil Hills, preparing for their September 20 departure. Soon thereafter, Chanute observed in a letter, "I am really sorry for Langley. He has had more than his share of mishaps, and the pesky reporters are giving him the reputation of a bungler." Unfortunately, Langley had seen only the tip of the iceberg. Wilbur replied to Chanute promptly on other matters but never mentioned his competitor.[38]

Wearing Out His Welcome

Chanute's assistance to the Wrights had been inestimable, but as time went on, he became more demanding and intrusive. Gradually, inexorably, like abrasive Kitty Hawk sand wearing down the wooden clapboards of their sheds, the elderly widower was wearing out his welcome. In returning to the City of Light in the spring of 1903, Chanute — now well into his 70s — began to dig his own grave regarding his relationship with the Wrights. In a speech before the Paris Aero-Club on April 2, he portrayed himself as the proud mentor to the Wrights, whom he characterized as "young, intelligent and daring, pupils," who worked under his supervision. A newspaper account of Chanute's address reported that the Wrights were essentially carrying Chanute's own work to completion.[39]

The effect of the speech on Chanute's relationship with the Wrights was a nuance lost on the audience. But what wasn't lost was the fact that two young Americans seemed poised on the verge of first flight. In the audience was a French artillery officer, Capt. Ferdinand Ferber, who had been so interested in the Wrights' project that he had flown in a model of their 1901 glider that he had ordered built for him. Hearing Chanute speak had caused his national pride to swell within him. The French, at all costs, must not allow America to claim the prize of first flight.

He immediately mounted a crusade among wealthy Frenchmen to win that title for France — such men as Ernest Archdeacon, a balloonist and lawyer of means. Archdeacon decided to make it his mission to "shake our aviators out of their torpor, and put a stop to French indifference concerning flying machines." He agreed to contribute 3,000 francs to a prize for glider flight and helped organize a band of aviation experimenters so dedicated to the cause that they called themselves "les aviateurs militantes."

The French, up to then foremost among European aviation pioneers, had now been stirred to action. But would they be too late?[40]

12

Down to the Wire

"They done it! They done it! Damn'd if they ain't flew!"—Johnny Moore of Nags
Head, N.C., December 17, 1903

ONE COULD ARGUE THAT THE RACE to the sky wasn't really a race at all. In a classic race, the contestants start from a predetermined point, using agreed-upon rules, and are aware of whom they're competing against. In the race between Langley and the Wrights, each party started independently, with Langley having a 12-year head start. No rules existed as to what constituted first flight, and each contestant wasn't completely sure who his competitors were or what equipment they were using. Yet if the essence of a race is focused energy brought to bear against rivals, the race to the sky has few equals for excitement.

Both sides understood that 1903 was do or die. The Wrights knew that Langley's symphony would reach its crescendo this year, for better or for worse. Friends were poised to alert them to the results of the October trial, and they'd learn of Langley's December flight from the newspaper.

Somewhat less clear is the extent of what Langley knew of the Wrights' operations. As early as 1902, Chanute had told him of the tremendous advances the Wrights were making in manned glider flight, and Langley clamored feverishly but unsuccessfully to see their work. Those who argue Langley and the Wrights weren't really in a race contend that the secretary knew only that the Wrights flew manned gliders and weren't aware that they would add an engine in 1903. Chanute assured the Wrights in October of 1903 that he hadn't told Langley about their new motor.

Yet it seems naïve to assume that Langley, as intrigued as he had become over the past year by the Wrights' work, wouldn't have inquired of Chanute or others whether they planned to motorize their craft. For if they had, then the entire federal crusade to become first in flight might be in jeopardy. A race would have suited

122

Chanute's purposes, since it would have stimulated the advent of flight, which had always been his overriding purpose. Although he may have said nothing explicitly to Langley, a nod or a wink might have told the professor all he needed to know.

The French Factor

We should add to the mix the resolve of France's Capt. Ferdinand Ferber. Octave Chanute had stirred the Frenchman's nationalistic juices earlier that year, and Ferber had already secured important financial backing to make sure France would reach the sky before America did. The French had only been at it for a short time, but who knows what progress they had made? It is simply not credible to think, as Washington's leaves began to turn in the third year of the new century, that Langley wasn't looking over his shoulder, too.

Both camps shared a common urgent objective, but the mood in the Smithsonian's South Shed was far different than that in a crude clapboard building on the dunes of Kill Devil Hills. Langley had run through his $50,000 government appropriation and had tap-danced through a rationale that his monumental project justified drawing $23,000 of additional Smithsonian money. His funders had nothing to show for their commitment, and the public was losing patience as well.

Press relations as a science didn't yet exist, although such public figures as Teddy Roosevelt and Thomas Edison had learned the dividends that come from care and feeding of the media. By contrast, their friend Secretary Langley had clamped an iron lid on his project, to avoid premature publicity, and shooed pesky reporters away with peremptory brusqueness. No wonder then that newspaper headlines cropped up reading:

PROF. LANGLEY ACCUSED OF
USING GOVERNMENT TIME AND
MONEY ON VISIONARY
FLYING MACHINE TESTS

CONGRESSIONAL INVESTIGATION
LIKELY[1]

At the very time he needed public support the most, Professor Langley was learning the hard way that the press has a few lethal bows in its quiver and has been known to use them when it feels unappreciated.

By contrast, the Wright brothers shared a contained self-confidence that was, in truth, a two-edged sword. Never had the brothers felt more sure-footed after a winter and spring of solving all mechanical problems thrown in their path. But in the wake of the rejection of their patent application, the vision of success on the horizon unsettled them, because they had no protection from those who might try to purloin their hard-won technological gains.[2]

A Gratuitous Letter

On the verge of leaving for Kill Devil Hills in September of 1903, Wilbur received a gratuitous letter from Octave Chanute, who was proving on more than one front a burr under the brothers' saddle. He now expressed dismay that the *Flyer*, as finally configured, weighed 675 pounds. "I am so much interested in your continued success," Chanute observed, "that I wish you had planned a lighter and more easily started machine, even at the risk of having to go a little faster through the air." Chanute had been sensitive enough in the past to know just when to buck up the brothers' spirits, yet now insisted on criticizing a design that it was too late to change. And if that wasn't negative enough, Chanute then raised the specter of the Wrights' new European competition, a threat that Chanute himself had done much to create. He reported that Capt. Ferber had built a machine weighing only 495 pounds. Was Chanute chafing over the Wrights not having taken his advice on certain matters, such as applying for patents? Or were the aches and pains of old age simply making him more crotchety?[3]

Wright biographer Tom Crouch says that, for all Chanute's sophisticated engineering knowledge and the great demand for his speaking and writing on aeronautics, he really didn't understand how the Wrights' craft worked. To have such a respected figure as Chanute spreading misinformation, as he nearly did in an article written for the French publication *Revue des Sciences*, was distracting at best and dangerous at worst. Fortunately, Chanute had sent Wilbur a draft for review. To an observation therein that "twines leading to the hands of the aviator" controlled the rudder or the operation of the vertical tail, Wilbur noted "Really, this is news to me."

For all Chanute's weeks spent at Kill Devil Hills, some of the brothers' most basic concepts continued to elude him. And in his desire to communicate progress in this emerging field lay the danger that he might overreach and say something that interfered with the patent process. Wilbur put pen to paper, to set down some guidelines for their friend:

> As the laws of France & Germany provide that patents will be held invalid if the matter claimed has been publicly printed we prefer to exercise reasonable caution about the details of our machine until the question of patents is settled. I only see three methods of dealing with this matter: (1) Tell the truth. (2) Tell nothing specific. (3) Tell something that is not true. I really cannot advise either the first or the third course.[4]

Yet if Wilbur harbored any resentment from the sentiments Chanute expressed, he didn't share them in his reply. Even at this juncture, the brothers plainly valued his friendship too highly. For the same Chanute whose inaccuracies caused them to tear their hair out was the man who, upon leaving Kill Devil Hills during a particularly cold stretch, stopped spontaneously at a store and bought warm gloves to ship back to his friends. Wilbur reported in his letter that he and Orville planned to reach

Kitty Hawk by late September, engage themselves for a week in building a new shed, and not to start testing much before October 25. He extended an invitation to Chanute to join them in their expanded camp.[5]

Captain Ferber wrote to Wilbur in September, at Chanute's urging, and reported troubles with his design caused by "too great depth of (wing) curvature," the same problem the Wrights had run into in the early going. Wilbur knew well that Ferber had vowed in 1902 that a Frenchman would be first in flight. How easy it would have been to rebuff Ferber as a potential competitor. Instead, he willingly and perhaps inexplicably shared with the French officer his solution to the curvature problem.[6]

The papers of Wilbur and Orville Wright contain hundreds of letters to and from Octave Chanute. But nearly all are between Chanute and Wilbur, not Orville. This is understandable at the outset, before Orville was involved deeply in the enterprise. As time went on and Orville became proficient at designing and flying aircraft, however, it is more curious that Chanute and Orville seldom wrote each other. Chanute often would ask Wilbur to remember him "to your brother," but without mentioning Orville's name. Yet no indication exists that Orville and the old man didn't get along. The anomaly is perhaps best explained by the fact that Chanute was an engineer, and Wilbur was involved more than Orville in the actual design of the crafts the brothers flew.[7]

What a Difference a Year Makes

As the brothers arrived in camp on September 25, it was hard to believe they had been away less than a year. A violent storm the previous February had blown their camp building clear off its foundation posts and moved it several feet nearer the ocean. Communicating its severity to sister Katharine, Orville demonstrated a gift for prose expression no less than Wilbur's when he talked about adverse conditions they had experienced in the past:

> ...when the mosquitoes were so thick as to dim the very brightness of the sun, exceeding in numbers all excepting those that devoured the whole of Raleigh's settlers on Roanoke and last year when lightning turned night into day, and burned down every telegraph pole between here and Kitty Hawk, we had supposed that nature had reached her limit; but far from it![8]

In spite of the primitive conditions they faced, Orville and his brother still insisted on some of the finer things in life. He devoted a full day to making a "French drip" coffeepot, to obviate the use of scarce eggs they had used to settle coffee grounds in the making of their daily brew.[9]

The camp would expand considerably this year. The brothers, with help from their friends the Tates and others, would construct a new 44 foot by 16 foot by 9 foot building immediately to the west of the existing living quarters, as a hangar[10] to house the *Flyer*, which was expected in camp in early October.

The Wrights' plan called for them to practice with the 1902 glider on days with good winds, saving the new machine for safer, less breezy conditions, to avoid damage that might set them back. The brothers had a good inkling that 1903 would be a pivotal year, they had only a handful of good weeks until deep cold set in, and a serious accident requiring major repairs might shut them down for the season.

Gliding was no endeavor for the out of shape. The brothers and whomever they could dragoon to help them trudged again and again up a 100-foot hill, sometimes 100 times a day, in sand up to their ankles. On September 28 alone, they made from 60 to 100 glides and continued to fly as weather permitted. By October 26, they had completed six glides lasting more than a minute, smashing their existing records by far.[11]

But all this was prologue to the *Flyer*. So Captain Franklin Midgett's sailboat, the *Lou Willis,* was a welcome sight on October 8, cruising down Albemarle Sound to Kitty Hawk landing, with crates containing the components of the *Flyer*. Locals hauled the heavy crates along the sandy four-mile road to Kill Devil Hills the next morning.[12]

While others put the finishing touches on the new shed, the brothers had resumed gliding on October 3, each making glides of up to 450 feet. As October wore on, heavy winds of up to 40 to 50 miles an hour plagued the team, relegating the brothers to household chores or reading.[13]

Waiting for Langley

Chanute had told the Wrights that Professor Langley planned to fly his machine that fall, so the brothers looked forward to that event with trepidation. On October 14 came word, relayed by a friend, that Langley's launch of the machine he called his *Great Aerodrome*, 150 miles to the north, had failed.[14]

The Wrights' diaries and collected correspondence is lively and engaging to read, written as it was at the time of the events it depicts. The Langley memoirs, finally completed in 1911 by Charles Manly, were written for posterity and generally lack the crackle of diary entries. However, even eight years later, the spirit of frustration pervades Charles Manly's account of the 1903 season, beset as his team was with bad weather, bad luck and technological mishaps.

With the *Aerodrome* completed, Langley's crew towed the houseboat down the Potomac 40 miles to Widewater, Virginia, a journey that hiked the cost of the financially-strapped project but helped avoid an aggressive press contingent that had dogged Langley's steps for months.[15] But then set in extreme dampness, which short-circuited the engine and loosened the glue holding the wings together. If that weren't enough, workmen poured too much gasoline into the fuel tank and failed to remove a launching track pin, which derailed one experiment. And erratic winds caused non-productive days, for which workmen still had to be paid.[16] Yet all that paled before the description of the aerodrome in flight, recalled by Manly, a man clearly in love with the machine he had helped create:

Professor Langley, left, confers with crew atop houseboat as infrastructure of *Aerodrome* looms above them, awaiting takeoff. National Air and Space Museum, Smithsonian Institution (SI Neg. No. 2002-16634).

> ...the graceful lines of the machine make it very attractive to the eye even when stationary, yet when it is actually in flight it seems veritably endowed with life and intelligence, and the spectacle holds the observer awed and breathless until the flight is ended. It seems hardly probable that anyone, no matter how skeptical beforehand, could witness a flight of one of the models and note the almost bird-like intelligence with which the automatic adjustments respond to varying conditions of the air without feeling that, in order to traverse at will the great aerial highway man no longer needs to wrest from nature some strange, mysterious secret, but only, by diligent practice with machines of this very type, to acquire an expertness in the management of the aerodrome not different in kind from that acquired by every expert bicyclist in the control of his bicycle.[17]

The challenge that Manly had faced was vastly different from the one that confronted the Wrights, in that Manly's craft lacked basic controls. The Wrights could steer their craft in three axes of motion, but Langley relied instead on whatever stability he had built into the machine. No matter how much Manly might try to anthropomorphize his man-made machine, it remained just that, a machine. Aloft and met

The formidable *Aerodrome*, viewed from the front, is poised for takeoff from its houseboat perch on Potomac River during the fateful 1903 season. Size of man at top left suggests craft's immensity. National Air and Space Museum, Smithsonian Institution (SI Neg. No. 2002-16639).

by changing conditions, he couldn't make the craft pitch, yaw, or roll. Surprisingly, the *Great Aerodrome* flown October 7 had never before been tested and certain features of the craft would make aeronauts wince.[18] For example, the pilot's fabric cockpit slung beneath the aerodrome, meaning that, in landing, he would hit the water first at 50 miles an hour and remain submerged until a rescue crew arrived.[19]

Langley's team built the aerodrome in the South Shed behind the Smithsonian castle, crafting it of tubular steel. The houseboat used to launch one-quarter sized models clearly wouldn't do, so the team built a boat big enough to sleep nine. On its roof, the crew incorporated a launching track 85 feet long and connected to a spring-loaded catapult.

A Wasted Effort

The extra cost Langley incurred to move the houseboat far away from the prying eyes of the media was wasted money. As a decoy, Langley had ordered his gardeners to let the weeds grow around South Shed to make it appear unoccupied, but somehow word got out; the Washington press corps was always on the lookout for a good story. Once reporters discovered the houseboat's location after it anchored there in July, they hounded Langley like Potomac mosquitoes and camped on the riverbank. They could pass up watching some wingnut jump off a barn roof, flapping home-made wings. But here was a national crusade, backed by Congress and the president. If flight indeed were possible, reporters knew it would most likely happen here. And if it failed, with such portentous backing behind it, well, that was a pretty good story as well.[20]

On the morning of August 8, Langley tested the quarter-model, which alternately rose and dipped for some 1,000 feet before crashing into the river. At that point, Langley curiously delegated to Manly the decision on when to attempt a manned flight, while the secretary resumed his quotidian duties at the Smithsonian. On the verge of the game's pivotal play, the quarterback had handed the ball to a lineman and walked off the field.[21]

Politics dictated the manner in which the manned craft would be launched on October 7. Although Manly favored a launching from the ground, Langley realized that a good chunk of the War Department's $50,000 appropriation represented its 15-ton houseboat launching apparatus. Langley was suddenly eager for press attention. When the engine roared to life that day, the crew fired a skyrocket to alert photographers on shore. What anticipation the secretary must have experienced 16 years after beginning his experiments, before age began to weigh heavily upon him.

With all in readiness, the *Aerodrome* roared powerfully down the track. But after leaving its tether, instead of soaring upward, it continued its downward trajectory until "it simply slid into the water like a handful of mortar."[22] The press clamored for an explanation, but Langley was not available. Manly gave a terse statement to the Associated Press, stressing the flight was only an experiment and stating, "My confidence in the future success of the work is unchanged."[23] Later in the day, the chagrined secretary told reporters a guy post had become caught in the launching track that dropped away when the craft left the track. Then, with one eye on his funders, he stressed that the structural integrity of the machine was not in question. The professor would later describe the fateful event in his 1904 annual report to the Smithsonian:

> ...The engineer (Charles M. Manly) took his seat the engine started with ease and was working without vibration at its full power of over 50 horse, and the word being given to launch the machine, the car was released and the aerodrome sped along the track. Just as the machine left the track, those who were watching it, among whom were two representatives of the Board of Ordnance, noticed that the machine was jerked violently down at the front (being caught, as it subsequently appeared, by the falling ways), and under the full power of its engine was pulled into the water...[24]

Back at the 8th Street wharf, 40 miles upstream, workmen fitted new wings to the craft and removed the offending lug on the guy post. Soon the hapless *Great Aerodrome* became the butt of the national vaudeville circuit, furnishing hilarious grist for the comedy mill.[25]

There but for the Grace of God

No one in the Wright camp seems to have gloated over Langley's failure. The golden figure they had once admired had now tarnished in their eyes, but the bishop's sons had to reflect on the scriptural dictum, "There but for the grace of God go I." Moreover, the mishap could redound to Langley's benefit if he learned from his failure and corrected it in time for later trials that year.[26] The brothers took no comfort in learning from Chanute, who talked with Langley after the accident, that his craft weighed 750 pounds (to their 775 pounds), yet had a 52 horsepower engine, four times more powerful than the *Flyer*'s.[27] If a machine lighter than theirs but four times as powerful sank like a stone on takeoff, what chance did they have? Unless, of course, their design was fundamentally superior to Langley's.

Wilbur felt like the man on the Olympic diving board after the competitor in front of him has just dived. "I see that Langley has had his fling," he wrote Chanute. "It seems to be our turn to throw now, and I wonder what our luck will be."[28] In the high-stakes gamble in which they were engaged, the brothers needed all the support they could get. In spite of the increasingly meddlesome presence that Chanute had become, Wilbur felt dismayed to learn in mid–October that their mentor might not be able to join them in camp. Urging Chanute to reconsider, Wilbur said, "We are expecting the most interesting results of any of our seasons of experiment, and are sure that, barring exasperating little accidents or some mishap, we will have done something before we break camp."[29] Rain and heavy wind plagued the Wrights as October wore on, each inactive day meaning one less opportunity for testing. By November 5, the *Flyer* was assembled, and the brothers cranked up the motor. Unexpectedly, the sprocket wheels on the propeller shafts had too much play, and they couldn't figure out how to tighten them. Further, they couldn't get enough spark from the magneto, and the engine vibrations twisted one of the propeller shafts. George Spratt had joined them now in camp, hoping to see the *Flyer* live up to its name. But when he learned that only Charlie Taylor back in Dayton could repair and strengthen the shafts, he realized his dream was not about to come true. Spratt volunteered to carry the shafts to Manteo and ship them to Dayton on his way home.[30]

Just as Wilbur alone almost always wrote to Chanute, Orville nearly always was the one to write to sister Katharine, their closeness perhaps explained by their being only three years apart in age, while she was seven years younger than Wilbur.[31] One hilarious exception came on October 18, when Wilbur recounted for her a Keystone Cops scenario involving Orville, who had climbed on a ladder in a 75-mile-an-hour wind, trying to nail down the shed roof to prevent its blowing off. He had borrowed the long raincoat of his taller brother, and its long tails blew up over his head while he tried to work, an image Wilbur tried to capture by drawing sketches in the margins, proving that for all his taciturnity, he had a lively sense of humor when the spirit moved him. Wilbur told his sister they decided in the midst of the howling storm to take the advice of a coach at Oberlin College, her alma mater, who told his team, "Cheer up, boys, there is no hope."[32]

Wilbur Wright, at door of hangar, center, admires his handiwork, the 1903 *Flyer*, which soon would make history. To the right are the crew's living quarters. Special Collections and Archives, Wright State University Libraries.

Octave Chanute hadn't spent years of his life and untold money to miss the first manned flight in world history. So he wrote the brothers on October 24 that he would be able to join them after all. In the meantime, he was on his way to the nation's capital, where he would stay at the New Willard's Hotel. The new mansard-roofed structure had become the epitome of luxury in Teddy Roosevelt's Washington. Chanute expressed surprise that the media had not found out that the Wrights were again in camp, particularly when they were on the cusp of a great breakthrough.[33]

The Cold Sets In

Chanute arrived in camp in early November, greeted by weather Orville's diary terms "too cold for work."[34] While self-confidence reigned, the brothers had little to show their patron. Instead, they sat around the wood stove late into the night, discussing how they should manage their success in 1904 if they achieved first flight in 1903. Chanute, who had become convinced the Wrights had a magic touch, tried to induce them to test other machines in which he had an interest. The rich wheeler-dealer was in negotiations to buy Clement Ader's steam-powered *Avion III*, with bat wings, and he wanted to send the Wrights the two-surface glider he and Augustus

Herring had developed, to prepare it for the St. Louis World's Fair of 1904. Noted Orville afterwards, "He doesn't seem to think our machines are so much superior as the manner in which we handle them. We are of just the reverse opinion."[35]

Chanute, now into his 70s, still maintained a heavy schedule. As much as he shared the brothers' anticipation of great things to come, his appointment book beckoned him on. He left the cold, rainy camp on November 12 and stopped in Manteo, where he picked up a few pair of gloves and sent them on to the grateful brothers.[36] There he ran into George Spratt, who bemoaned the Wrights' technical troubles and doubted they would fly this season. Chanute had a very different take. "I believe the new machine of the Wrights to be the most promising attempt at flight that has yet been made...," he told Spratt.[37]

The optimism Chanute expressed to Spratt is curious, given the doubts he voiced earlier to the brothers about whether a machine weighing 675 pounds could fly. As the Wrights refined their operation at Kill Devil Hills, they found the actual weight topped 700. In a letter to his father and sister, Orville himself questioned whether the *Flyer* would be airworthy. "Mr. Chanute says that no one before has ever tried to build a machine on such close margins as we have done to our calculations."[38] With propellers expected to deliver 90 pounds of thrust at 330 revolutions per minute, the Wrights concluded that somehow they would have to find an extra 10 pounds. The machine was already designed, however, and they could do little in camp to change its capacity. But they also knew that mechanical expectations are sometimes wrong. With any luck, their estimates would have erred on the down side.[39]

Mum's the Word

The Wrights had long had a penchant for cloaking their operations in relative secrecy, and never before had they needed so much to keep their operations close to the vest. In June, Orville had warned George Spratt, "Please do not mention the fact of our building a power machine to anybody. The newspapers would take great delight in following us in order to record our *troubles*." Left unexpressed was the fear that such information might reach the ears of Professor Langley.[40]

Speaking again at Chanute's invitation to the Western Society of Engineers on June 24, the audience put Wilbur on the hot seat. One questioner asked him, "Have you made any experiments in propelling a machine with a motor?" Without hesitation, Wilbur replied, "We have not applied a motor to any of our machines. The driving force has been gravity."[41] This was technically true at that moment but illustrates the delicate tightrope walk that led the Wrights to try to avoid as much public contact as possible.

Octave Chanute had always encouraged the free flow of ideas among the early aeronauts in the interest of science. But showing that he understood how vulnerable his friends were with no patent protection, he also wrote Spratt: "...If you get into communication with Prof. Langley, please be very careful that you do not intimate to him that the Wrights are proposing to apply a motor, as they do not want this known. You will of course be on your guard as to the other features of the apparatus...."[42]

The Whopper Flying Machine

With Chanute's departure, the Wrights were alone again and spent most of their time refining the test track and attaching the craft to it. The weight of the *Flyer* led the brothers to find a new way to launch it, since hauling a 700-pound craft to the top of Big Hill (the tallest of the three hills making up Kill Devil Hills) repeatedly for scores of glides was obviously out of the question. So they built a 60-foot takeoff monorail made of 2 × 4s, set endwise and topped with a narrow iron bar 1½ inches wide. The "whopper flying machine," as Orville and Wilbur had come to call the *Flyer*, would fit onto a small launching cart with two wheel hubs cadged from old bicycles, positioned one behind the other. The cart, in turn, would ride along the iron bar. When the craft reached the end of the rail, it would soar and the cart would fall off the rail.[43]

They first installed the track on an 11-degree slope at the foot of Big Hill. In a letter to his father, Wilbur wrote, "Our track for starting the machine (total cost about $4.00) amused Mr. Chanute considerably, as Langley is said to have spent nearly $50,000 on his starting device which failed in the end to give a proper start, he claims. At least this is the reason he gives for the failure last month."[44] Wilbur, at least, had grown more and more disenchanted by the man who had been their initial inspiration.

As the end of the year approached, the cold intensified, and by mid–November, the brothers had to rub their hands together briskly upon arising before cracking the ice in the puddles outside their bunkhouse. An abundance of time on one's hands leads one to concoct silly games, such as the rating system the Wrights developed for night-time comfort. As Wilbur related in a letter home to Katharine and their father: "We now have 5 blanket nights, & 5 blankets & 2 quilts. Next come 5 blankets, 2 quilts & fire; then 5, 2, fire & hot-water jug. This is as far as we have got so far. Next comes the addition of sleeping without undressing, then shoes & hats, and finally overcoats. We intend to be comfortable while we are here."[45]

On November 20, Captain Midgett returned to the brothers the propeller shafts they had sent home for Charlie Taylor to repair. But on testing them after dinner, they found the sprockets wouldn't stay tight on the propeller shafts. Time, they knew, was closing in as the weather grew colder, and the oncoming Christmas season beckoned them home to Dayton. Orville's diary reported, "Day closes in deep gloom."[46]

But some jury-rigged repairs the next day restored the engine to working order. Again borrowing on their bicycle enterprise, the brothers applied to the sprockets some Arnstein's Hard Cement, which they used in Dayton to fasten bicycle tires to the rims, and they held tightly. After a test, the brothers found to their surprise that the propellers generated 132 to 136 pounds of thrust, far more than the 90 pounds they had figured. Never had they been happier to be wrong.[47]

Back to Dayton

In a letter to Charlie Taylor, Orville reported the 1902 glider had become quite dilapidated and would probably be retired, with its duration record standing at one minute, 11⅘ seconds. In late November test runs, the brothers discovered with dismay a cracked propeller shaft, the same one that had broken weeks earlier. The Wrights now decided that, with time so short, they could no longer risk trying to repair it in camp. With the clock ticking and the temperature dropping, Orville left for Dayton on November 30 to build shafts made of spring steel.[48]

Left alone and growing colder as he waited for Orville to return, Wilbur tended to his correspondence. Taking off the aeronaut's hat and replacing it with the psychiatrist's, he replied to their good friend and failed doctor George Spratt. Suffering chronically from depression, Spratt was in constant need of reassurance, which Wilbur seemed willing to provide. He suggested on December 2 that Spratt's low spirits came from "living and working too much alone." Spratt had decided he wanted to work at the Smithsonian and wondered if this would compromise the Wrights, given their competition with Professor Langley. Graciously, Wilbur encouraged him to proceed: "The fact that you are acquainted with some of our ideas need not stand in the way so far as I can see, for it is now too late for Langley to begin over again, and besides we may possibly publish our tables, &c., before long anyhow."[49]

Langley's Moment of Truth

Unknown to the Wrights, Langley was rapidly nearing his moment of truth. Langley's *Great Aerodrome*, pulled by two steam tugs, left from the Eighth Street wharf in Washington on December 8, passing ice floes and barren leafless trees as they motored down to the point at which the Potomac joins the Anacostia River. The team had resolved to make its flight, for better or for worse, today. The operation was broke, with no money remaining to pay the crew or to refine the craft further. So even with an ominous dark sky, heavy gusts of wind and dusk approaching, the crew decided to try their luck. Even perfect conditions wouldn't have changed the result. Prepared for the worst, pilot Manly wore only a cork-lined jacket over his union suit, so as not to be waterlogged during a rescue mission if the craft sank.[50]

Later, Langley would write his account of the fateful flight:

> ...The engine being started and working most satisfactorily, the order was given by the engineer (Manly) to release the machine, but just as it was leaving the track another disaster, again due to the launching ways, occurred. This time the rear of

the machine, in some way still unexplained, was caught by a portion of the launching car, which caused the rear sustaining surfaces to break, leaving the rear entirely without support, and it came down almost vertically into the water.[51]

Dignitaries watching the launch from a tugboat in the river and other small boats provided for the occasion saw the nose of the machine tip up sharply on takeoff before the wind pushed the craft over onto its back, so the tail entered the water first. Manly, the pilot, found himself looking at the sky.[52] Trying to right the craft, Manly flipped its wings rightside up before trying to extricate himself. His jacket had caught on a piece of metal and, in his desperation to escape, he tore it in two, only to find himself trapped below a sheet of ice.

His breath nearly exhausted, Manly dove under and escaped the ice cake only to watch a crew member, unaware Manly was safe, dive from the houseboat to rescue him. Back on the boat, Manly was so frozen his clothes had to be cut from his body. Safe but furious, he unleashed a "most voluble series of blasphemies." For as his fellow crew members knew as well, they'd soon be receiving their last paychecks. To add insult to injury, the crew had hitched a line to the aerodrome's tail, but in yanking it, they broke the frame in half. It served as an exclamation point to Langley's star-crossed aeronautical career.[53]

Mistaken Jubilation

Ironically, as gloom pervaded the houseboat and the Langley crew, the mood back at the Smithsonian was one of jubilation. Those staff members left behind, whom one newspaper called "the stuffers of birds and rabbits," had climbed to the tower of the castle, where they trained binoculars on the houseboat anchored at Arsenal Point from atop its roof. Since the castle roof could accommodate only a few of the workers, they arranged an oral relay, passing on any happenings they observed to the troops below. After all, this day's event was of more than passing interest to staff members. So tightly had Secretary Langley been tied to aeronautics after his 16 years at the Smithsonian helm, these well-publicized experiments placed the very reputation of the institution itself at stake.

At dusk, one worker spied the aerodrome shoot off the end of the houseboat and disappear behind a clump of trees. Inferring that the craft was still rising, dipping, and circling out of his sight, the staffer concluded the trial was a success and shouted jubilantly to his colleagues below, who passed around the 1903 version of high-fives. It was only the arrival of Secretary Langley back at the castle that brought the sobering news.

Not only did Langley have to comfort his staff members, but a skeptical press waited outside his doors with its collective arms folded, waiting to pounce on whatever statement the secretary chose to offer. In a prominent headline, *The Washington Post* called the disaster a "mystery to Langley" and estimated $5,000 would be required

Samuel Langley's *Aerodrome* destructs dramatically upon takeoff on Potomac River on December 8, 1903. It would be Langley's last flight. National Air and Space Museum, Smithsonian Institution (SI Neg. No. 2002-16637).

to fix the broken machine. That the respected scientist couldn't say definitively why his crucial test had failed wouldn't be encouraging to his funders. Still holding out a glimmer of hope that his beloved aerodrome would yet fly, Professor Langley put a game face on the disaster and estimated he could fix the craft for $2,000. Manly, recovered from his attack of profanity in the aftermath of the crash, told the press that "Something caught the airship on the launching track, as we went over the edge, the rear portion of the aeroplane was pulled down, the front portion was shoved up, and then I felt we were going over."[54]

Long-time Langley supporter Theodore Roosevelt, who had attended one of Langley's early trials with Rudyard Kipling , missed the Arsenal Point launch. Although Roosevelt, as president, now headed the national crusade for first flight, he was up to his ears in both foreign and domestic policy crises. *The Washington Post* that day reported that American troops had landed in Panama to prevent an invasion of the Isthmus, where the Panama Canal was being built. As the president listened to that news with one ear, his other one was on the machinations of GOP Boss Mark Hanna. No Roosevelt fan in the early going, Hanna had called together Republican leaders in Nashville to plan for the 1904 presidential campaign, and the president wanted to insure the conclave would back him to run for a full term.[55]

A Congressional Shellacking

The venerable Professor Langley was clearly in for a shellacking from Congress and the public. Langley had cloaked his project in a veil of secrecy and treated the press with contempt. Now the Fourth Estate returned the favor with scathing indictments of its own, calling the ill-fated launch "a fiasco." Langley's hometown newspaper, *The Washington Post*, showed little mercy:

> In the past, we have paid our respects to the humorous aspects of the Langley flying machine, its repeated and disastrous failures, the absurd atmosphere of secrecy in which it was enveloped, and the imposing and expensive pageantry that attended its various manifestations. It now seems to us, however, that the time is ripe for a really serious appraisement of the so-called aeroplane and for a withdrawal by the government from all further participation in its financial and scientific calamities.[56]

A *New York Times* editorial on the event mingled pity with derision: "It would serve no useful purpose to say anything which would increase the disappointment and mortification of Prof. Langley at the instant and complete collapse of his airship. The fact has established itself that Prof. Langley is not a mechanician, and that his mathematics are better adapted to calculations of astronomical interest than to determining the strength of materials in mechanical construction."[57]

Langley, as he had done in October, felt the launching mechanism rather than the aerodrome's structure itself had probably caused the mishap. In making his analysis, Langley had a choice between two unpalatable explanations. If he faulted the aerodrome itself five years after contracting with the Board of Ordnance to build a flying machine and two years beyond the point at which he promised he'd have it in the air, he'd look like a fool. But did he come off any better by pointing to a defect in the launch mechanism two months after the same kind of problem had derailed his experimental flight?

Secretary Langley's explanations to the contrary, biographer Fred Howard holds that "...it is generally conceded today that inherent structural weakness was the cause." The only extant photograph of the aerodrome in flight, taken by an alert *Washington Star* photographer, shows the wings bent and the frame twisted, well before the craft ever hit the water.[58]

Heated debates raged throughout the 20th century over the extent to which the *Great Aerodrome* was, in fact, airworthy. It had a superbly-designed engine, capable of turning out 52 horsepower yet weighing only 125 pounds, but one historian has called the aerodrome "a travesty of aerodynamic design" and one that "could not possibly fly."[59] Further, Langley discounted the kind of preliminary experiments the Wrights performed, such as the use of a wind tunnel. This device might have told Langley that wings using curved leading edges produce less drag than flat ones or that double-decker wings offer more lift than wings placed one behind the other. And rather than conducting trials of his aerodrome itself, Langley flew quarter-sized unmanned models, believing that would sufficiently replicate conditions in the full-sized manned aerodrome.[60]

But Langley had his defenders, and some were passionate. One such was Glenn Curtiss, the aeronautical pioneer who believed so strongly in Langley's *Great Aerodrome* that he would have one rebuilt in 1914. He flew it in Hammondsport, PA to help vindicate the by-then tarnished name of the late Professor Langley, albeit for personal reasons.[61] Ironically, Langley's greatest legacy may have been the 1896 flights of his 30-pound models, if for no other reason than that they inspired Wilbur and Orville Wright to take up flying. Years later, Wilbur wrote generously of Langley's 1896 test: "It had a great influence in determining my brother and myself to take up work in this science and without doubt it similarly influenced others."[62]

Cynicism Tars the Wrights

Langley's dramatic failure generated a wave of public cynicism that washed over the Wrights as well. Following only by days the failure of the vaunted *Great Aerodrome*, the prospects for the Wrights' forthcoming flight would be a hard sell — that is, even if it were a success. Orville read of the Langley debacle while returning from Dayton to Elizabeth City on December 9. He knew this likely meant the end of the line for Langley, but when the next-to-last high jumper fails to clear the bar, it by no means assures victory for the last competitor.

By December 11, Orville was back in camp, and the brothers wasted no time setting the propeller shafts and running the machine along the crude track. Warm air for December augured well for their experiments. Everything depended on favorable weather and, at last, the perfect day arrived, with a 15 mile-an-hour balmy wind. But December 13 was also a Sunday. Devoted to their minister father, the brothers had promised him they would not work on the Sabbath. During a day filled with reading and quiet walks, they kept their pledge.[63]

Hard-bitten crew of U.S. Life Saving Station at Kill Devil Hills greeted Wrights with curios-ity and skepticism on their arrival in 1900. But before long, they would become fast friends and helpmates. Special Collections and Archives, Wright State University Libraries.

On December 14, they put out a red flag signal for five of the hard-bitten men from the Life Saving Station to help them test the engine. Over the four seasons the Wrights had come to Kitty Hawk, they had become good friends with these seafarers. Since the founding of the Life Saving Station in 1847, its men had acquired a proud reputation in the Outer Banks, which had seen some 600 ships lost and thousands of shipwrecks in a region some call the Graveyard of the Atlantic. The stations, set seven miles apart along the 60-mile sandbar, often became community centers in the sparsely-settled area, housing residents in emergencies and supplying them fresh water from the large tanks into which they gathered rain runoff. The lifesavers were heroes to the children as well. Their daily drills included one man walking north along the beach from the station and another walking south. Upon reaching a small halfway house between the stations, the first to arrive would wait for the rescuer coming from the other direction. Then they would exchange badges and carry them back to their original station as proof they had completed their work.[64]

Carrying a 700-pound machine 150 feet up Big Hill in ankle-deep sand and installing it on the track was arduous work, even for rescuers whose day job was sav-ing lives at sea. Four long sections of 2 × 4s, laid end to end, comprised what the crew soon nicknamed the "junction railroad." To move the craft up the hill, they had to remove the hind section of rail, move it to the front, push the *Flyer* along it, remove the new hind section, place it at the front, and continue the process.[65]

In operation, the *Flyer*'s pilot lay prone, facing forward, just as with the 1902 glider. His right hand held an upright strut while his left hand pushed the lever for the elevator. The pilot's hips lay in a cradle, so that when he moved sideways, wires affixed to the cradle caused the ends of the wings to warp while simultaneously turning the rudder as well.[66]

Wilbur the First to Fly

Wilbur drew by lot the right to take the *Flyer* up. With everything in readiness, the engine shuddered to life and hurtled down the track at a nine-degree incline, as Orville guided the craft along the track 35 to 40 feet until it completely outran him. The first trial, lasting 3.5 seconds, carried Wilbur 105 feet. The trial would have been longer, Wilbur figured, except he mistakenly steered the craft upward too soon after leaving the track, causing it to slow down and land prematurely. The left wing hit the ground first and a number of members broke upon impact, largely because Wilbur, in the excitement of the moment, forgot to shut off the motor when it began to sink. The flight was a lot shorter than many of their unmotorized glides, and a lay observer might have shaken his head in disappointment. But the brothers were jubilant. What the short flight had shown them was that the launching system was reliable, the motor was sufficiently powerful, and the craft was strong enough structurally to withstand the rigors of flight.[67]

Knowing everything the Wright family as a whole had invested in this venture, in which the bishop, Katharine, and Lorin had already participated, Orville drafted a telegram to Dayton, documenting the trial: "Misjudgment at start reduced flight to hundred and twelve. Power and control ample. Rudder only injured. Success assured. Keep quiet." The terse warning at the end was to prevent the kind of "pesky" reporters who had plagued Langley and who could be unforgiving in the event of failure.[68]

The brothers decided to ditch the downhill launch they had used the day before, feeling it made the launch more difficult, not less. But more than that, they had argued early that the mantle of first flight would belong to one who launched a craft from a flat surface, soared into the sky, and then landed again. How could they claim that prize for themselves if they took off from a downward-sloping launching track? So they relocated the junction railroad to a level stretch not far from their living quarters.[69]

The crew spent December 15 repairing the *Flyer* and December 16 in a futile wait for wind. Thursday, December 17, began auspiciously, with a northerly wind of 20 to 25 miles per hour greeting them on awakening. The local life savers sensed anticipation in the air and responded quickly to the beckoning of the Wrights' red flag. Trekking to their camp came five men, including John T. Daniels, a giant of a man who could not have sensed the importance of the historic role he was about to play; Will Dough, a witness to Wilbur's flight three days earlier; Adam Etheridge, who had brought his wife and children to camp several days earlier to share the excitement; W.D. Brinkley, a Manteo lumber dealer; and Johnny Moore, a Nags Head teenager.[70]

Wilbur Wright surveys damage to front horizontal rudder and skid after abortive flight on December 14, only six days after Professor Samuel Langley suffered a similar fate, although on water, not sand. Special Collections and Archives, Wright State University Libraries.

Fancy-Dressed Flyers

One might have thought the Wrights were dressed for a special occasion, with ties, white shirts and starched collars, unless one also knew they dressed that way every day. Orville drew the lot to pilot the first trial. He would be flying into a brisk wind, which a hand anemometer measured at 24 to 26 miles per hour. A crew member dripped a tiny amount of gasoline into each cylinder of the crude engine and lifted the battery box to hitch it to the engine. As they prepared for Orville to take the helm, a touching tableau unfolded, as the crusty seamen watched the brothers, who had been inseparable for years, hold each other's hand. As one of the crew observed, "...sort o' like two folks parting who weren't sure they'd ever see one another again."[71]

After a formal handshake with his brother, Orville climbed aboard and eased himself into the cradle. Before Orville was a horizontal lever pointed to the rightmost of three positions, meaning that the fuel line was closed. He pushed it to the center and started the engine, welcoming its vibration and deafening roar. Finally, he moved the lever to the left, slipping the release rope at 10:35 A.M. The craft eased down the track, gaining speed to seven or eight miles an hour as Wilbur ran along side it, before it lifted from the track. Conscious that this could be an historic moment, Wilbur

Outer Banker John Daniels, taking his first photograph ever, snaps one for the ages as he chronicles Orville piloting the *Flyer* on its first flight, lasting 12 seconds, as Wilbur runs encouragingly alongside. Special Collections and Archives, Wright State University Libraries.

had corralled John Daniels to become the official photographer of the Big Moment. Though Daniels had never taken a photograph in his life, Orville situated a box camera atop a tripod, inserted a 4" × 5" glass plate in it, and positioned Daniels at the end of the rail, his head shrouded by a black cloth, his hand on a rubber bulb. Daniels's instructions were to snap the shutter the moment the *Flyer* was free of the rail. He did so dutifully, if nervously. In the now-famous shot, which framed the action perfectly, Wilbur can be seen running slightly behind the craft in the right foreground.

The rudder control seemed to malfunction, causing the craft to exaggerate its lift and drop, and the flight ended in 12 seconds, some 100 feet after leaving the track. Orville discovered, as Wilbur had three days earlier, that the control lever was extremely sensitive, and moving it only slightly caused an exaggerated rise or dip.[72] In the mild crash, the landing skid beneath the rudder cracked. As biographer Crouch observes, "You could have thrown a ball farther but, for the Wrights, it was enough. For taking off from level ground, a powered aircraft under control of a pilot, had risen aloft and landed no lower than the ground on which it had started — all under the complete control of the pilot." A century later, Americans would still celebrate their triumph.[73]

As eager as the team was to try again, the cold and whipping wind numbed the limbs, and the Wrights invited the rescuers all to stand around the wood stove in their shed for a few minutes before the trials resumed. Ironically, the one local everyone expected would be there wasn't. Since 1900, the Wrights had found no bigger supporter than Bill Tate, the postmaster and man who first welcomed the brothers to Kitty Hawk in 1900. When he awoke on December 17, Tate concluded the weather was too cold and windy for the Wrights to make the attempt and chose to stay home.[74]

Twenty minutes later, the repairs made, Wilbur climbed aboard to make the second trial. This attempt lasted 175 feet, far shorter than many of their earlier glides. By 11:40 A.M., Orville began the third trial, but a strong gust hit the craft from the left side after 200 feet and brought him down. He probably went farther than his first flight because of his experience with the sensitive control lever.

Would Anyone Believe It?

At this point, the brothers knew that using their own standards, they had achieved flight. But could they convince anyone else? In describing the criteria for flight, Wilbur Wright had already written that engine momentum alone could carry a craft a fair distance in the air: "…we estimate that it is possible to jump about 250 feet, with a machine which has not made the first steps towards controllability and which is quite unable to maintain the motive force necessary for flight." Clearly, if they were to develop credibility in the aeronautical community, a 200 foot flight would never do. And so a fourth trial would be necessary.[75]

The fourth attempt, with Wilbur at the controls, began at high noon, and just as Orville had, Wilbur benefited from his earlier flight that day. Just as with the previous three trials, the *Flyer* rose and fell like a bucking bronco. Fortunately, it didn't hit the ground as the previous ones had, although at one point it dipped to a foot from the earth before Wilbur could correct it. Some 300 to 400 feet out, Wilbur seemed to have it under control. Had the craft landed at that point, jubilation would have broken out, for the Wrights clearly would have achieved first flight. But the *Flyer* continued to cruise about 15 feet above the ground, 600 feet out, 700 feet, until reaching a small hummock some 800 feet from the launching point. At this point, it began pitching again, perhaps because the sand formation had disrupted the wind pattern, and dove to the ground. The impact shattered the front rudder frame, but that reality paled beside the fact that their craft had flown 852 feet in 59 seconds, by far he longest trial they had made.[76]

The brothers removed the damaged rudder and, celebrating all the way, carried the *Flyer* back to camp. But while they all were congratulating each other on the successful flight, a wind gust picked up the historic machine and upended it. John Daniels and Orville grabbed hold of uprights at the rear of the *Flyer* but couldn't right the craft, which turned over upon them. Daniels hung on from the inside, but the craft knocked him down, and the huge man cartwheeled over and over, while he held on for dear life. Since the man-made tumbleweed included a heavy engine and chains, Orville termed Daniels' survival "miraculous." The calamity severed the engine legs, smashed most of the rear ends of the ribs and the uprights, and bent the chain guides. Although, the *Flyer* would be the subject of story, film, and display for the next century, it would never fly again. Daniels would joke years later that he had been the pilot of the fifth Wright flight that day and had survived the first aircraft crash in history.[77] "I was plumb scared," he told the crew. "When the thing did stop for half a second I nearly broke up every wire and upright getting out of it."[78] The Wrights had abandoned their earlier gliders at Kill Devil Hills, but their sense of history impelled them to ship the broken *Flyer* back to Dayton.

Later that day, after calling on some stalwart supporters in Kitty Hawk to share the news, Orville fired off to the Bishop what would become one of history's most heralded telegrams: "Success four flights Thursday morning all against twenty-one mile wind started from level with engine power alone average speed through air thirty-one miles longest 57 seconds inform press home Christmas."

A helpful Western Union operator offered to contact the local press, but the Wrights sternly forbade it. They had worked out their press strategy ahead of time and had designated their older brother, Lorin, as their press agent. His energetic assistant proved to be the boys' father, the genial bishop. To Katharine Wright fell the task of telegramming the first notification outside the family, to Octave Chanute. The old man could not have helped bemoaning the fact that, after nurturing the conception of the project in so many ways, he wasn't present at the birth.[79]

An axiom of press-agentry is that if all else fails, you can always fall back on your home town. But when Lorin Wright puffed out his chest and strode proudly through the doors of the *Dayton Journal* that evening, the local Associated Press representative dismissed the story out of hand. Frank Tunison told Lorin, "Fifty-seven seconds, hey? If it had been fifty-seven minutes then it might have been a news item." However, the *Virginian-Pilot*, not far from the Outer Banks, broke the story the next day, although in wildly-exaggerated fashion, claiming the craft had soared three miles. Of 21 newspapers the Associated Press contacted to determine their interest in carrying the story, only five responded. But after the *Cincinnati Inquirer* ran an article the next morning, the afternoon Dayton dailies reluctantly picked it up, and the rest, as it is said, is history.[80]

The Wrights' triumph proved many things to the aeronautical community. To the public, it proved that technological breakthroughs don't necessarily take barrels of money. Professor Langley's national crusade had cost the American government and Smithsonian benefactors some $73,000. When the Wrights sat down to tally the expenditures they had made from 1900 through their successful flight on December 17, 1903, their total came to less than $1,000.[81]

13

Grudging Acceptance

"Imagine a locomotive that has left its track and is climbing up in the air right toward you — a locomotive without any wheels, we will say, but with white wings instead … a locomotive made of aluminum. Well now, imagine that locomotive with wings that spread 20 feet each way, coming right toward you with a tremendous flap of its propellers, and you will have something like what I saw…. I tell you friends, the sensation that one feels in such a crisis is something hard to describe." — A.I. Root, writing in *Gleanings in Bee Culture*

From the day that the fine white sand of the Outer Banks tickled the toes of the first human, no, before that, long before, an abundance of wildlife soared, swam, and slithered along this 60-mile-long sandbar edged with jungle. Overstocked is the word that best describes nature's bounty here in the years when the calendar turned to the 20th century, a milestone for which hundreds of local people took passing notice and many thousands of crawling, flying, and swimming creatures did not.[1]

Years later, 90-year-old Mary Midgett would talk about the life of a young mother in the days when two polite but strangely formal young men came to town to try out what they said was a machine that could fly. So underfished were the waters of Abermarle Sound, Mary said, that a housewife needed only to wade in at Kitty Hawk landing with a kitchen pan and harvest her family's supper with her bare hands.[2]

Local wildlife — canvas-back ducks, redhead ducks, teals and Buffleheads, wild geese and swans, migratory Canadian geese, marsh ducks — their numbers "exceeding all conception of any person who had not been informed," had learned to tolerate the scattering of people.[3] No settlement on the Outer Banks had more than a few hundred people. Gulls, crows even a kind of pelican that dwelt there might have felt, literally, above it all, since the meanderings of the two-legged folk had less to do with them and more with the wild horses, hogs, sheep, and cattle with which homo sapiens shared this vast expanse of sand. William Tatham surveyed the coast in 1810 and reported that "The Banks are justly valued for their advantages in raising stock; horses, cattle, sheep and goats etc. are raised in considerable numbers without the least expense or trouble to the proprietors more than that of marketing."[4]

A New Flying Beast

But then came the 20th century and a new flying beast no bird or animal had ever seen before. It rose from the ground, with sand swirling about it, great white wings not flapping but dipping up and down at their tips, and with a deep, persistent roar at its center, a sound no creature of the land, sea, or sky had ever made. Writer Byron Newton described several years later his idea of what that local menagerie must have experienced:

> Often as the machine has buzzed along above the sand plains, herds of wild hogs and cattle were frightened from their grazing grounds and scurried away for the jungle, where they would remain for hours looking timidly out from their hiding places. Flocks of gulls and crows, screaming and chattering, darted and circled about the machine as if resentful of this unwelcome trespasser in their own and exclusive realm. There was something about the scene that appealed to one's poetic instincts—the desolation, the solitude, the dreary expanse of sand and ocean and in the center of this melancholy picture two solitary men performing one of the world's greatest wonders.[5]

Such bounty would not go unnoticed for long, for local providers made their living fishing the warm coastal waters and hunting the dense semi-tropical forest. Breadwinners soon learned they could earn as good a living in commercial hunting as they could in fishing. And so the frequent crack of double-barrel, breech-loading shotguns rang out along the Banks. By the last quarter of the 19th century, so large was the demand for fowl that hunters packed them in huge barrels, alternating the winged carrion with layers of ice, to ship to fine restaurants in Philadelphia, New York, and Boston. Russell and Van Griggs set a local record in 1905 by dispatching 892 ruddy ducks in a single day, keeping a bucket of cold water nearby to dip their gun barrels into whenever they overheated.[6]

Race to the Sky Continues

With the triumphal flights at Kill Devil Hills on December 17, 1903, had the race to the sky ended? Or had it only just begun?

It wasn't the profit motive that lured Wilbur and Orville Wright to the quest to become first in flight. Scientific curiosity and the youthful desire to go where no one else had gone was sufficient incentive to make them gradually relegate a thriving bicycle business to the status of an avocation while allowing aeronautics to consume the rest of their life. But what they had learned since 1899 about foreign policy as well as science had made them wiser men. With Professor Langley's abject failure, Washington had yet to gain the leading edge in aerial surveillance. Now the governments of competing European nations had begun sponsoring aeronauts who, they hoped, could give them just that. Whoever invented an airship that nations would compete to buy would clearly gain financial independence for life.

The brothers were too realistic to delude themselves into believing that they alone would lead the race that lay ahead — the competition to exploit the commercial and military possibilities of flight. First of all, they hadn't yet received the public acceptance that would be their red carpet when they sought contracts from national governments. And even if public recognition came in due time, they knew some of their European competitors, and particularly the French, had vowed not to sleep until they overtook the Dayton bicycle mechanics.

Europeans were no Johnny-come-latelies to aeronautics. As early as 1874, Felix du Temple had launched a plane outfitted with a hot-air engine. In 1884, Russia's Nikolai Mozhaiski deployed his steam-powered craft from a ski jump. Neither craft, however, allowed the pilot to control his craft in all three axes of movement, the single feature which the Wrights believed essential for military or commercial use.[7]

The French government, which shared the same imperial designs as the United States, shared also Washington's commitment to spend public funds to achieve its goal. The French military, for example, made sure Clement Ader had all the money he needed to build his *Avion II* and *III*, after he caused a stir in 1890 by launching his batlike, steam-powered *Eole*, with its four-blade propellers.

The Wrights had achieved their goal without a penny of government aid, and other European pioneers had managed so far without tapping the public till. Horatio Phillips's 1893 craft sported 20 wings; but once launched, he could scarcely control it. A decade later, Germany's Karl Jatho built and flew a biplane with a nine-horsepower gasoline engine.[8]

Chanute had urged the brothers repeatedly to exhibit the *Flyer* at the 1904 St. Louis Exposition, which generated even more hoopla than the 1893 Chicago Columbian Exposition. Sponsors even wrote a popular song for the event, entitled "Meet Me in St. Louis, Louis." (Decades later, Judy Garland would record the song in a motion picture based on the fair). But patent concerns led the cautious and secretive Wrights to beg off.

The Inside Track

Without the Dayton brothers as an attraction, experts considered the airship of France's Alberto Santos-Dumont to have the inside track for the widely-advertised $100,000 first prize. If anyone was predisposed to dominate the media spotlight, it was this small and wiry Brazilian. A flashy dresser with a penchant for Panama hats, Santos-Dumont lived with a swaggering panache. He had inherited enough money from his Brazilian family's coffee plantations to allow him to pursue his aeronautical hobby full-time. Santos-Dumont had met with the eager St. Louis committee, which treated their likely top draw with kid gloves, even reconfiguring their race course to make it more to his liking. The parties agreed the competition would feature a race covering three flights over a 10-mile path at the fairgrounds.

Watching the attention that the French contender had drawn to himself, the Wrights began to wonder whether they had missed a golden opportunity. They traveled to St. Louis to examine the fairgrounds and sensed quickly that the race had been rigged to favor the charismatic Frenchman. They concluded the rules were too restrictive and favored longer flights, even ones that didn't allow the kind of control the Wrights had mastered and which they believed was the reason one flew. However, they were sufficiently intrigued that upon returning to Dayton that they agreed they would enter the St. Louis contest if their experiments this season were successful.[9]

On June 17, Santos-Dumont landed in New York with a splash. Flashbulbs popped as stevedores unloaded the three two-ton crates carrying his flying machine and attachments. Meeting him with open arms at the White House was President Theodore Roosevelt. The Rough Rider, leader of the Langley mission in the race to the sky, had chosen to honor an aeronaut from another nation before even acknowledging the men who had succeeded in the national crusade. So eager was the St. Louis committee to have a stellar attraction that when Santos-Dumont arrived at the fairgrounds, it again bent to the wily Frenchman's requests for changes in the course, now reducing it to a six-mile round trip between two points.

The Santos-Dumont craft was a dirigible-balloon, shaped like a sausage and filled with hydrogen. On the eve of the exposition's opening, the guard attending it reportedly left the craft unattended while he took a break. The next day, the Santos-Dumont team reported that someone had slashed the silk skin of the gasbag in four places. A report in the morning papers quoted the negligent guard as alleging Santos-Dumont's own crew had damaged the balloon so they wouldn't have to compete. Getting wind of this, the dapper little aeronaut flew into a rage, stalked away from the Exposition, and took the next steamship home.[10]

Kitty Hawk No Big Deal?

In 1903, the news that an air-filled balloon had spent a full minute aloft wouldn't merit even passing mention in a newspaper. Lighter than air balloons, some equipped with propellers, engines, even rudders, were everywhere. So we shouldn't be surprised that the *Dayton Journal* newspaperman Lorin Wright approached dismissed the report of his brothers' 59-second flight as trivial. Lorin had visited Kitty Hawk only once and was involved with his own life, so he may not have been able to give the perspective to his brothers' accomplishments that it deserved. If Lorin had compared the flight to the unsuccessful mission of Professor Langley nine days earlier, that might have

Colorful Brazilian-born Alberto Santos-Dumont sits at controls of flying machine that he flew for France. Woman to his right is unidentified. National Air and Space Museum, Smithsonian Institution (SI Neg. No. 2002-16632).

given newsman Frank Tunison some reference point. But even then, consider that Langley was known worldwide, was backed by the federal government itself, and had failed. You're saying that your brothers, whom we've never heard of, even here in Dayton, succeeded where Secretary Langley hadn't? Sure, and pigs fly too, fella.[11]

City editors with college degrees were rare in 1903, and the amount of misinformation spread about was rampant. Some editors, such as those at the *Dayton Daily News,* alleged the Wrights had simply copied the work of Santos-Dumont, who had in fact used a gas-filled bag rather than biplane wings.[12]

Actually, Wilbur Wright had put his de facto press agent in a difficult position. While he hungered for the world to take notice of his and Orville's achievement, he had good reasons for not wanting to share with the press the important details of how they had accomplished their great feat. They had even sworn to silence the Kill Devil Hills lifesavers, who were the only direct witnesses to the flight.

All this, of course, was because they hadn't gotten around to securing a patent for the *Flyer.* The press can hardly be faulted for neglecting a story that it wasn't given enough facts to write intelligently. As soon as the 1903 holidays were behind them, the Wrights would make patent protection their top priority. But not until 1906 would they win their patent. Until then, the brothers would try, sometimes unsuccessfully, to shield their work behind a curtain of secrecy.[13]

When the Wrights sternly forbade the telegraph operator at Norfolk from passing on word of their triumph to a friendly reporter, it may not have occurred to them that he might disregard a command from someone he didn't know. H.P. Moore, friend of the Norfolk operator and a young reporter on the *Virginian-Pilot*, had already become aware of the work the Wrights were doing at Kitty Hawk. Simultaneously Ed Dean, another *Virginian-Pilot* reporter, learned of the story from different sources and began making telegraph inquiries. Eventually the two reporters learned that they were sniffing the same scent and combined their efforts, both working under hard-driving Keville Glennan, the *Virginian-Pilot*'s 23-year-old city editor.[14]

Even though the Wrights would wince at the headline, the *Virginian-Pilot* gave the story the bold-faced banner headline that the brothers undoubtedly felt it deserved:

FLYING MACHINE SOARS 3 MILES IN TEETH OF
HIGH WIND OVER SAND HILLS AND WAVES
AT KITTY HAWK ON CAROLINA COAST

The Wrights couldn't have written it better themselves, except for the distance covered. And in words the brothers would especially welcome, the editors added the subhead,

ACCOMPLISHED WHAT LANGLEY FAILED AT.

In a day before journalism schools were prevalent, the line between fact and fiction wasn't strictly observed. Frenzied reporters, under deadline pressure to unearth tales that would sell papers, did their best to write authoritative scoops with the meager facts they had. The *Virginian-Pilot*'s front-page piece explained definitively that "The problem of aerial navigation without the use of a balloon has been solved." Would they have felt that way had they known the flight was only 852 feet instead of 15 times as long? Among innumerable inaccuracies, the article asserted that the *Flyer* climbed to 60 feet above the ground instead of 15 feet and never mentioned that the brothers made four separate flights.

The description of the landing was dramatically fanciful: "He (Wilbur) selected a suitable place to land and gracefully circling, drew his invention slowly to earth, where it settled like some big bird, in the chosen spot." The reporters claimed that, upon landing, Wilbur had shouted "Eureka!," an assertion that provided belly-laughs for the brothers in the days ahead. Among newspapers carrying the story prominently were the *Cincinnati Enquirer* and the *Kansas City Star,* although Boston, New York and Washington, D.C. newspapers relegated it to the inside pages.[15]

By now, the Wrights had managed to kindle the public imagination, and on December 19, the *New York World* and *Century Magazine* sought exclusive rights to the Wrights' story, along with *Women's Home Companion* and *Scientific American,* which clamored for photos. Perhaps surprising to those esteemed publications, the brothers turned down all requests.[16]

Food for a Hungry Press?

Their reticence didn't satisfy a hungry press. Desperate, with driven editors at their backs, some reporters fabricated stories and used photographs of previous aeronautical trials by others, describing them as the flight at Kitty Hawk. *The Independent,* a weekly magazine, went so far as to piece together Wilbur's two speeches to the Western Society of Engineers with a Wright press release, pull out some factoids from newspaper coverage of the flight and slap on Wilbur's byline before publishing it. Things were clearly getting out of hand.[17]

Wilbur and Orville didn't arrive home until late on December 23. What a mixture of emotions must have greeted them, as Dayton was awash in Christmas preparations, with carolers celebrating a blessed birth quite apart from any awareness that they were awash in the birth of a new age as well. Bishop Wright, as the head of both community and household flocks, tended to the preparations for Christmas festivities. The proud contribution of Carrie, the Wrights' cook and part-time housekeeper, was the porterhouse steak she cooked for Mr. Orv. and Mr. Will on their arrival, welcome contrast to the cuisine they had enjoyed for the past few weeks. One might have forgiven the brothers if they had given short shrift to holiday gifts. Yet at a Christmas gift exchange at Lorin's home, Wilbur and Orville bestowed a micrometer on Charlie Taylor, by now one of the family, and gave Katharine a set of steak knives with pearl handles.[18]

The holidays behind them, the brothers felt the need to clear the clouded air the media had stirred up. They issued a simple statement, characteristically terse in tone, which concluded, "As all the experiments have been conducted at our own expense without assistance from any individual or institution, we do not feel ready at present to give out any pictures or detailed descriptions of the machine." Had they yielded to Chanute or others who suggested they accept backing from others, Wilbur and Orville might have been pushed into the limelight against their will. Their stubborn insistence on independence now guaranteed they would control the story of their fateful flight.

Still Living at Home

As generations of young people have discovered, living as an adult in one's parent's home may frustrate the independent spirit but does wonders for the bank account. During the Kitty Hawk years, the brothers neglected their bicycle business during an industry downturn, yet their savings grew to nearly $5,000, although much of the money came from their share of the sale of a family-owned farm in Iowa. This financial cushion let the brothers consider entering the nascent aeronautical industry full-time.[19]

If the Wrights harbored any illusion that the *Flyer* was instantly marketable, the coming season would destroy it. Yet they were confident that they had taken the lead ahead of all others who sought to make flight commercially possible. The time had come to seize the day. Oh, they'd still keep the bicycle business, which Charlie Taylor would run. And the seventh-grade dropout had become so indispensable to their fledgling aeronautical enterprise that he'd have to shuttle between the two businesses.

Wilbur Wright's innate conservatism shone through when the 36-year-old wrote about the life plan he envisioned for him and his brother, then aged 32: "...we believed that if we would take the risk of devoting our entire time and financial resources we could conquer the difficulties in the path to success before increasing years impaired our physical ability."[20]

Their immediate tasks were three: First, to smooth the rough edges off the design of *Flyer I*, then to retain an attorney to protect their hard-won gains by obtaining a patent on their work. Finally, they wanted to find a place closer to home to test their invention; one shielded, insofar as possible, from a rude and invasive press. Kill Devil Hills was an ideal locale for testing flying machines, but living year-round in a crude shed amid sand dunes was evidently a bleak prospect.

Orville, Wilbur, and Charlie Taylor put their heads together and soon decided that *Flyer II* would have a slightly-enlarged rudder, somewhat more wing surface, a shallower wing camber, and wing spars of white pine instead of spruce. The elevator control, they concluded, should move to the rear of its original location, to make it easier to handle. Increasing capacity of the gas tank echoed their success, since it meant a more refined craft could make longer flights. And a new engine, with a bigger bore, could crank out 15 horsepower and eventually 20 horsepower, as they broke the new cylinders in. In all, the changes added 100 pounds to the *Flyer*, which would have worried them to death six months earlier, before they knew they would have a much more powerful engine.[21]

A Nemesis Reappears

A timely appearance by the Wrights' old nemesis Augustus Herring, this time as a wolf in sheep's clothing, came only nine days after the Kill Devil Hills flight and the day after Christmas and underscored, as few things could, the pressing need for patent protection. Herring presented the brothers his own Christmas present: a figurative gun to the head. He offered to let them participate in a three-way partnership in an aeronautical venture. After all, he stressed, he was the "true originator" of the 1896 Chanute-Herring glider. He thought the brothers ought to know, by the way, that unnamed parties had offered him a "substantial sum" to buy his rights in what might, in other hands of course, become a patent infringement suit against the Wright brothers.[22] As often as Herring would peek into his mailbox in the weeks that followed, he'd never find a reply from Orville and Wilbur.

Which is not to say that the Wrights did not respond. For, without delay, they hired Atty. Henry A. Toulmin of Springfield, Ohio, who predictably advised them to clamp the lid of secrecy on their operations, something that would surely offend

Octave Chanute. The old man was hoping that news of the Wrights' accomplishment would germinate seeds of progress throughout the world. Toulmin told them they would gain more effective protection by patenting the system of control in all three axes of movement than by patenting the machine itself.

Chanute, not an attorney, had a different take. He forecast the brothers would obtain, at best, a very narrow patent on their invention and urged them to gather their rosebuds while they may, in the form of earnings through demonstrations and competitions. They decided that Chanute's advice was worth exactly what they were paying for it (nothing) and, instead, listened to the counsel they were paying.[23]

The brothers were polite to a fault by training, and this factor papered over some basic disputes that would eventually bring their relationship with Chanute to an end. The Wrights felt the breakthrough they had made was pacesetting new technology that would spawn a whole new industry. Their elderly mentor, on the other hand, felt only that "they had put old ideas into new bottles." The Wrights couldn't have disagreed more and would make the remarkable assertion to intimates that Chanute, in spite of his close relationship to the Wright camp, really didn't understand how the *Flyer* worked.[24]

Each ambitious applicant seeks a patent written so broadly that anyone who builds anything like his machine would infringe on it. A quarter-century earlier, engineer and attorney George Selden of Rochester, New York, obtained a patent for *the idea* of a motored land vehicle, with a small internal combustion engine, attached to a four-wheel frame, connected to a drive shaft and containing a fuel source. The fact that Selden produced no working model of the automobile didn't prevent him winning his patent.[25] The Wrights were considerably ahead of Selden in that they had created a machine that actually performed.

Government the Most Likely Buyer

The most likely buyer of their machine, the brothers felt, would be a national government. How they envisioned governments using the *Flyer* is revealing of their own values. While Teddy Roosevelt, as president, was looking for the kind of "splendid little war" that had made him the Rough Rider, the Wrights saw aerial surveillance as contributing to the end of war altogether. If warring armies could spy on each other from the air and detect their every move, unmasking enemy plans would prevent either side from gaining an advantage and would render warfare practically impossible. In so believing, they followed American pacifists' assessment of Hiram Stevens Maxim's invention of the machine gun. They actually hailed the development, believing the machine gun would cause such terrible carnage as to make nations recoil from war altogether.[26]

If the news of the Wrights' triumph didn't create front page headlines in America, the European aeronautical community saw it as a significant event. Yet the conventional wisdom, even on the continent, seemed to be that one 57-second flight didn't call for history books to be rewritten. In France, where aerophiles had vowed to prevent America from gaining primacy in flight, the tendency was to soft-pedal the accomplishment. Captain Ferdinand Ferber, who learned the news from Octave Chanute, wrote the Wrights in January, asking whether his own experiments might have been the spur that led them to motorize their craft. Such was not an unfair question under the aura of secrecy in which the Wrights had operated. Ironically, it was the French government that would grant the Wrights their first patent in July of 1904.[27]

A stroke of luck came the Wrights' way in early 1904 when they approached Dayton banker Torrance Huffman, owner of a 90-acre pasture, to rent his field for their experiments. The pasture, part of his dairy farm, wasn't otherwise in use, and he agreed to let the brothers use it without charge as long as they steered clear of his small grazing herd. Not that he was a supporter of the Wrights. Huffman had read the range of opinion circulating in the press about the brothers in wake of the Kill Devil Hills flights, and his terse assessment was, "They're fools."[28]

In configuration, the pasture measured roughly a half-mile by a quarter-mile, with high trees on two sides, to screen it for privacy. But every half-hour, the interurban railway (a high-powered trolley) passed through, on its way to and from Dayton, meaning the secretive brothers would have to time their flights to fall in the intervals. Even if someone saw them in flight, they'd be 200 feet or more away from the tracks, preventing any close-up photographs.[29]

The pasture, only eight miles outside of town, was undeniably convenient, but the differences in climate and altitude from that on the Outer Banks would take some getting used to. Wright biographer Harry Combs compares conditions at Kitty Hawk on the day of their fabled flight with the first day of testing *Flyer II* at Huffman Prairie. On December 17, 1903, the temperature at the sea-level testing site of Kill Devil Hills was 34 degrees, with clear, dry air and a 27 mile-an-hour wind — prime flying conditions. By contrast, Huffman Prairie is 815 feet above sea level, the temperature was 81 degrees and humidity 66 per cent, all adding weight to the wings. The wind, cut by the trees at either end of the pasture, was variable at best. Outweighing the less than ideal conditions? The Wrights' workshop was nearby, they didn't have to maintain a full camp, and they could sleep every night in their own beds. The brothers proceeded to scythe down the tall grass and build a shed like the one that housed the *Flyer* at Kitty Hawk. To adapt to the variable winds, they lengthened the 60-foot track used at Kitty Hawk to 100 feet and eventually 240 feet.[30]

Chasing the Wind

The brothers developed a routine of checking the likely wind pattern early in the morning, staking down several 20-foot sections of track in its direction, preparing the *Flyer* to roll, then settling in like hunters behind a duck blind and waiting for the grass to stir in the distance, indicating the wind was rising. Then they would sprint to the *Flyer* and hope that the wind didn't suddenly abate, which it often did.[31]

Folklore has it that the Wrights planned an elaborate subterfuge on May 25, to keep the press away. First, the story goes, they'd invite the media en masse and stage two failed flights. Gradually, the press would lose interest and leave them alone. The flames of this rumor are fanned by statements Wilbur made long afterward about how he fooled the press during those first weeks at Huffman Prairie. The Wrights are not known for dissembling, and the weight of evidence is that they were flying a newly-designed craft in unfamiliar conditions and simply sustained the kind of technical failures they had at Kitty Hawk. The difference is that at Huffman Prairie, they had gone to great lengths to invite a dozen reporters and other dignitaries, the way their rival Langley did. Knowing the savage treatment the press gave Langley, the Wrights may have worried that reporters could conclude their Kill Devil Hills flight had been a fluke and simply felt the need to save face.[32]

At last, the Wrights could get down to business. For all the attention and celebration, the reality remained that the four fabled flights of December 17 had given them barely two minutes in the air. They each needed much more time at the controls to learn their own craft, quiet time alone in the air, unmonitored. By June 10, they had entrusted the bicycle shop to Charlie Taylor once more and were taking the interurban daily to the pasture, which some called Huffman Prairie. They soon discovered that the downside of the large trees screening the pasture for privacy was that they also constituted an unnecessary windbreak. This contrasted markedly with the great open expanse of dune at Kill Devil Hills, where the Wright crew was exposed to wind from all directions.[33]

During their first two weeks, the brothers couldn't fly more than 300 feet and found the grassy hummocks of Huffman Prairie far less forgiving to a crashing aircraft than the sandy expanses of Kitty Hawk. After a number of early mishaps, causing twisted and broken members, bent rudders, and smashed propellers, Wilbur decided to move *Flyer II*'s center of gravity somewhat to the rear, which required rearranging supporting members. The hard landings were tough on the brothers as well, and a compassionate neighbor named Mrs. Beard used to dispatch one of her children to the pasture with a bottle of liniment each time she saw them take off.[34]

Spectators a Lucky Few

The pasture was officially off-limits to the curious, but a few lucky or unobtrusive folks managed to witness the tests at Huffman Prairie. Daytonians had heard that Wilbur and Orville had flown some kind of a machine down in North Carolina, but most newspapers didn't run the story and many felt it was just a rumor. The Griep family lived only doors away from the Wrights' bicycle shop and were family friends. When the architect father announced he was taking the family to Huffman Prairie to see history made, great excitement ensued. Like so many people at the turn of the century, Griep was in love with change, and the new home out in the country that he had designed for his family would have electric power throughout.

They hitched Old Nip, the family horse, to a surrey and rode to the prairie on the dirt road that paralleled the interurban railway. Griep urged his horse to the pasture's highest point for the best view. "Are you paying attention to this?" he asked his fidgety children. "Now listen to me, you're going to remember this to your last day." Eight-year-old Mabel wrote later that her father had to keep a tight hold on the reins "because the noise from the flying machine's motor was so terribly loud." She recalled:

> When that plane took off the ground, I just can't describe how I felt. I think I held my breath the entire time, and I'm sure an awful lot of people said a prayer. It was spectacular — just unbelievable. That's all I can say. The plane lifted sort of level at first and then started to rise up. I don't know just how far they went. The whole flight couldn't have lasted longer than a minute, but it proved that it could be done. When the plane landed, the whole field just exploded with applause. And then it got strangely quiet. Nobody could believe what they had just seen.... It was like witnessing a miracle.[35]

On August 6, Wilbur remained aloft, 10 feet above the ground, for about 600 feet and a week later, bested their Kill Devil Hills record by exceeding 1,000 feet. He cut nearly 20 seconds off his time in doing so. In the early going, the Wrights simply used a much longer version of the Kill Devil Hills launching track. But conditions augured for a way to give *Flyer II* more of a boost. By August, the brothers decided to stack four 30-foot poles into a tower. Pulleys and ropes ran from a 1,600-pound weight inside the tower down to the track and alongside it to its front end, crossed a pulley, and then doubled back to the aircraft. When the pilot was ready to fly and the propellers started to whir, he'd reach over the wing's leading edge and unfasten a clip holding an A line that anchored the weight. The dropping weight would exert a 300-pound pull on *Flyer II*. This, together with the thrust of the propellers, would propel the machine to flying speed by the time it reached the end of the track. Just as at Kitty Hawk, the non-flying brother would run alongside the track to balance the craft. And critically, the new system would work without wind power.[36]

With the new launching mechanism functioning well, the brothers turned to circling in the air to perfect control. Wilbur flew in half-circles to learn and to feel how to bank the *Flyer*, but the craft seemed prone to slide sideways with centrifugal force as it turned. Luckily, Wilbur turned his first perfect circle during the first visit of a legitimate outsider, as opposed to loyal locals and family members. The intense visitor, beekeeper A.I. Root, had motored nearly 200 miles over dirt roads to witness the flight. Root came away so enthused that he wrote a first-person recollection of the experience.

Failing to interest *Scientific American* in it, he published the piece in the January, 1905, issue of his trade magazine, *Gleanings in Bee Culture*, not the kind of publication the Wrights would have sought for publicity. With Root's eyes trained on the sky, Wilbur took off and after soaring 1,000 feet north, dipped the left wing a short distance from the pasture fence. *Flyer II* circled around a tree and, before completing the circle, leveled out and dipped the other wing, making an "S" turn before landing. The 65-second flight covered a half mile.[37]

Following an afternoon downpour, Wilbur decided to take the *Flyer* up again. He followed the same trajectory as the previous flight, turned around a large tree, and this time, continued turning until the craft had made a full circle, flying some 4,000 feet in 90 seconds. Root called it "one of the grandest sights, if not the grandest sight of my life." It "outrivals the Arabian Nights," he told the readers of his magazine:

> Imagine a locomotive that has left its track and is climbing up in the air right toward you — a locomotive without any wheels, we will say, but with white wings instead ... a locomotive made of aluminum. Well now, imagine that locomotive with wings that spread 20 feet each way, coming right toward you with a tremendous flap of its propellers, and you will have something like what I saw ... I tell you friends, the sensation that one feels in such a crisis is something hard to describe.[38]

Weighing an Option

The Wrights had left open the option of entering the aerial competition at the Louisiana Purchase Exposition, known popularly as the St. Louis Fair. But as the entry deadline of September 30 approached, they still hadn't sent in their $250 entry fee. During the summer, a series of mishaps, including one that nearly left Orville seriously injured, convinced them that success in the St. Louis contest was far from assured. Now that Santos-Dumont had walked off in a huff and the Wrights had grounded themselves, the contest organizers found themselves in a fix. The remaining entries were of poor quality, with Germany weakly offering a map-making demonstration, and Britain demonstrating how to produce hydrogen for airships. Somehow, France's airship entry ruptured in the move to its hangar (shades of its countryman Santos-Dumont's experience), and the best America could do was to charge a fee for two passengers to rise aloft in a balloon tethered to a 1,000 foot rope. Chanute entered his double-decker glider in the competition. He recruited carpenter William Avery, who had been so instrumental to the success of his 1896 trials, to demonstrate it. But a variety of mishaps sidelined the entry.[39]

In desperation, fair organizers extended the entry deadline to October 31 and pinned their hopes on the *California Arrow*, piloted by American Thomas Baldwin. On October 25, he managed to fly a figure "S" over the fair, as hopeful fair organizers patted each other on the back. But then Baldwin's engine died, and he drifted clear out of the fairgrounds and across the Mississippi River before alighting 15 miles away in Illinois. In a fitting end to a disastrous escapade, fair organizers were forced to admit that they had fallen woefully in debt. As authorities moved in to impound what money was left, it became clear that no prize would ever be awarded.[40]

Octave Chanute arrived in Dayton on October 15 with great anticipation, having missed the brothers' epochal flight the previous December. Orville had made his first circling flight on October 14 and wanted Chanute to see him do it again. After he made his first turn, a crosswind blew sharply against Orville's raised right wing, forcing the plane to make smaller and smaller arcs. He finally took the only practical course open to him and crash-landed *Flyer II*, landing with such force as to shatter both propellers and damage the engine. Alas, Chanute would leave the Wrights once more without witnessing a landmark flight that others had seen. Repaired at their Dayton shop, the propellers broke once again on November 3 and made their way back to the Dayton workshop, where Charlie Taylor worked overtime in reconstructing struts, spars, and other members that had smashed onto the unforgiving terrain.[41]

A Victory Flight

Theodore Roosevelt had ascended to the presidency after an assassination, and on November 8, he won election for the first time in his own right. The day after, the Wright brothers and their father, all Republicans, held what they called a "victory flight," as Wilbur stayed aloft for five minutes, circling the pasture four times and covering a distance of three miles. Had the engine not shown signs of overheating, the flight would have been longer.[42]

On December 9, the first anniversary of Professor Langley's swan song, the late autumn chill told Wilbur and Orville it was time to suspend operations for 1904. They could look back on a season of more than 100 flights, logging altogether a full hour in the air, and with two flights of more than five minutes. Yet much of the time, as historian Tom Crouch observes, they were really flying out of control. They still had far to go before they could proclaim to the world that they had built a practical flying machine. *Flyer II* was unsalvageable and would be discarded, except its engine and transmission.[43]

Yet before they could achieve the perfection they sought, the brothers Wright became players in an international chess game that held in the balance their fortunes and the fortunes of the major nations of the world.

14

Aircraft for Sale

"The American government has apparently decided to permit foreign governments to take the lead in utilizing our invention for war purposes."— Orville Wright to Octave Chanute, before offering the Flyer for sale to foreign governments

WITHOUT QUITE KNOWING IT, IN 1905 the Wright brothers became players in an Alice in Wonderland-like board game, in which one could win by losing. Like the race to the sky, the game had no published rules. The players were the national governments of America, England, France, and Germany, and those gifted inventors who sought to sell them motored aircraft. The Wright brothers loomed large on that stage, but they had company, most prominently Capt. Ferdinand Ferber and Alberto Santos-Dumont, both of France. Soon a newcomer, an American motorcycle racer named Glenn Hammond Curtiss, would join their ranks. His career would intertwine with those of the Wrights long after Ferber and Santos-Dumont were forgotten.

One might expect an aeronaut with a product designed for aerial surveillance to sell it to his own nation. The Wright brothers had earnestly tried to interest Washington. Yet they stressed repeatedly as a rationale for guarding their secrets that they had taken not a dime of public money during their aeronautical careers. Why should they feel bound to the United States government when it came to selling their finished product? Certainly, they'd prefer America to buy their product. But they had worked too long and hard on powered flight to simply sit by and let the next inventor win financial independence by selling his aircraft to a national government.

But how, then, does an inventor win this game by losing? The governments of the four contesting nations all were keenly interested in doing aerial surveillance. America, through Professor Langley, and France, through Clement Ader, had been sufficiently proactive to further that goal by sponsoring their own aeronauts. That process set up a dynamic that pushed people and politics together in curious ways.

In 1904, the four governments and several credible inventors circled each other warily, keeping their cards close to their chests. Government wanted to be sure it wasn't paying too much for a product that wasn't airworthy. The inventor wanted to secure top dollar for his product while not revealing his trade secrets prematurely. At some point, an inventor would contract with a government to supply it with a motored craft. With X having won, would Y and Z retreat to the sidelines to lick their wounds? Far from it. For three national governments needed aerial surveillance even more urgently now that one of them had already achieved it, and one less inventor could sell it to them, since presumably the successful inventor would have given the contracting government an exclusive. The products of the remaining inventors, therefore, would become even more attractive, and their price to the nations remaining would increase. Better, perhaps, to be the second to sign a contract than the first.

Orville Loses Control

In June of 1905, the Wrights began their fifth year of testing and the second at Huffman Prairie. Far from having refined their technique to lessen or eliminate dangerous conditions, they suffered a severe crash on July 14, when their French competitors were presumably taking a break to celebrate Bastille Day. Orville, as pilot, somehow lost control of the elevator, sending the craft crashing to earth at 30 miles an hour. The incident may have proved the adage that what doesn't kill you makes you stronger, since the mishap led the Wrights to modify the elevator, pushing it farther in front of the wings and enlarging it.[1]

Successful flights rewarded the Wrights for their efforts during September and October. On October 3, with 26 glorious minutes aloft, they broke all previous records and the next day boosted their record to 33 minutes. They covered more than 24 miles on October 5, in staying aloft 39 minutes at an average speed of 37 miles per hour. The press had largely ignored the Wrights' earlier flights. But now, word funneled in from readers to newspaper city desks that they had seen the brothers stay aloft a half hour or more, and Cincinnati and Dayton newspapers began to take notice.[2] Yet even then, the story received little play. *Dayton Daily News* city editor Dan Kumler acknowledged many years later that his paper largely ignored the story. "I guess the truth is that we were just plain dumb," said Kumler.[3]

Historian Stephen Kirk argues that Wilbur and Orville often seemed to be their own worst enemies. Octave Chanute, upon learning of their escalating triumphs, had urged the brothers to exhibit the *Flyer*, release photos of it aloft or even eyewitness statements from those who had seen it fly, but to no avail. From late 1905 through the end of 1907, the Wrights worked tirelessly to sell planes in the United States, Great Britain, France, or Germany, usually to governments but sometimes to private syndicates. In each case, they refused to reveal details, drawings, or to stage demonstrations until they had a signed contract. They were wary of giving away secrets, to be sure, but Kirk observes that as honorable men, the brothers naively expected to be taken at their word. How could the Wrights, of all people, not realize that after having been burnt by the Langley debacle, Washington wasn't likely to buy an aeronautical pig in a poke any time soon?[4]

Take That, Octave!

Over the Christmas holidays of 1904, Octave Chanute learned the peril in criticizing the efficiency of the Wrights' machines. In a December 26 letter to Wilbur, he observed, "I am under the impression that birds use less power than you have found necessary." Soon a hapless crow in Dayton learned it was being sacrificed to science, as Wilbur measured its body to rebut Chanute's assertion. By return mail, he sent Chanute the measurements: "Weight — 14 oz. Spread — 35 inches. Width of wing — 7½ inches. Surface — about 1½ sq. ft. Diameter of body — 3 inches. Thickness of wing at front edge — about ¼ inch." He concluded by saying, "...I am far from believing that it expends less power, In proportion to weight and speed, than is readily attainable in a dynamic flying machine of large size." Take that, Octave![5]

In early March, the Wrights learned that the German patent office had held up their application because "the principle of *twisting the wings*" had already been disclosed in a patent by German Major Herman W. L. Moedebeck. Proving himself not beyond guile, the strait-laced Wilbur confessed to Chanute that he and Orville had been aware of Moedebeck's patent and had crossed their fingers that the Germans would overlook it. "We fear that it may interfere with our being granted a broad claim on twisting the wings," he wrote. To keep their claim alive, the Wrights resorted to German dictionaries and a hair-splitting analysis of German semantics, turning on translation of the word "twisting." More practically, Chanute happened to know Major Moedebeck, as he did most players in the aeronautical community, and agreed to ask Moedebeck to vouch for the Wrights, if necessary.[6]

Europeans Come Up Short

In 1905, as the Wrights perfected the third version of the *Flyer*, Europeans were still coming up short. Captain Ferdinand Ferber, who had vowed in 1903 that France would put a man in the sky before America did, could do no better than to fly a powered glider tethered to an overhead cable. While most European experimenters pirated the Wrights' basic biplane design, others such as France's Ernest Archdeacon, Louis Bleriot, and Gabriel Voisin, introduced box-kite crafts.

One of Octave Chanute's most insistent themes was that aeronautical experimenters everywhere must pool their findings for the good of all, an appeal the Wrights found easy to resist. Yet on reflection, they would realize that they had learned of ailerons from M.P.W. Boulton of France and of wing-warping from Germany's Otto Lilienthal. The brothers' decision after the 1905 season to go underground until they had won their patent was indeed a setback for science as a whole.[7]

The U.S. War Department was obviously disappointed at the failure of the national crusade it had hoped would yield a machine for aerial surveillance. Without question, it was still interested and might begin shopping around. Even though the Wrights still lacked patent protection, they decided to approach Washington on their own behalf.

They first contacted their congressman, Robert M. Nevin, and agreed to his suggestion that they make their proposal through him to War Secretary William Howard Taft. In their submission, the brothers explained they had made two five-minute flights at speeds of 35 miles per hour and offered to build such a craft for the federal government.[8] The Board of Ordnance and Fortification had received so many proposals since the bitter Langley escapade that they sent the Wrights a form letter composed to save time in answering a flood of inquiries. They particularized the reply only to say that they'd entertain a proposal from the Wrights once they had brought their craft "to the stage of practical operation...."[9]

In a rueful letter to Chanute in May, Wilbur observed, "The American government has apparently decided to permit foreign governments to take the lead in utilizing our invention for war purposes." Not bothering to counter the board's fallacious assumption about what they had accomplished, the Wrights approached the British War Office. In 1902, they had become acquainted with Patrick Y. Alexander, a member of the Aeronautical Society of Great Britain, and invited him to witness the 1903 flights, but he was unable to attend. An associate, Lt. Col. John B. Capper, had come to America for the St. Louis Fair of 1904 and came away convinced that American aeronauts were ignorant know-it-alls, but someone advised him to stop by the Wrights' on his way home. Reluctant to show off too much to a stranger, Wilbur and Orville showed him photographs instead. "We were much pleased with him," Wilbur wrote Chanute, "and also Mrs. Capper, an unusually bright woman." In spite of not having witnessed the *Flyer* aloft, the Wrights impressed Capper enough for him to suggest the Wrights make a written proposal to the British government.[10]

The proposal they made to the British War Office in March of 1905 offered to build a machine carrying two men 50 miles on a tank of gas and offered to do it for 500 British pounds (about $2,500) for each mile the craft covered in its longest test flight. Reluctant to dip its toe in the water, the British government insisted instead on visiting Huffman Prairie to see a test flight.[11] As the Wrights waited, the British failed to appear.

Debut for Flyer III

The Wrights considered the Huffman Prairie site less than ideal, but it certainly was convenient and the brothers were eager to try out their newly-redesigned *Flyer*, once again having modified the craft to reflect lessons learned in the past season. The 1905 version would hold a heavier payload and be better able to crash without damage. Its tail was longer, to increase stability and control. Larger engine cylinders now developed 25 horsepower. Total weight of the craft, when piloted, would be 845 pounds.[12]

Orville and Wilbur didn't begin to fly until late June, and none of their first 10 flights exceeded any they had made at Kill Devil Hills. Then came weeks of torrential rains, burying Huffman Prairie under water. They used the down time to design a new set of propellers, wider and thinner than those used on the *Flyer*. The brothers had feared the old propellers bent in flight, causing a loss of thrust. They designed the new propellers with a backward sweep to prevent that.[13]

With the pasture largely dried out, the Wrights made a breakthrough on September 6, when Orville flew three miles, not in a week but in a single flight! The next day, he flew the first figure-8 either of the brothers had ever flown. Three weeks later, Wilbur flew 11 miles and circled the pasture 16 times. Orville boosted this record to 20.7 miles a week later and, a day after that, Wilbur averaged 38 miles an hour in flying 24.2 miles, and he stopped only when he ran out of fuel. But each longer flight increased unwanted public attention. On October 6, the brothers decided to suspend all further flights until Washington approved their patent application. Historian Harry Combs believes their decision was motivated, in part, by their own government's apparent rejection of their sales offer.[14]

A Letter to Taft

With British prospects seemingly dimming, Wilbur wrote in October once again to the corpulent War Secretary Taft, who had sent their proposal to the Board of Ordnance and Fortification. The board, Wilbur informed Taft, "seems to have given it scant consideration." Holding the offer open a while longer, he observed, "We do not wish to take this invention abroad, unless we find it necessary to do so."[15]

In a memo to himself on the 1905 flights, Wilbur gave insight into the practical reason why the *Flyer* characteristically stayed low in the sky: "With only one life to spend, we did not consider it advisable to attempt to explore mysteries at such great height from the ground that a fall would put an end to our investigations and leave the mystery unsolved."[16]

The season's trials behind them, the Wrights turned to the task of marketing the *Flyer* abroad. In late November, they wrote French Ambassador J. J. Jusserand and offered to share the results of their Huffman Prairie trials which, they noted, a dozen or more neighboring families had witnessed. The brothers weren't yet willing to lay their plans and specifications on the table, but the French could prove their veracity by talking to people who had seen the actual flights.[17]

While guardedly inviting foreign governments to take a closer look at their machine, the Wrights still distanced the rest of the world. But they found it impossible to plug all the holes in the information dike. In the fall just past, two men the Wrights didn't recognize appeared at the pasture and asked to look around. Wilbur cautiously agreed, as long as they took no pictures. The men went into shed housing the *Flyer* and seemed very knowledgeable, calling each aircraft part by its correct name.

The Wrights later learned that Charles Manly, Langley's chief engineer, had given a speech in which he mentioned the Wrights had made 100 circuits of a field, something the press hadn't written about up to that point. Wilbur wrote Chanute in early November, asking if he could guess the identity of the mystery men. Chanute wrote back that he suspected either Manly himself or Augustus Herring.[18]

December proved an auspicious month for the Wrights. Wilbur learned from the brothers' attorney that "all our claims have been allowed in the U.S. patent."[19] Final approval would come on May 22, 1906, with the granting of Patent No. 821,393. This fact induced them to guard their interests a little less closely, and they agreed to allow limited publicity of their flights. Octave Chanute greeted the news warmly and suggested they send information to President Roosevelt as well.[20]

The French Visitor

Just before the year turned, they received a visit from a man identifying himself as Arnold Fordyce. France's Captain Ferber told them Fordyce was an agent for a private syndicate charged with buying the *Flyer* and then turning it over to the French government. On the afternoon of December 30, Orville and Wilbur signed over an option to the French government. If France exercised it, the Wrights would build a replica of the *Flyer* for a million francs (about $200,000),[21] not a bad return on investment for the $1,000 the frugal pair had spent on aeronautics to date, including their Kitty Hawk encampments.

Like nature, technological advancement abhors the kind of vacuum that the Wrights created by their self-imposed sabbatical, and the dashing Alberto Santos-Dumont saw his opportunity to fill it. It was becoming clearer in the aeronautical world that control was the holy grail, and the Frenchman achieved a semblance of control in 1906 in his *14-bis*. The craft, in which Santos-Dumont stood upright in a wicker basket, featured double box-kite elevators in front, large biplane wings in the shape of box-kites with a substantial dihedral, and multiple side-curtains. In October of 1906, he flew 150 to 200 feet, no great feat. But three weeks later, Santos-Dumont lengthened that to 726 feet.

Aeronautical energy in Europe seemed concentrated in France. Historian Stephen Kirk reports that French aeronauts studied photos of the Wright flights that Chanute had published in European publications and used them as a launching point for their own experiments. In 1907, with the Wrights still absent from the scene, French aeronauts put on a push to set still more distance records. Leon Delagrange flew 1,600 feet in November. His countryman Henri Farman stretched the record to 4,900 feet, as he flew just short of a full circle during a demonstration at which one quiet spectator was Orville Wright. As they grew more puffed up by their advances, some French aeronauts began to assert that the Wrights were fakes.

Samuel Pierpont Langley (in forefront, hands on lapels) meets with rival Alberto Santos-Dumont of France (third from right, hands on hips) and their respective entourages in 1906. National Air and Space Museum, Smithsonian Institution (SI Neg. No. 2002-16635).

The brothers, not about to demonstrate why that wasn't true, suffered in silence.[22] Actually, they had a method to their madness. Such aeronautical backers as Ernest Archdeacon had taunted the Wrights to come to France and demonstrate their triumphs for all to see. Perhaps, he said, they could give the French lessons. With the Wrights' French patent application hanging in the balance, the brothers declined to take the bait. As Wilbur explained in a letter to Chanute, he wanted "to give the French ample time to finish and test any discoveries of the secrets of flying which any Frenchman might possess, and thus shut them off afterward from setting up a claim that everything in our machine was already known in France."[23]

A Sobering Reality

The Wright brothers had come to realize that flying an aircraft for a mile might be a grand spectacle, but that feat by itself didn't insure the machine was viable for military or commercial use. Wilbur wrote Chanute in October that "no one will be able to develop a practical flyer within five years."[24]

But this didn't stop them from continuing to market the *Flyer* for sale. The Wrights had been knocking on the door for nearly four long years when Uncle Sam answered in December of 1907, agreeing to put out to public bid a heavier-than-air flying machine. The Wrights had been poised for this moment for several years and had a proposal back to the government within a month. In fact, they had five new airplanes in various stages of construction.

The 1908 season would bring the brothers an embarrassment of riches, as the Wrights' European agent in March closed a deal to sell the *Flyer* to a private French syndicate. Such contracts required demonstration flights, so after a 2½ year layoff, the Wrights would take to the sky again. Rusty as they were, they'd need a lot of practice first. To achieve relative isolation, they decided to return to the Outer Banks. By the time they finished their season there, four other Americans would have flown.[25]

Their Just Deserts

"Nous sommes battu" ("We are beaten")— Comment of French aeronaut Leon
Delagrange to press after watching Wilbur Wright fly at Le Mans

THE PROSPECT OF BECOMING A celebrity that entrances and excites some people only
made Wilbur and Orville Wright wince. In the off chance that having their names in
the headlines might have turned his sons' heads, the bishop added a few words of
warning: "Enjoy fame ere its decadence, for I have realized the emptiness of its trum-
pet blasts."[1] At the least, the brothers would have to grin and bear it, for the year 1908
was to be a very public year.

Not having flown for some 30 months, the brothers felt the need to work out
the kinks before engaging in the all-important trials of the *Flyer*, on both sides of the
Atlantic, which would, if successful, fulfill their contracts with the French and American governments. In preaching the gospel of control to the aeronautical community,
the Wrights had shown extraordinary faith in the ability of the pilot to manipulate
his aircraft quickly and correctly when unexpected conditions arose, as they invari-
ably would. The corollary to this principle is that a pilot flying a control-dependent
machine has to have razor-sharp reflexes and preparation exceeding that of the pilot
of a craft depending largely on its own internal stability.

Huffman Prairie had become a zoo by the time they left it in 1905, with a spectator section drawing hungry reporters, curious competitors, and would-be customers alike. They recalled, with nostalgia, the relative solitude of Kill Devil Hills
and decided to return there in the spring of 1908. But the Kill Devil Hills they recalled
was the one they left in 1903 as nobodies. They would come to realize in 1908 that
they had left solitude behind forever.

What a difference a decade had made. For a group of fellows to form an aeronautical club in 1898 would have risked charges of insanity. To do so a decade later

was to mark its founders as cutting-edge pioneers. So it seemed natural that Alexander Graham Bell and his formidable wife, Mabel Hubbard Bell, gathered in the fall of 1907 the kind of like-minded people who had attended his Wednesday evening salons on Connecticut Avenue in the late 1890s, this time to form the Aerial Experiment Association. Bell had buried his friend Professor Langley a year earlier, dead some said of a broken heart. In the association, he hoped to unite his love of kites with Langley's faith in launching aircraft from water. Mabel believed enough in the idea to advance $20,000 for the venture from her family trust fund.[2]

Curtiss Enters the Fray

Now in his early 60s, Bell had a knack for spotting talent and invited two promising young men to join the venture: Lt. Thomas E. Selfridge, a San Franciscan and West Point graduate, who some thought spent too much time on aeronautics to the neglect of advancing himself as an Army officer. Bell saw that Selfridge's intent was to gain so much expertise in flying machines that when governments bought them for military use, he'd be in great demand. Motorcycle racer Glenn Hammond Curtiss specialized in building engines and had already sold one to Bell, who was so impressed he asked Curtiss to stay on as chief engineer for the AEA. But after indulging Bell in a round of kite experiments in early 1908, the younger members of the team agreed that kites were passé. Bell, outvoted, withdrew to his beloved Beinn Breagh to continue kite experiments on his own.[3]

During its brief existence, the AEA built and flew several models that drew substantial interest. In the spring of 1908 it unveiled its *Red Wing* model. Shortly thereafter, the Wrights read with irritated surprise an ad in the *Scientific American* for the AEA's *White Wing* model, equipped with ailerons, for $5,000. Not only did the brothers consider this blatant infringement of their 1906 U.S. patent, but the Alexander Graham Bell they had known by reputation was a man of honor. As it turned out, the ad was an apparent hoax, but it helped teach the Wrights that applying for a patent was only half the battle. Once granted, its holder had to defend it. The AEA experience had stoked Curtiss's fires, and he set out to construct models of his own design. By Independence Day, he flew the *June Bug*, and won a trophy from the *Scientific American*.[4]

The directives of the Wrights' American and French contracts helped crystallize their two goals for 1908: to complete two 50-kilometer flights within an hour in France, and to carry two men 125 miles at an average speed of 40 miles an hour in America.[5] The brothers would not realize these objectives at Kitty Hawk. They had shipped down only *Flyer III* from 1905, to which a larger motor and passenger seating had been added, with the pilot's controls moved to a space between the two seats. Their purpose in the Outer Banks was simply to gain more time in the air. The *Flyer*, for better or worse, was control dependent, requiring the brothers to be extra sharp when the time for the French and American trials arrived.

The return to Kill Devil Hills was a little like coming home after what must have seemed like five very long years. The Wrights stopped in Elizabeth City to buy gasoline and lumber and sailed across Albemarle Sound, arriving at Kitty Hawk landing on April 9. The five-year interval might have been an eternity on the harsh, windswept sandbar. Wilbur and Orville trudged through four miles of sand from Kitty Hawk landing to the site of their Kill Devil Hills camp, only to find a ghost town. The roof had blown clear off the camp building, leaving only three walls standing, and the hangar next door had almost completely collapsed. Residents of Kitty Hawk, probably concluding the Wrights had abandoned the camp, had pawed over and removed much of the camp's contents.

An unexpected addition to camp this year was the arrival of Dayton mechanic and friend Charlie Furnas, who stayed through their sojourn. Charlie's visit turned out to be fortunate, in that he unknowingly solved a dilemma for the brothers. They had rashly promised their father that, since two could fly together now, they would never do so themselves. It was enough that the bishop had been widowed at an early age. He accepted that his sons were engaged in a dangerous field that risked the loss of life. But to lose two sons at once would simply be too much to bear. Orville and Wilbur hadn't planned just how to avoid that eventuality. Charlie, in an instant, became the permanent passenger.

Word had filtered to the media that the Wrights had embarked for the Outer Banks, and the brothers would have been foolish to think that hungry reporters wouldn't dog their every step, spurred on by demanding editors. Soon after their arrival, a stringer for the *New York Herald*, D. Bruce Salley, showed up in camp. Salley was under special pressure, since his paper's owner, James Gordon Bennett, was a rabid aeronautical enthusiast. Given a brusque brush-off by the Wrights, Salley decided to hide in the weeds and report in secret.

Nearly three years had passed since the brothers had last flown. Yet in their first 1908 attempt, Wilbur soared more than 1,000 feet in 22 seconds. Recognizing they would have strong Kitty Hawk winds on their side, the brothers had left the Huffman Prairie catapult at home and used instead a 120-foot rail of the rather crude type they had employed in 1903. Salley, chased away from the first flight, reported on it through a report relayed to him by phone. His one glaring error, which would have made Bishop Wright's heart sink, was to report that the brothers had flown together. The *Herald* picked up the story and put it on the telegraph wire to other newspapers, while its owner decided his paper was on to something big and dispatched one of his A-team reporters to the Outer Banks.[6]

"A Chattering Clattering Sound"

Enough aircraft were flying publicly by 1908 that reporters covering them had come to compare and contrast their structures, aesthetic appearance, and even the sounds they made. Some reporters likened the sound of the *Flyer* to that made by a

Glenn Hammond Curtiss shown winning the *Scientific American* trophy in 1908 at Hammondsport, N.Y. in his "June Bug." National Air and Space Museum, Smithsonian Institution (SI Neg. No. 2002-16644).

grain reaper in a distant field at harvest time. Harry Harper, a British journalist, noted how much quieter it sounded than the French flying machines, which had much more powerful motors. Harper said the crossed chains driving the propellers, an innovation derived directly from the Wrights' bicycle shop, made a "chattering, clattering sound."[7]

Editors across America no longer yawned when told the Wright brothers had flown. Newspapers now clamored to send reporters to Kitty Hawk. New Yorkers Byron Newton of the *Herald* and Bill Hoster of the *American* checked into the Manteo's Tranquil House, which soon would be anything but. Newton, who had covered the Spanish-American War, was the kind of swashbuckling veteran who in later conflicts might fashion himself a "foreign correspondent," wearing a flak jacket and swapping tall stories over straight bourbon in hotel bars with overhead fans. He had worked at the *Herald* since 1902 and cast a cynical eye on the Wrights' record.

Newton portrayed Outer Banks residents as hayseeds at best, "well nigh as ignorant of the modern world as if they lived in the depths of Africa," coverage that wouldn't endear him to the locals if they read his dispatches, which they likely didn't. But local residents, most of whom remembered the brothers' exploits when they were unknowns, now felt they were watching history being made. Typical of the Outer Banks spectators was the Midgett family, ironically a stocky, broad-shouldered breed, who had lived in the area since the 1700s. Many of their members served in the prestigious lifesaving service and were still prominent in Kitty Hawk as of the writing of this book. The dissonance between their name and the sturdy appearance of many of the clan led their neighbors to call them the Mighty Midgetts.[8]

Florid prose was de rigueur in the days when newsboys in knickers screamed from city street corners, "Extra, Extra, Read All About it!" Newton might have been trekking through an Amazonian jungle, as he described his walk to the Wrights' camp. He and his companions, he reported, passed among "thousands of moccasins, rattlers and blacksnakes, the blinding swarms of mosquitoes, the myriads of ground ticks and chiggers, the flocks of wild turkey and other fowl, the herds of wild hogs and cattle and the gleaming white sand mountains." Newton had a scholarly mien, with a square jaw and long, straight nose on which perched rimless pince-nez glasses, above which his forehead rose to a thinning head of hair, severely parted in the middle. Apropos to his profession, Newton's lip line turned down at the corners into a skeptical sneer.

Converting the Press

But watching the Wrights soar more than a half-mile into the blustery Kitty Hawk winds turned Newton, a show-me type, into a believer. He now began to promote flight and the Wrights with the passion of the converted. "Thinking men and women of our generation have in store a great treat when they shall have the good fortune to witness this marvel of man's creation.... It brings a special exhilaration," Newton gushed. "It is different from the contemplation of any other marvel human eyes may behold in a life time." If Newton showed that response to a half-mile flight, his reaction was predictable when, later that day, Wilbur flew a full two miles.[9]

Salley sent home the same kind of enthusiastic dispatches. His hard-bitten editors, perhaps thinking their reporter had bought a bill of goods, greeted them with harrumphs. The *Cleveland Leader* was so disbelieving that it refused even to pay the story's telegraph charges. Newton, now hooked on aeronautics, submitted stories of the wonders he had seen to magazines, but none expressed any interest. "It does not seem to qualify either as fact or fiction," one editor sniffed.

However, other newspapers and magazines, including *Collier's* and the *London Daily Mail*, sent their own people to the scene. One of the reporters complained about the conditions encountered on the four-mile walk through the woods from Kitty Hawk landing to Kill Devil Hills. "Geographically, this may be only four or five miles," he complained, "but measured by the sand into which your shoes sink and which sinks into your shoes, the pine-needles you slip back on, the heat, and the 'ticks' and 'chiggers' that swarm up out of the earth and burrow into every part of you, it seems about thirty-five."[10] And once they arrived, since the Wrights assiduously kept reporters at arm's length, they had to create a secret encampment a mile away from their camp.

The brothers made four flights on May 13, one stretching 2½ miles. On May 14, Charlie Furnas became the first passenger in airline history, sitting next to Wilbur and enjoying a half-mile ride that took a bit less than 30 seconds. Later that day he flew with Orville more than 2½ miles in a circular trajectory. After dinner, they logged, at five miles, the longest flight ever on the Outer Banks.

The otherworldly scene of a human being soaring with the birds challenged reporters' powers of description. Hoster wrote of the *Flyer* that "her motions were like clock work, and she sailed along serenely under the bright blue skies like a thing endowed with life. Behind her floated a flock of gulls and crows that seemed at once amazed and jealous of this new thing in the air." Unfortunately, that 7½ minute flight ended in a crash, which broke the craft's upper wing and ended the Wrights 1908 season at Kitty Hawk. The brothers had professed lack of interest in the presence of the newspapermen, but they still stopped to peruse the guest register at Manteo's Tranquil House on their way out of town, to learn just who it was who had been spying on them.

With some solid practice behind them, designed to make their reaction to all contingencies second nature, the Wrights now could hear the clock ticking on their contract deadlines. Fulfilling major contracts with two nations simultaneously posed logistical challenges, since the brothers couldn't be in two places at once. They decided that Orville should stay in America and Wilbur would travel to France. On his way to Paris, Wilbur stopped in Norfolk, Virginia, and agreed to have dinner at the Monticello Hotel with Bruce Salley, now a reporter for the *Norfolk Landmark*. Byron Newton, who wasn't lucky enough to gain a personal interview, wrote the Wrights upon his return, praising their efforts. The letter he received in reply seems odd at best, given the cloak of secrecy the Wrights had drawn around themselves. Orville wrote, "...I am only sorry that you did not come over to see us at our camp."[11]

Taking Europe by Storm

Flint & Co., the Wrights' American agent, booked passage for Wilbur for May 18 aboard the R.M.S. *Campania*, bound for London via Liverpool. Meeting him at Euston Station was Flint's European agent, Hart O. Berg, a beefy fellow with a walrus mustache and a twinkle in his eye. Berg recalled later that Wilbur carried only one suitcase, "about the size of a music roll." On a mission in which the older Wright brother would be meeting dignitaries and prospective buyers, Berg knew this would never do. Oblivious to fashion as Wilbur was, it was obvious that Berg would have to become his sartorial consultant as well, just as Orville and Katharine had been years earlier. He took Wilbur from the train station directly to a tailor to measure him for a new suit and dinner jacket.[12]

On the eve of the landmark unveiling, the condition of the crates Wilbur received in Paris caused him to fly into a rage against Orville. In what seems to have been a Custom's Office job of unpacking and sloppy repacking, many of the components of the *Flyer* were dirtied and broken. It would take Wilbur six weeks to rebuild and assemble the craft.

A public relations wizard couldn't have planned any better the Wrights' public introduction to the world. By agreement, the trials were to be held at the Hunaudieres race course, 100 miles from Paris, near Le Mans. Wilbur was to perform in August the trials required by the French contract, two 50-kilometer flights in an hour. But Wilbur's vision was trained far beyond that one contract — he had decided to stage an extended aeronautical clinic for the public. On the appointed day, Wilbur started with two circuits of the field, a short two-minute flight on August 8, and then eight more flights from the following Monday through Thursday, flying as many as seven circles of the track. Most impressive were his figure-8s and deeply banked curves, showing the extent to which he could control his craft. For skeptics in the crowd, who had ridiculed the Wrights as "bluffeurs," the exhibition was an eye-opener. The daily repetition was strategically important, for French skeptics could raise their eyebrows in reading about a successful flight and still have time to travel to the trial site to see for themselves what the fuss was all about. Each day, new banner headlines and photos filled such publications as *Le Figaro* and the *London Daily Mirror*. The exhibitions, *L'Aerophile* said, "have completely dissipated all doubts." Yet grumbling persisted among French flyers, who saw all their hard work going down the drain. But Bleriot sniffed that the Wrights demonstrated only a "momentary superiority."[13]

By September, when the American trials were due to begin at Fort Myer, Virginia, the American press — deluged with the European coverage — didn't dare not cover the event. Ironically, it was largely the positive European coverage that finally made Orville Wright an overdue hero in his own country.[14]

Only by 1908 had the Wrights become savvy and confident enough to publicize their efforts. Though Wilbur was the more experienced writer, circumstances forced Orville to undertake reluctantly a major piece, entitled "The Wright Brothers' Aeroplane," for *Century Magazine* in the spring, an article which has become a classic in its field. Their exploits had now led others to feed off their accomplishments, by copying their plans and techniques. Aeronauts on both sides of the Atlantic were now accomplished enough to fly distances and durations that would have stunned the Wrights had they done it themselves only three years earlier.[15]

The Wrights' biplane design was instantly recognizable to French flyers, but other configurations had succeeded in flying as well. Notable among them was the box-kite design, pioneered by another pair of brothers, Gabriel and Charles Voisin; as well as designs by Ernest Archdeacon and Louis Bleriot. Santos-Dumont's eclectic designs and his rakish manner drew interest wherever he went.

To the modern eye, Bleriot's monoplane is perhaps the most striking, looking so similar to contemporary airplane designs. In it, the pilot sits upright at the plane's highest point, flanked by one set of wings, as a long, tapered tail and rudder trails behind. Takeoff and landing wheels slung underneath the craft. Bleriot would win the *London Daily Mail*'s 1,000 pound prize the next year for his 37-minute flight across the English Channel from Calais to Dover, England, at an average speed of 75 miles an hour, a feat the newspaper couldn't induce any of its countrymen to perform. In the words of historian A. Scott Berg, "The economic, social, and political implications of that flight were boundless."[16]

Control vs. Stability

The Europeans had long put stability on a higher pedestal than control. Now that theory, that a pilot didn't need extensive controls if his craft was structured to withstand all stresses and contingencies, was being put to the test. Gradually and graphically, the enduring importance of control emerged, as the throngs watched Wilbur fly up to 78 miles in 140 minutes and demonstrate how a pilot could move his machine up and down and side to side by manipulating metal rods next to his seat.[17]

After Wilbur's stunning triumph in Le Mans, French aeronaut Leon Delagrange came to see for himself. Earlier that year, he had triumphantly logged two 15-minute flights, but reading the daily press, he now found himself overshadowed. What did this American have that he lacked? After watching Wilbur Wright perform at length, he understood at once the profound importance of what he had experienced. Asked by a reporter for his reaction, Delagrange offered the concise summation, "Nous Sommes battu." (we are beaten).[18]

LeMans would be, without doubt, a watershed event in the Wrights' careers. The overwhelming public acclaim showering down on them spread from the European continent across the ocean to America, so that Wilbur, a man who could have strolled down Fifth Avenue utterly unnoticed a year earlier, was now greeted as a hero wherever he went.

Back to America

If only Orville could score such a triumph in America as Wilbur had done in Le Mans! The American trials were to take place at Fort Myer, Virginia. Orville stopped in Washington on his way. When he clambered off the steam train, there to meet him was Dr. Albert Zahm, an intimate of Graham Bell, one of the original Langley brain trust, and now teaching physics at Catholic University. Finding that Wright had reserved a room at the St. James Hotel, Zahm moved him to accommodations befitting his newly-exalted status, at the posh Cosmos Club, whose prestigious members were eager to meet him. Orville was finding, as Wilbur had before him, how much time and energy a celebrity must spend meeting people that otherwise could be devoted to practicing his craft.[19]

Wilbur's successes outside Paris had made Orville's life both easier and harder. The enormously favorable press coverage meant less criticism to overcome, but it heightened expectations as well. Publicity, good or ill, didn't change the American contract requirements at all. Part of the Wrights' American contract called for them to train pilots who could fly the craft. Orville's students were to be Army Lts. Benjamin Foulois, Frank Lahm, and Thomas E. Selfridge, who had already worked with the Wrights while they were part of Alexander Graham Bell's Aerial Experimental Association.

Orville's first trial came on September 3, when he flew a circle and a half of the field in 71 seconds. Witnessing the flight was Theodore Roosevelt, Jr., the president's 21-year-old son. Much as in France, the media and spectators flocked to the course as word spread. Hundreds, if not thousands, saw Orville set new world records, including an endurance mark of 57 minutes and 13 seconds. He would break his new record later that day and, within a week, remained aloft for 70 minutes.[20]

The American media interest was far greater than had greeted the Wrights in the past but still a far cry from the banner headlines featured in European publications. *The Washington Star* ran the story of Orville's first flight at Fort Myers on page three, indicating editors saw the trial as worthy of coverage but not earth-shattering. One possible reason for the contrast was that well-known flyers such as Delagrange, Bleriot, and Farman had witnessed Wilbur's flights and could validate their importance for the press. But no American experts at Fort Myer schooled the press on why a flight aloft in a biplane is much more significant than one in a balloon.

On September 10, as Orville continued to set world records day after day, Charlie Taylor climbed to the top of the *Flyer*'s shed at Fort Myer with a can of white paint. After Orville had been up for 50 minutes, he slathered a giant "50" atop the roof, then five minutes later "55." When Orville had been up for an hour, Charlie raised both hands triumphantly over his head, and car horns tooted. Orville had not only flown 66 minutes but had set a world altitude record at 200 feet. Altogether, the younger brother had set nine world records in four days.[21]

The First Fatality

On September 17, Orville was to fly with Lt. Selfridge, not only a pupil now but also a member of the Board of Ordnance. Orville had developed an intense dislike for Selfridge and wrote Wilbur, in words that would come back to haunt him, "I will be glad to have Selfridge out of the way. I don't trust him an inch. He is intensely interested in the subject and plans to meet me often at dinners, etc, where he can try to pump me. He has a good education, and a clear mind. I understand that he does a good deal of knocking behind my back."[22]

After a normal takeoff and three circuits of the parade ground, Orville was alarmed to hear a tapping at the back of the machine, followed by two audible thumps and violent shaking, causing the craft to lose control. The left wing continued its downward trajectory and pointed the craft towards the ground, where it hit at top speed and "nosed over," burying both men in a tangle of debris. Both were knocked unconscious and carried off the field. Orville sustained several broken ribs, deep gashes to his scalp, a broken left thigh, and injured back. Selfridge, suffering a fractured skull, was rushed into surgery.[23]

By then, the number of crashes Orville had survived might put him in competition with young Hungarian escape artist Harry Houdini, who was just becoming well known in America. Lt. Selfridge, the ambitious Army officer, set his only aeronautical record as he became aviation's first fatality in the era of powered flight.[24]

Wilbur had been too busy in France to return home in time to see Orville fly at Fort Myer. But one day in September, he received a communication the French had learned to dread. It was a *papier bleu*, usually reserved for families of servicemen killed in battle. Fortunately, the news it brought Wilbur could have been worse. At home, where Katharine was devoted as ever to her brothers, she quit her teaching job upon hearing the news and nursed Orville back to health. She would never set foot in the classroom again.[25]

Knowing Orville was in good hands, Wilbur remained in France. Capping off his summer triumph, he flew 77 miles on the last day of 1908, setting an aviation distance record. The next month, a recuperated Orville and sister Katharine joined him in France. Flashbulbs popped upon the trio's arrival home, where they were welcomed now as a family of celebrities.[26]

Little did Wilbur know that his 1908 French exploits would mark his high point on European soil. In August of 1909, an international air exhibition would take place in France at Rheims. Its leading draw, with the Wrights now back on U.S. soil, was the American Glenn Hammond Curtiss. Soon France would overtake America as the world leader in aeronautics.

The U.S. government accepted the cause of the propeller problem that had led to the crash at Fort Myer and didn't let that derail the contract. The Wrights rebuilt the *Flyer*, and Washington accepted it on June 28, 1909, after it flew two miles an hour faster than the 40 mph contained in the specifications, earning the Wrights a bonus of $5,000. In November, they used their windfall to incorporate the Wright Company, to be distinguished from the Wright Cycle Company, which would continue to exist. While building a factory in Dayton, the company set up corporate headquarters in Manhattan, the country's financial center then, as it is now. Predictably, Wilbur became president. The corporate entity bought all patent rights from the brothers, giving them $100,000 cash plus 10 percent royalty on sales. By the end of that year, the authoritative transportation publication, *Jane's*, reported the company had manufactured 10 airplanes and had another dozen on order. By 1911, they would turn out two planes a month.[27]

By their early to mid-40s, Wilbur and Orville Wright had both insured their places in history and achieved financial independence. They looked forward to another generation or more of sharing each other's friendship and scaling new aeronautical mountains. But waiting for them around the bend was a future very different from the one they had anticipated.

Epilogue

T<small>HE</small> 1908 F<small>RENCH AND</small> A<small>MERICAN</small> trials of the Wright *Flyer* cemented Wilbur and Orville Wright firmly into the aeronautical pantheon for all time. But owning the basic aircraft patent and achieving worldwide recognition did little to settle claims for primacy by those who sought to topple the Dayton brothers from their throne. Rest from that struggle, in fact, came only in the death of the last Wright brother in 1948. It is beyond the scope of this book to describe the growth of the airplane industry and the profound effect that air travel has had on American life. Yet much of it plays out in the rest of the lives of the major players in the race to the sky, and the author would grievously shortchange the reader by not finishing that story.

The first part of this epilogue follows the remaining lives of our characters and, in so doing, offers at least a peek at the astounding growth of the phenomenon that is air travel. The key players will be familiar by now to the reader: Charles D. Walcott, the Langley deputy who persuaded President McKinley in 1898 that his boss offered the world's best hope to put a man in the sky; Glenn Hammond Curtiss, who would seek to rehabilitate Professor Langley's reputation posthumously as a way to win his ongoing patent litigation with the Wrights; the talented but conniving Augustus Moore Herring; and the Smithsonian Institution, which Professor Langley had infused with an aura of rectitude before his death in 1906 but which now willingly joined in a despicable cabal to destroy the Wright legacy.

Part of this epic involves the development of the major airlines and aircraft manufacturers. Volumes would be required to do justice to that saga. But it is possible in a chapter, through telling the story of one corporate giant, to give the reader a sense of how the industry developed into one of the American economy's chief engines of growth. Accordingly, the second part of the epilogue tells the story of Pratt and Whitney Aircraft and its successor, United Aircraft Corporation.

The idea of building a luxurious dream house seems antithetical to the ethos of

Wilbur and Orville Wright, after their straitlaced upbringing and their Spartan approach to aeronautics. One is at a loss to explain their decision to do it except to quote Supreme Court Justice Oliver Wendell Holmes's dictum that "Consistency is the hobgoblin of little minds." The Wright family had lived at 7 Hawthorn Street for 42 years, and the brothers wanted to build a bigger house in the city. But they acquiesced to the wishes of sister Katharine and, in May of 1912, bought a 17-acre tract of land in the upscale suburb of Oakwood, on a rise overlooking the city of Dayton. There, the family would construct a magnificent structure it would call Hawthorn Hill, not in nostalgic recollection of their boyhood home but after a proliferation of old hawthorn trees on the property. Orville would design the plumbing, heating, and electrical systems himself and even incorporate a central vacuum into the mansion.[1]

Wilbur had been dogged by a fever since a recent trip to Boston and tried to shake it off over the next few days while working on company business. By May 8, he had grown weaker, and the family doctor, D.B. Conklin, suspected typhoid fever. This deadly disease, often caused by contaminated food products, was a scourge of urban communities in that era and had afflicted Orville in 1896. Wilbur felt sick enough to call in Mabel Beck, his personal secretary, and dictate his last will and testament. Two days later, he slipped into unconsciousness. The 45-year-old aeronautical genius, otherwise in good health, lingered on for three more weeks and died "without a struggle" during the night of May 30. His grief-stricken father communicated his thoughts of the moment to his daily diary:

> This morning at 3:15, Wilbur passed away, aged 45 years, 1 month and 14 days. A short life, full of consequences. An unfailing intellect, imperturbable temper, great self-reliance and as great modesty, seeing the right clearly, pursuing it steadfastly, he lived and died. Many called — many telegrams (probably over a thousand.)[2]

Wilbur was no longer only the bishop's son; fame had made him a son of the world. Flowers poured in from scores of individuals and organizations the family had never heard of. On Saturday, June 1, his body lay in state, like that of a potentate, at the First Presbyterian Church. When it was all over, Wilbur's father, who had buried so many parishioners himself, could still scarcely believe it. "Wilbur is dead and buried!" he told his diary. "We are all stricken. It does not seem possible that he is gone."[3]

The Wrights had endured bad times during their Kitty Hawk and Huffman Prairie days. But father Milton, an iconoclastic preacher often criticized and censured, knew about the winds of outrageous fortune and had taught his family how to circle the wagons and wait until the storm blew over. Few families were closer in adversity than the Wrights, and Wilbur and Orville knew they could always draw upon the strength of the bishop, certainly of Katharine and, even though he no longer lived at home, of Lorin. But as he grew into middle age and finally old age, Orville — through death and unexpected family estrangement — would end up fighting off his attackers and storming his own barricades as a lonely old man. If somewhere Wilbur

Flanking family patriarch bearded Milton Wright are Orville Wright and sister Katharine on the lawn of Orville's new Dayton mansion, Hawthorn Hill. The two men at left are unidentified. Next to Katharine is Earl Findley and to his left, nephew Horace. Library of Congress.

could have witnessed the spectacle, he would have burst his buttons with pride for his little brother.

Capitalizing on Success

Applying even a modicum of imagination to the results of the Wrights' 1908 trials, the commercial and military implications were too great, too immediate, to ignore. The brothers' creation of the Wright Company in 1909 was a logical next step. That within a year it would turn out two planes a month was reasonably foreseeable. But the growth in the industry that World War I would produce was beyond anyone's wildest imagination.

French aeronauts have argued that Gabriel Voisin actually set up the first aircraft company in 1907, even though his firm built only experimental airplanes. Glenn Curtiss, of course, would debate that, echoing the earlier dispute about what constitutes flight. In any event, 16 firms built airplanes for sale in 1914, but altogether, they produced only 49 machines. Their owners were largely seat-of-the-pants entrepreneurs

Winter scene at Hawthorn Hill, the opulent mansion Orville and Wilbur had built in 1912.
Normally conservative in taste, Orville threw himself into creating a state-of-the-art home,
designing the plumbing and heating systems himself and incorporating a central vacuum.
Library of Congress.

who had stitched together a wood and metal skeleton that managed to fly well enough
for a buyer to take a chance on it. Few were formally educated; a fair number were
school dropouts—the dreamy kids in the back row of class who couldn't wait to
escape the classroom to get back to their garage workshops. Hardly any had been
trained as professional managers, although in 1910, few in any line of business had
professional training.

But the era of "scientific management" had dawned with the new century, and
its chief tenet — that businesses ought to be organized systematically — was sweeping
the country. Until then, the "great men" had controlled business, the Carnegies, Rocke-
fellers, and Morgans, whose vision and energy were enough to propel their enterprises
to unparalleled success. Scientific management relied instead on organization of
enterprises and produced a new breed of managers. Before long, this managerial class,
trained in universities, would muscle out the raw, dirt-under-the-fingernails geniuses
who had created aeronautical companies in the first place.[4] The trend was hardly surprising. To expect a brilliant, creative engineer also to exhibit the skills of a top-flight
manager once his company began to grow geometrically was clearly too much to
expect. "The Wrights possessed no inclination to actively manage their company,"

observes business historian Donald Pattillo, "and Curtiss's business judgment was at times nearly disastrous."[5]

Becoming an Industry Overnight

The aeronautical world in 1918 would be unrecognizable to one such as Wilbur Wright who had left it only six years earlier. As late as 1914, the worldwide aircraft industry employed only a few hundred workers. By 1918, some 350,000 people drew paychecks from the new industry, which had by then manufactured 50,000 aircraft.[6] The difference was World War I.

By the time the United States entered World War I, other countries had pulled far ahead in production. As early as 1913, a year before European hostilities had even begun, France appropriated $7.4 million for aviation. By contrast, America's spending of $125,000 about equaled that of Bulgaria. By 1914, when the Sarajevo assassination catapulted European nations into war, they had several hundred airplanes ready to take to the skies, even though they had little idea of what to do when they got there. Gradually, while fulfilling their original task of spying behind enemy lines, aircraft also came to be used for direct combat against one another, and the concept of the "dogfight" was born. To withstand the higher stresses of combat, metal began to replace wood in aircraft construction and open cockpits yielded to enclosed ones. From such conflict emerged such legendary aces as America's Edward V. "Eddie" Rickenbacker and Germany's Baron von Richtofen ("the Red Baron").[7]

By the war's end, seasoned pilots flooded into peacetime industry to man the faculties of aeronautics schools that popped up across the country, serving as a lure for young ambitious men drawn to the cutting edge. One such individual signed up after learning that the Nebraska Aircraft Corporation's school had placed three men in jobs paying up to $500 a month. Friends of the rosy-cheeked lad from Little Falls, Minnesota, called him Slim. His given name was Charles Lindbergh.[8]

Money Is the Key

A huge stumbling block for any new industry, then or now, is financing. Few banks want to underwrite a product yet untested in the market when other proven products are available to finance. The years bracketing the turn of the 20th century, which some have called the age of invention, was a cornucopia of production, a financier's smorgasbord. Such aeronautical pioneers as William Boeing and Sherman Fairchild happened to be independently wealthy. Donald Douglas, Claude Ryan, and John Northrop each had rich sponsors. But most were like Glenn Hammond Curtiss.[9]

Curtiss created what could probably be called the world's first aircraft manufacturing company in 1909, even though his enterprise lasted only a year. Back home now in Hammondsport, New York, after his flirtation with the Aerial Experiment

A Wright *Flyer* engaged in one of the first European air battles in World War I, which would soon give rise to the word "dogfight." National Air and Space Museum, Smithsonian Institution (SI Neg. No. 2002-16645).

Association, Curtiss busily designed new flying machines. But ahead of him lay a huge stumbling block — how to raise the capital needed to build aircraft on a larger scale. Until he could scale that hurdle, Curtiss would remain just a man with many ideas.

One day, a well-spoken man approached Curtiss with a business proposition. Curtiss found him especially attractive, since he claimed financial connections in New York and said he owned patents to practical aircraft that predated the Wrights'. This was Curtiss's lucky day! If this fellow's patents were older than the Wrights', they might well take precedence over them. Not only could the older patents allow their holder to manufacture aircraft without interference from the Wrights; they might just force the brothers out of business. As Curtiss listened, he became more and more impressed. His visitor, it seemed, had worked with Langley, Chanute, and the Wrights, all the leading lights of aviation's birthing days. And he was willing to join in partnership with Curtiss. In deference to his depth of experience and contacts, the visitor felt it was only fair that his name should come first in the company title. Given what his guest brought to the table, how could Curtiss object?

The man's name, which meant nothing to Curtiss, was Augustus Moore Herring. On March 19, 1909, the two men formed the Herring-Chanute Company, to manufacture designs borrowed from the AEA for $7,500 apiece, and recruited two former directors of the association for their board. Curtiss gladly folded into the operation his manufacturing company, which in 1908 had employed 100 while earning a healthy net profit of $120,000. But for all Herring's talk of New York financial contacts, the only person other than Curtiss to invest was former AEA director Cortland Field Bishop, who anted up $21,000. During 1909, the company delivered only six planes.[10]

Soon the truth caught up with the silver-tongued Herring, as it had years earlier in his dealings with Langley, Chanute, and the Wrights. Herring claimed patents, it turned out, that simply didn't exist. Curtiss needed capital to build a factory in Hammondsport, and Herring assured him he would sell enough stock to raise it, but nothing came of the offer. At last, the board of directors bearded the elusive Herring, demanding that he produce his patents or, failing that, show evidence that he had applied for them. Herring could produce nothing. Finally, Curtiss offered Herring $10,000 to surrender his interest and get lost. "At best he exaggerated his knowledge and accomplishments," says business historian Pattillo. "At worst he was an outright fraud."[11]

The Herring-Curtiss Company eventually filed for bankruptcy on April 10, 1910, and, in December, the unencumbered Glenn Curtiss formed the Curtiss Aeroplane Company. With the Herring albatross off his back, Curtiss obtained a patent for an "improved flying machine" in 1911 and soon was a major player in the new industry. He built the A-1 Triad for the U.S. Navy and, in 1914, hired B. Douglas Thomas as his first design engineer. War orders led the company to move to Buffalo in 1914, and the following year, it received a $15 million order from Great Britain. In short order, the Curtiss Aeroplane Company had become America's largest airplane manufacturer.

In this questing age, races and exhibitions proliferated, as aeronautical promoters played to the public imagination. Curtiss took a steamship to France in the summer of 1909 and won the $10,000 Gordon Bennett speed trophy. That October, Wilbur Wright lived a photographer's dream by flying up and down the Hudson River, with the New York City skyline in the background. To top that, rival Curtiss flew 151 miles from Albany to Manhattan the next May and won another $10,000.[12]

Flying pioneers had spent the first decade of the 20th century just gaining public acceptance; their task in the second decade was to create faster, more maneuverable planes while building an industry to manufacture them. The scores of new aircraft rolling off production lines were useless without skilled pilots to man them, so the Wrights, Curtiss, and Glenn Martin all set up flying schools.

Records fell daily. By August of 1911, the world altitude mark, which three years earlier was only 300 feet, soared to 11,642 feet. Three months later, Calbraith Rodgers flew cross-country, from Long Island to Long Beach, in 49 days in his Wright Vin Fiz, making more than 80 stops along the way. In 1912, a plane received radio signals for the first time, and a year later, a pilot flew across the Mediterranean sea. Still, by 1914, only 200 planes had been built in America. The Wrights and Curtiss earned more from exhibitions and contest prizes than from manufacturing contracts.[13]

Had America been surrounded with hostile foes, as were many European countries, its aircraft industry would unquestionably have grown faster than it did. The U.S. Signal Corps, which bought the first *Flyer* in 1908, didn't purchase a second plane until 1911, when it spent $125,000 to buy five more aircraft. The Corps had bought the *Flyer* solely for reconnaissance, but that mission expanded in 1910, when Corpsmen used the machine during an air conclave in San Francisco to drop a bomb on a field below, opening up frightening new possibilities.[14]

The Patent Wars

Like so many successful entrepreneurs of their time, the Wrights guarded their patents like crown jewels. Those who sought information for experimental or scientific use were welcome in the Wright Company, but woe betide one who put to commercial use anything learned there. Lt. Thomas Selfridge, then of the AEA, asked the Wrights for and received technical data in early 1908. When the Wrights learned that Curtiss—then still working with Bell—wanted to use the information commercially, they charged he was infringing on their patent. Curtiss denied it, but in fact, he had sold a $7,500 plane, constructed from the Wrights' plans, to the Aeronautical Society of New York. Curtiss strongly defended the claim, arguing that the plane's ailerons, developed by his then-partner Herring, were an innovation that demonstrated that he wasn't simply copying the Wrights' patented concepts.[15]

The patent dustup with Curtiss was no isolated case. The Wrights would keep their lawyers in clover for years by bringing a dozen patent suits in America and 20 abroad. In this age of innovation, inventors and entrepreneurs constantly fended off those less imaginative types who tried to steal their ideas. Patents even became a commodity to be traded, for if you sold me the patent rights to build a widget, I could build tollgates barring other widget makers until they paid me a royalty.

It was not surprising that the Wrights sued Curtiss for infringing upon their patent. In 1910, a federal court enjoined the Herring-Curtiss Company and Curtiss himself from building or selling planes.[16] Some industry watchers, including automaker Henry Ford, felt the Wright patent was too broad to be upheld, and the irascible tycoon spoke from experience.

In 1903, just as the Wrights and Langleys were getting ready to play out the last act of the race to the sky, Henry Ford set up shop in Michigan to manufacture economy automobiles. He soon received a notice from the Electric Vehicle Company of Hartford, Connecticut, that he was violating its basic patent on the automobile. EVC, headed by bicycle magnate Colonel Albert Pope and former Treasury Secretary William Collins Whitney, had paid only $10,000 to buy an 1895 patent from Rochester, New York, attorney and engineer George Selden. The shrewd, flinty Selden had secured a broadly-worded patent on a device he dreamed up in 1879 but never built. When automakers saw his patent covered any vehicle with four wheels, an engine, drive train and fuel supply, they scoffed at the idea that it would ever hold water in court. But when Ford sought to attack Selden's patent in court in a draining six-year battle, he lost. Ford achieved a Pyrrhic victory when he won an appeal two years later, although Selden's patent ran out a year later anyway. During the lengthy saga,

Glenn Curtiss, left, and Henry Ford confer while examining Curtiss's *Flying Boat*. Ford lent the experience of his blistering eight-year court battle over the Selden automobile patent to Curtiss, who was engaged in a similar bitter contest with Orville Wright. National Air and Space Museum, Smithsonian Institution (SI Neg. No. 2000-9687).

however, Ford had shrewdly cast himself as David, going up against a wealthy cadre of Goliaths. What he won from public sympathy far outweighed anything he lost in legal fees.[17]

Ford saw how much energy and money his patent fight had consumed, resources that could have been put to work in advancing the industry. He saw the Wrights' patent as preventing the aviation industry from moving ahead and advised Glenn Curtiss to stick by his guns. Curtiss returned to the same Buffalo, New York judge who had ruled against him in 1910 and argued that the Wrights' patent was too broad to be upheld. But on February 27, 1913, the judge ruled against Curtiss once more. Unlike Henry Ford's experience, the appeals court upheld the Wrights' patent in 1914. As a result, anyone building a plane using the Wrights' basic configuration would have to pay royalties to the Wrights.[18]

In holding that the Wrights owned exclusive rights "to all known means to laterally stabilize an airplane," the court even held that their patent extended to improvements anyone made to the Wrights' basic design. This was more than an academic point, since while Curtiss considered his ailerons (French for "little wing") a new invention, Orville argued it simply tinkered with the Wrights' wing-warping principle. No matter. For technology galloped fast enough to render the Wright patent obsolete by the time Curtiss could appeal. Ironically, notes Curtiss biographer Seth Shulman, the Wright Company began abandoning wing warping in favor of ailerons, within months of the court decision.[19]

The ongoing litigation between Wright and Curtiss, now as personal as it was professional, had so embittered Orville Wright that he announced he would deal with any airplane maker willing to pay him a 20 percent royalty on its revenues from sales or exhibitions. But under no circumstances would he deal with Curtiss. In a front page interview with the *New York Times,* Orville minced no words. Not only had Curtiss stolen the Wrights' designs, he said, but the stress he had caused Wilbur led to his death.[20]

Curtiss's options had narrowed radically. Further court appeals seemed pointless, and Orville wouldn't deal with him. Aeronautics was his life. What was he to do, move to a country that didn't recognize the Wright patent? At this point, Henry Ford whispered into young Curtiss's ear. Soon Curtiss hired a tenacious litigator named W. Benton Crisp, the attorney who had helped Ford win his case on appeal, and named him chief counsel of the Curtiss company. Curtiss and Crisp invited A. F. Zahm of the early Langley brain-trust to a strategy session and together hatched a plan that would resonate in court and in the public press for the next 30 years.[21]

See You in Court

Litigation brings out the worst in people,[22] as they test their moral boundaries in seeking the hold that will pin their adversary to the mat. As the aeronautical industry grew like wildfire, one might think the enormous profits produced would have left all the players rich enough. But in the quest for gold, no prize ever seems enough. The 1914 court decision had given Orville what he called "absolute control" of the industry, leading such financiers as August Belmont, Cornelius Vanderbilt, and Robert Collier to flock to his door.[23] The winner of the Wright vs. Curtiss patent feud would become the wealthiest person in aeronautics. Glenn Curtiss vowed to find a way to become that person.

It haunted Curtiss that Professor Langley's craft had failed eight days before the Wrights' December 17, 1903 flight, apparently only because the catapult launch mechanism malfunctioned. What if the aerodrome could be reconstructed and flown again, to demonstrate that the craft itself was entirely airworthy? If this were so, wouldn't Langley's aerodrome, rather than the Wrights' *Flyer,* have been the first flying machine? This might put a new twist on the patent litigation. But first he'd have to approach the Smithsonian.

The secretary of the Smithsonian Institution in 1914 was Charles D. Walcott, the Langley deputy who had convinced President McKinley in 1898 that he should back the professor's quest as a national crusade. He had been crestfallen at Langley's failure, along with the rest of the Smithsonian staff, had watched him decline and die, and had witnessed the effect the debacle had had on the Institution's reputation. So he warmed immediately to Curtiss's proposal, since rehabilitating the Langley name would benefit the Smithsonian as well. Zahm now headed the Langley Aerodynamical Laboratory at the Smithsonian and had signed on as a witness in the

Curtiss vs. Wright litigation. All agreed he would help Curtiss with his mission. Walcott entrusted Zahm with the original fuselage, some wing ribs, propellers, tubing, and the engine of the original craft and put up $2,000 to assist the project.[24]

Curtiss and Zahm released the news that they were rebuilding the Langley machine to its original 1903 condition. But in fact, the 1914 aerodrome would be far different from the 1903 product. A world of advancement in aeronautics had taken place since that fateful December of 1903. Whether Curtiss and Zahm knew at the outset that the original craft wasn't airworthy or whether they decided to employ more modern advances just to be on the safe side is a fact lost to history. But in fact, they changed the camber and shape of the wings, modified the trussing wires for the wings, altered the configuration of the guy posts, added wooden struts, reinforced the wings' center spar, and varnished the cotton covering the wings. Zahm and Curtiss decided to launch the craft from river-borne pontoons rather than from the top of a houseboat, which necessitated some of these changes. Nevertheless, the reconstructed aerodrome simply wasn't the same craft Charles Manly tried to fly in 1903.

Had Curtiss and Zahm deemed those changes unimportant, they presumably wouldn't have hesitated to discuss them. However, they kept the alterations a closely-guarded secret, but one which Orville Wright was determined to crack. On his trips to Europe, Orville had met an enterprising British attorney, Griffith Brewer. He now commissioned the lawyer to journey sub rosa to Curtiss's factory at Hammondsport, spending as much time there as he needed to get to the bottom of things. The task daunted even this sophisticated counsel. He wrote later that he felt "like a detective going into hostile country, where I should get rough handling if my mission was known."[25] But it wasn't, at least while he was there. Brewer managed to catalog a lengthy list of changes Curtiss had made to the aerodrome and included it in a letter carried prominently by the *New York Times*. Orville didn't stop there; he dispatched brother Lorin to take photographs at the Hammondsport trials in 1914. When the Curtiss minions saw what he was up to, they surrounded Lorin and confiscated his film.[26]

The redesigned aerodrome did fly at Hammondsport. Smithsonian and Curtiss issued a joint statement that the flight proved that "Professor Samuel P. Langley had actually designed and built the first man-carrying flying machine capable of sustained flight."[27] Curtiss sullied himself irrevocably within the aeronautical community by the deliberate deception involved in restructuring the Langley craft so it would fly. But even though the Smithsonian Institution wanted desperately to rehabilitate the reputation of its esteemed former secretary, it is difficult to understand why it was willing to stoop to such a level.

A Warm Relationship Sours

As time went on, the tense relationship between the Wrights and Octave Chanute, with whom they had been through so much, developed an even sharper edge.

The Wrights had always considered wing-warping one of their signal contributions. Chanute, politely at first and less so later, had always disagreed, holding that aeronauts as far back as Leonardo da Vinci knew of the concept.[28] Now that wing-warping had become a central element in their patent lawsuits, the Wrights were dismayed to find Chanute speaking openly to reporters and taking their opponent's side. Disagreement within the aeronautical family they understood, but for Chanute to broadcast his contrarian views they felt was embarrassing, potentially damaging, and most hurtfully, disloyal.[29] When they confronted the elderly engineer with their feelings, the subsequent letters back and forth dredged up all manner of real and imagined slights of one against the other. The Wrights were eager to reconcile with Chanute, but before they could figure out how to do so came word that he had died at home of pneumonia on November 23, 1910, at the age of 78. Upon receiving the news, Wilbur took the first train to Chicago to attend his funeral.

Orville had become more distant and detached from his company's board of directors after the passing of his alter ego. In July of 1914, he bought out the interests of all his investors except his close friend Robert J. Collier, so that the two of them now owned the Wright Company together. That October, Orville sold his share for $1.5 million to a New York investment syndicate. Orville would remain active in the industry for rest of his life, but as an advisor, not an active player. The Wright family continued to blame Curtiss for hastening Wilbur's untimely death. But the well-publicized litigation had cost the Wrights public support too, while Curtiss seemed to gain public sympathy. Meanwhile Curtiss perfected the aileron, the technological successor to the Wrights' wing-warping system; invented the seaplane, and became known as the father of naval aviation.[30]

Before he died, Orville Wright saw an airplane fly at supersonic speed. Less than a decade following his death, a spaceship orbited earth. Only two decades later, a man walked on the moon. Historian Harry Combs observes of that flight that, "In the same time it took Wilbur Wright to cover 852 feet in the first full flight of a powered airplane, the first expedition to the moon *flew a distance of four hundred and thirteen miles.*"[31]

Death Weeds Out the Pioneers

With the death of Chanute and Wilbur Wright, the field of original aeronautical pioneers had begun to thin. Samuel Pierpont Langley had lived to see the Wrights eclipse him, winning the race to the sky, but succumbed in February, 1906, to a stroke at age 72. Accolades poured in from throughout the world for this decent, if flawed, gentleman. One of the more poignant remembrances was contained in a letter Wilbur wrote to Octave Chanute, who had been a fast friend of both men:

> No doubt disappointment shortened his life. It is really pathetic that he should have missed the honor he cared for above all others, merely because he could not launch

his machine successfully. If he could only have started it, the chances are that it would have flown sufficiently to have secured to him the name he coveted, even though a complete wreck attended the landing. I cannot help feeling sorry for him. The fact that the great scientist, Prof. Langley, believed in flying machines was one thing that encouraged us to begin our studies....[32]

By the time he died in 1930, Glenn Hammond Curtiss had divorced himself from aviation completely, just as he had abandoned motorcycle and engine production to enter aeronautics. In a monumental irony, his Curtiss Aeroplane and Motor Company merged with the Wright Aeronautical Corporation in 1929, several months before the stock market crash. That the new company placed "Curtiss" ahead of "Wright" enraged the proud Dayton family.[33] And Augustus Herring went on causing trouble.

After Curtiss put the Herring-Curtiss Company into bankruptcy, Herring revived it and became its new president. During Herring's tumultuous life, someone else, not he, always seemed to be responsible for his misfortunes. It surprised few that he sued Curtiss for damaging him by filing for bankruptcy. When the court ruled against him, he appealed. Herring would not live to see the lower court ruling reversed in his favor in 1928, for a stroke had claimed him two years earlier. Hart Berg, the Wrights' colorful European agent, lived on to age 76, dying two days after Pearl Harbor ushered in a new age of aeronautics in wartime.[34]

What of the others, this breed of fearless adventurers whose lust for life outstripped their desire for self-preservation? Not all of them died quietly in their beds. Although his brother Gabriel lived until 1973, France's Charles Voisin died in an automobile accident the same year as Wilbur. Just as Alfred Nobel rued the day he invented dynamite after seeing the destruction it had unleashed, the colorful Alberto Santos-Dumont took his own life in 1932 at age 59 after pondering his role in developing the airplanes that became a combat force in World War I. Captain Louis Ferdinand Ferber, who vowed an American would not fly before a Frenchman did, and Leon Delagrange, who told reporters "Nous sommes battu" after watching Wilbur Wright fly at Le Mans, both died in airplane mishaps. Louis Bleriot, the first man to pilot an airplane across the English Channel, sustained crippling injuries, though surviving a 1909 airplane crash into a house, and never flew again.

Of the bit players: Bill Tate, the Kitty Hawk postmaster and the first to welcome the Wrights to Kitty Hawk, died at age 84, missing out narrowly on his goal of attending the celebration of the flight's 50th anniversary. Charlie Furnas, the Dayton neighbor who became the first airplane passenger, died in 1941 in Dayton. He had abandoned his desire to become a pilot, sobered after Lt. Thomas Selfridge became powered aeronautics' first fatality at Fort Myer in 1908. Charlie Taylor, the intrepid mechanic who held together the Wrights' bicycle enterprise with one hand while building and improving their aircraft with the other, lived to the age of 88. Henry Ford prevailed upon him to help restore the Wright home and bicycle shop he moved to his museum in Greenfield Village in Dearborn, Michigan. Yet this truly indispensable factor in the Wrights' success died penniless.[35]

As for the Wrights: Bishop Milton Wright lived to age 88 and died in the same month that America entered the Great War in 1917, never living to see the aeronautical cottage industry transform itself into a mighty force in the American economy. His sons' biggest cheerleader and moral exemplar, the bishop was laid to rest next to his wife Susan after services at Orville's spanking new mansion at Hawthorn Hill. Orville's older brother Reuchlin died three years later, and Lorin, who had good-naturedly pitched in at Kitty Hawk as his brothers' helpmate and sometime press agent, lived on to 1939.[36]

It is hard to overestimate Katharine's influence on the family, particularly after her mother died in 1889 while her offspring were still children. Even as the youngest child, she radiated capability but also supplied a leavening femininity that softened a household dominated by focused, purposeful men. Katharine had left her teaching position in 1908 to nurse Orville back to health after his plane crash at Fort Myer and instigated the family's move to Hawthorn Hill, remaining there with Orville after their father's death. Whether or not their pact was ever spoken, Orville evidently assumed that he and Katharine would grow old together like a happily married couple. Imagine his reaction when his spinster sister announced in 1926, at age 52, that she was engaged to Henry J. Haskell, with whom she had attended Oberlin and later served on that college's board of trustees.[37] The elegant Hawthorn Hill had served as the lavish wedding site of choice for much of the family since Orville had built the mansion, but Katharine announced that her nuptials would take place at her beloved Oberlin College.

Orville could have bitten his tongue, swallowed the reality that he was about to become a much lonelier bachelor, and wished his sister and her new husband well. Instead, he chose to regard his sister's decision to marry as a betrayal and a rejection. Katharine and Henry moved to Kansas City, where Henry became editor of the *Kansas City Star,* while Katharine sought repeatedly and unsuccessfully to reconnect with her wounded brother. Only two years later, she developed pneumonia, an often fatal disease in the days before antibiotics. Even after the family learned that Katharine's condition was hopeless, Orville was determined to sit at home with his arms folded. But perhaps he recalled the regret he and Wilbur had felt after Chanute's death in 1910, at not having been able to reconcile with their old mentor. When Lorin prevailed upon Orville to rush to his sister's bedside, he did and was with her when she died.[38]

Katharine's death left Orville largely alone. A 1930 profile in The *New Yorker* found him "a gray man now, dressed in gray clothes. Not only have his hair and his moustache taken on that tone but his curiously flat face ... a man whose misery at meeting you is obviously so keen that, in common decency you leave as soon as you can."[39]

Orville's Master Stroke

The year before Katharine died, Orville, in a deft political stroke, took an action that would shake the aeronautical community to its roots. Having fought for nearly two decades with the Smithsonian establishment to gain the respect he knew the Wrights' legacy deserved, he announced in 1925 that he was shipping the 1903 *Flyer* to the Science Museum of London. For the jewel of America's technological crown to reside from then on in a foreign country smacked of heresy to some. But as Orville explained it publicly, his motives became clear:

> I believe that my course in sending our Kitty Hawk Machine to a foreign museum is the only way of correcting the history of the flying machine, which by false and misleading statements has been perverted by the Smithsonian Institution. In its campaign to discredit others in the flying art, the Smithsonian has issued scores of these false and misleading statements.... In a foreign museum this machine will be a constant reminder of the reasons for its being there, and after the people and petty jealousies of this day are gone, the historians of the future may examine the evidence impartially and make history accord with it.[40]

Orville's coup de grâce could have backfired. Critics could have blasted him for making an unpatriotic gesture in a fit of pique. Instead, it had the very effect Orville had desired. *Aviation* magazine spearheaded a drive to have the *Flyer* returned to the United States. Charles D. Walcott, who risked his fine reputation as a geologist by going to unscrupulous means to defend Langley's memory, had died in 1927. Once Charles Greeley Abbot succeeded him, the Smithsonian began to yield to public pressure and soften its attitude toward the Wrights. First the institution revised the caption on Langley's aerodrome display to make his claim of his primacy in flight more ambiguous. Then its board issued a resolution conceding the Wrights deserved credit for making the first powered, heavier-than-air flight.[41]

All this wasn't enough to satisfy Orville. The Smithsonian had plainly lied when it said that Langley's 1903 craft was airworthy. Its board could split hairs until the cows came home, for all he cared. Until it retracted that misstatement of fact and admitted that the Curtiss/Zahm team had altered the 1903 aerodrome substantially before flying it in 1914, they could forget about the Wrights' iconic machine being returned to America. Finally, Abbot sold Orville on appointing a committee, headed by Colonel Charles Lindbergh, to mediate the dispute. Lindbergh's heralded 1927 transatlantic flight in his *Spirit of St. Louis* had made him a national hero. It would have been difficult for Orville to say no.

Arguments raged back and forth for many months over the ground rules for the mediation until a party not at the table weighed in. That party was the American public, which now began, through letters to newspapers and the Smithsonian itself, to side with Orville. Citizens put pressure on their congressional representatives to bring the matter to an honorable conclusion. Congressmen, feeling the need to respond in some meaningful way, did what congressmen do when put on the hot seat. They called for an investigation, and national magazines ran such story titles as "Bring Back Our Winged Exile." But even public pressure failed to move the protagonists. When Orville Wright drafted his last will and testament in 1937, he directed that the *Flyer* remain in Britain after his death.[42]

By then, Orville was approaching his biblical allotment of three score and 10 years. The Smithsonian realized only too well that simply waiting would invite the Grim Reaper to impose a final solution. If Orville died before the matter was resolved, the *Flyer* would likely remain in Britain forever. Ironically, it was not a scientist or a politician but a journalist who ended up mediating a solution to the dispute which by 1942 had raged for more than a decade. For decades, Orville had fended off requests to allow one writer or another to become the Wrights' authorized biographer. Finally, he gave the honor to Fred C. Kelly, whom he had known for more than a quarter-century. Kelly, in his research, became so immersed in the story of the 1914 alterations that he wrote to Secretary Abbot on his own and offered to mediate the long-simmering dispute, and Abbot agreed. What emerged wasn't much different from earlier attempts at settlement. Maybe the Smithsonian by now was simply war-weary. But by agreeing at last to publish the ways in which the 1903 aerodrome differed from the 1914 machine and to repudiate Professor Zahm's 1914 report that they were the same, the Smithsonian broke the logjam.

History records no embrace between Orville Wright and Charles Abbot on the steps of the Smithsonian castle, but Orville set about quietly to arrange for the *Flyer* to return to Washington. But a war was raging in Europe in the late 1930s, and because of the resultant danger in transporting this historic cargo, the parties agreed to delay its shipment until the war's conclusion. The flying machine remained on exhibit at the Science Museum until the July, 1940 Blitz sent it into deep storage for safekeeping.[43]

The Final Chapter

The heart attack that claimed Orville's life occurred on January 27, 1948, fittingly in his laboratory, only three months after he had survived an earlier one while bounding up a set of stairs. Since neither side had made public the resolution of the dispute over the *Flyer*'s final resting place, reporters tried frantically to discover the fate of the historic machine in the days following Orville's funeral. Only later in the year did the Smithsonian and Orville's executors publish the agreement. On December 17, 1948 — 45 years to the day after their first flight — a large ceremony in the Smithsonian Arts and Industries Building enshrined the Wright *Flyer*. As an American historical artifact, it had good company, surrounded as it was by such national icons as George Washington's military uniform and the war-battered flag that had inspired Francis Scott Key in 1814 to pen the Star Spangled Banner.[44]

Orville and Wilbur Wright had achieved first flight against overwhelming odds. But the odds of Orville's gaining vindication of that accomplishment against the forces that sought to destroy it had been equally long. As he fought on from 1914 through 1948, largely alone in the later years, how easy it would have been to compromise on a plan to display the Langley *Aerodrome* and the Wright *Flyer* together. How easy it would have been, in the weariness of his old age, to finally accede to a display that might have given the two aircraft equal billing. But his strong-willed father had taught his equally strong-willed sons to stand up for what they thought is right, and so Orville did. As a result, the first artifact today's visitor to the nation's Smithsonian Air and Space Museum sees on entering its door are the spreading white wings of the Wright *Flyer*, below which is prominently displayed the following wording:

THE ORIGINAL WRIGHT BROTHERS AEROPLANE
THE WORLD'S FIRST POWER-DRIVEN,
HEAVIER-THAN-AIR MACHINE IN WHICH MAN
MADE FREE, CONTROLLED, AND SUSTAINED FLIGHT
INVENTED AND BUILT BY WILBUR AND ORVILLE WRIGHT
FLOWN BY THEM AT KITTY HAWK, NORTH CAROLINA
DECEMBER 17, 1903
BY ORIGINAL SCIENTIFIC RESEARCH THE WRIGHT BROTHERS
DISCOVERED THE PRINCIPLES OF HUMAN FLIGHT
AS INVENTORS, BUILDERS AND FLYERS THEY
TAUGHT MAN TO FLY, AND OPENED
THE ERA OF AVIATION

One day in late April of 1925, as nature's first green kissed the trees of Hartford, Connecticut, the hulking black locomotive of a New York, New Haven and Hartford Railroad steam train chugged into the city's brownstone Union Station and heaved to a stop. Among those disembarking was a tall, thin, jobless man, 37 years old, who had come to Connecticut's capital city to look for work. It was the age of flappers, bathtub gin, Al Capone, short skirts and a rising stock market. Yet the visitor to Hartford had few prospects, no job references in his tattered suitcase, and only one letter of introduction from a family friend. Not that he was without skills. For nearly a decade now, he had been building aircraft engines.

His name was Frederick B. Rentschler, and his destination was the Pratt & Whitney Division of the Niles-Bement-Pond Company. Once there, he had directions to proceed to the offices of Clayton Burt, Pratt & Whitney's general manager. Fortunately, young Rentschler had a friend in high places. James K. Cullen, Niles-Bement-Pond's president, had been a close friend of his father, George A. Rentschler, who had died several months earlier. When his late friend's son called on Cullen in his corporate offices in Manhattan, he said of course he'd visit with him. On meeting, Cullen cut a striking figure, with white hair combed severely back, a broad, expansive face, and a whiskbroom mustache.

Knowing Rentschler's background helped Cullen evaluate his merit, for he recalled that the Princeton graduate could have had a white-collar job in his father's manufacturing plant but chose instead to enter factory life and become a molder — a hard, physical undertaking. He then became qualified as a machinist, intuiting that knowledge gained on the factory floor would make him a better executive.

Rentschler had been drawn to automotive engines at first. But his experience as a first lieutenant in World War I placed him in the U.S. Signal Corps, charged with producing and inspecting Hispano-Suiza engines made by the Wright-Martin Aircraft Corporation in New York and New Jersey. Once released from active duty, Rentschler was hooked on aviation and, in 1919, helped found the Wright Aeronautical Corporation, which he headed as its president. Orville Wright had sold his shares in the original Wright company several years earlier along with the right to use the respected Wright name. Rentschler's decision dismayed his father, who called aviation a "damn fool business, mostly for sportsmen" and worried his son was frittering away his talents and expensive education.

Six years later, Rentschler resigned from Wright and, in the six months since, had held a half-dozen conversations with Cullen. But instead of distancing him from aviation, the hiatus had only made him homesick for it. To Rentschler, an aircraft was no better than its engine, and he now knew his passion was to build the best engines ever. The prize, he felt, belonged to the company which could construct the best and biggest air-cooled radial engines. But building them wasn't nearly as big a hurdle as financing their manufacture.[45]

The wheels of Cullen's mind had begun to whir. Not only did he wish to find a job for the young man, as a favor to Frederick's father, but he also calculated that his company's plant, which had expanded so rapidly during the Great War, now had acres of empty space needing to be filled. What particularly excited Cullen and then Rentschler was that this vast idle space was located in Hartford.

The Riches of Hartford

The city of Hartford, one of the richest per capita in America, was awash in skilled labor. From the 1840s on, it had been home to the Colt Manufacturing Company, where Samuel Colt had machined the rifles and pistols that opened up the American West. As tool and die making became a sought-after art, both workmen and companies gravitated toward the capital city of Connecticut. Colt died prematurely at age 47 in 1862, and his widow Elizabeth continued to operate the huge factory. But many of the skilled men who had worked under the blue onion dome of the Colt armory on the banks of the Connecticut River ended up on Capitol Avenue a mile away. There, a succession of manufacturing companies had built a sprawling, four-story brick plant, on a 17-acre site next to railroad tracks.

The Weed Sewing Machine Company, then in pitched competition with such giants as Elias Howe and Merritt Singer, had been a victim of its own success. By the late 1870s, the industry had saturated the market for the wildly popular sewing machines, which had revolutionized domestic life. Succeeding Weed at that site was Colonel Albert A. Pope's manufacturing company. Colonel Pope by the mid–1880's had become the world's largest manufacturer of high-wheeled velocipedes at first and later, safety bicycles, whose wheels were of equal size. From the mid–1890s on, the grey-bearded Civil War colonel had built electric and gasoline automobiles, becoming America's largest automaker by 1900. But the giant shakeout in the automobile industry in 1907 caused the firm to founder. By the teens, Pope's Capitol Avenue plant sat largely idle.[46]

Southern New England was the hotbed of the machine tool industry. In Lowell, Massachusetts, young Francis Pratt had begun as an apprentice under a seasoned journeyman named Warren Aldrich. At age 25, he decided to test his wings and, beckoned by the national reputation of Samuel Colt, settled in Hartford. He won a job at the Colt Armory, which many considered a finishing school for mechanics. After two years there, he became the superintendent of the Phoenix Iron Works. The move was more significant for a contact he met there than for the experience itself. For at Phoenix, Pratt made the acquaintance of the young skilled workman Amos Whitney.

The Whitney name already resonated in New England, for Amos's cousin was Eli Whitney, whose Hamden, Connecticut, factory 30 miles south of Hartford was turning out his own invention — the cotton gin. Amos Whitney had learned by the seat of his pants like Pratt and so many mechanics of the age. He apprenticed at age 14 with the Essex Machine Co. in Lawrence, Massachusetts. Like Pratt, he had served an apprenticeship in the Colt Armory before moving to Phoenix. On one key point, Pratt and Whitney agreed: that accuracy was the sine qua non to manufacture machined products. The greater the accuracy, the smaller the tolerance, the finer the product. As he moved ahead in his career, this school dropout was able to buy a sprawling Victorian mansion in the city's fashionable West End.

Ambition drove both men. By 1860, when Francis was 33 years old and Amos 28, they decided to go into partnership together, setting up a modest shop on Potter Street, near the city's downtown. One of their first contracts was to design and produce automatic silk winders for Manchester's Cheney Mills, then spinning textiles for customers throughout the world. Evicted by a fire from their humble shop, they moved to the rear of the building housing *The Hartford Times,* one of a half-dozen daily newspapers in the city. Needing more money to help meet expanding orders, they took Monroe Stannard into partnership in 1862. Among the three of them, they had a mere $3,600 in capital, but galloping orders would cause that figure to skyrocket to $75,000 within four years. Needing even more resources to stay abreast of orders, they added partners Roswell S. Blodgett and Seth A. Bishop. When they incorporated in 1869, the Pratt & Whitney Company showed capital of $300,000, a staggering amount, given what they had started with. But even that would grow tenfold in the next six years.[47]

An Industrial Legacy

In the third quarter of the 19th century, the concept of interchangeable parts, pioneered by Eli Whitney among others, marked the cutting edge of technology. The need to make the same part do varied jobs within a machine meant the dimensions of each like part needed to be not approximate, but exact. Pratt & Whitney made sure they were in the vanguard of those industrialists stressing standard measurements.

On the edge of downtown Hartford, they built a four-story factory which, by 1888, would become a whole complex of buildings, snaking along a freight railroad track. By 1906, after adding a small tool plant, the complex hugged the tracks from both sides. The penchant for accuracy that Francis Pratt and Amos Whitney shared led them to create precision gauges to monitor industrial production. By 1885, its Standard Measuring Machine could measure tolerances accurate to .00001 of an inch. Predictably, the company entered contracts with manufacturers of such trailblazing items as the sewing machine, typesetting machines, typewriters, and weighing machines. Others called them to manufacture machine tools as diverse as drills, dies, lathe chucks, counting devices, and envelope-making machines.

When the Pratt & Whitney Company issued its illustrated catalogue for 1899, it sold its most expensive ad, on the page facing the title page, to Atty. Francis H. Richards of New York City, a patent attorney and mechanical engineer. The prominence of the ad suggests how important patent concerns were to the early industrialists in the "age of invention." Photograph after photograph proudly showcased the company headquarters, then employing some 1,200 workers, on the north bank of Hartford's Park River. The factory floor was a spiderweb of belts, pulleys, and gears, while in corporate offices on the upper levels, scalloped-bowl chandeliers with the arm span of a man dominated offices packed with rolltop desks, swivel chairs, and regulator clocks.[48]

By 1901, the name Pratt & Whitney resonated strongly within the industrial firmament. With the automobile industry now offering the next new product, the Niles-Bement-Pond Company bought out Pratt & Whitney, as P&W's founders receded into retirement. So fast did that industry grow that an industry shakeout killed off legions of manufacturers. One, the 17-acre Pope Manufacturing Company, sat nearby on Hartford's Capitol Avenue. In 1914, Niles-Bement-Pond moved into Pope's capacious quarters, keeping the name of the Pratt & Whitney Division. During the Great War, it would supply tools, gauges, and machines for the war effort, and by 1939 would encompass 23 multi-story buildings. The company's employee roster reflected America's diverse growth in its formative years of the early 1900s. Joining such Yankee surnames as Holcomb, Wilcox, and Parsons were Quattropani, Johnson, Homicki, Kelly, and Silverman.[49]

Natural Partners

Even as a New Yorker, Rentschler expressed amazement at the scope of Pratt & Whitney's headquarters when the taxi let him off at the Capitol Avenue curb. Rentschler's father was a principal in the Hooven-Owens-Rentschler manufacturing plant in Hamilton, Ohio, and Frederick was surprised to learn that his company had also bought small tooling services from Pratt & Whitney.

Giving Rentschler a walking tour of the premises, the beefy Clayton Burt studied his young visitor through tortoise-shell glasses. He told him of his interest in the future of aviation, but Burt was even more interested in finding a tenant to help absorb the crushing overhead the company had been amassing in the years following World War I. When Rentschler fixated on a four-story building on the premises, his proposal met a willing ear. The building was then used to store tobacco, a fact that stunned Rentschler, not used to the idea of tobacco being grown north of Virginia. In fact, Connecticut then prided itself in being "tobacco valley," home of broadleaf tobacco, used to fashion fine cigars.

Back in Burt's office, Rentschler spun out his vision for the Pratt & Whitney brass, gesticulating with his "big mechanic's hands." Demand was transforming aviation from a cottage industry to a big business, he argued. To succeed at that level, new companies had to have muscular research and development arms that would constantly reinvent their company's product as technology progressed. He respected liquid-cooled engines, such as those made by Curtiss and Packard, but Rentschler felt the future belonged to the air-cooled engine, which he thought he could build in the 400 to 500 horsepower class.

The U.S. military had generally favored liquid-cooled engines, but the Navy encouraged competition among technologies. Several weeks before, Rentschler had fascinated Rear Admiral William Moffett with a description of his air-cooled engine, and the Navy representative conceded it just might fill the bill for the 200 aircraft planned for its new *Saratoga* and *Lexington* carriers. To succeed, Rentschler would have to persuade the Navy to give him a development contract, so he wouldn't have to bear the up-front cost of evolving the engine from an idea to a product. But Moffett made clear the Navy wasn't about to take on that risk. This meant Rentschler would have to amass private capital on his own , along with skilled workmen.

"Naturally, we had no assets," Rentschler recalled in his memoirs, "nothing but plans on paper, and obviously nothing which a commercial bank could possibly do for us. I rejected any thought of going to an investment banker for the flotation of a company. This was the type of company I had just left at Wright Aeronautics. And I did not propose again to get back into any such position."[50]

Rentschler told Burt and his colleagues that he could supply the skilled labor, but he would need $250,000 to $500,000 to back him. That was just the beginning, he said, mincing no words. If the experimental engine proved out, he'd need another $1 million to produce it. Rentschler's proposal would be a major challenge to Pratt & Whitney, and he left Hartford uncertain of its response. But several weeks later, Cullen called Rentschler in New York and told him Pratt & Whitney would make $250,000 available to him as soon as he could get his men together. In spite of his years manufacturing more sophisticated engines, Rentschler had developed great respect for the minimalist motor that mechanic Charlie Taylor had developed for the Wright brothers. After automotive engine makers declined because they couldn't build an engine as light as the Wrights wanted, Taylor had built a 170-pound, liquid-cooled engine that could turn 16 horsepower, even though he had never built an engine in his life.

The United States had been through a world war now, and conflicts in Europe and elsewhere suggested future armed missions were likely. Yet unlike European nations, America had no aviation policy that would develop specific aircraft to match the country's military needs. Rentschler saw an opportunity in this crisis, for the only players in the quest to develop both domestic and military aircraft would be those adept at raising capital. He felt confident he could do that. By 1917, the only American company developing aircraft was Glenn Curtiss's company, the Curtiss Aeroplane and Motor Corporation. Its 90 horsepower OX engine represented the state of the art, in powering the military's *Jenny* trainer. Rentschler's controversial plan was to build on European designs which had already proven themselves in combat during World War I. His position horrified some proud nationalists, who felt an American plane should have an American design.

After the Great War, only Curtiss and Packard remained as major aircraft companies. But Rentschler, an Army captain, had been assigned in the aftermath to help wind up the affairs of the Wright-Martin Company. During the war, it had churned out 5,816 French Hispano-Suiza engines and 51 airplanes, under its wartime president, George Houston, a partner in Goethals Engineering Company. The company's assets were sold after the war to the Mack Truck Company, with a $3 million pot set aside in case its principals decided to set up a small aviation company in the postwar era.[51]

Houston, who had come to know Rentschler during wartime, now offered him a dream scenario. If he became Goethals' vice president and general manager, Houston would put the $3 million wartime set aside at Rentschler's disposal, to create a new aviation company that would go up against the big boys, Packard and Curtiss. The new operation would take over Wright-Martin's manufacturing license for the Hispano-Suiza engines. Rentschler found a plant in Paterson, New Jersey, and began refining these models and formulating new designs, both in liquid-cooled and radial air-cooled engines.

There, Rentschler began assembling a crack team. He targeted George Mead, an MIT graduate and experimental engineer from Wright-Martin, and asked him to head temporarily a power plant lab at McCook Field in Dayton, Ohio, to deepen his testing abilities. He would ultimately become the new company's vice president for engineering. Filling out his brain trust were tooling expert Charles Marks, Andrew Van Dean Willgoos, an engineer who could "think with his fingertips"; and to superintend his machine shop, John Borrup, who would work to tolerances of one-thousandth of an inch. The vestigial assets of the Wright-Martin company included the license to use the respected Wright name, so the new company would be called the Wright Aeronautical Company. By 1921, orders were being placed for its Hispano engines. The same year, Wright's T liquid-cooled, 575 horsepower engine emerged and would serve as the standard Navy seaplane power plant until 1926.[52]

Rentschler's first air-cooled radial engine was the R-1, a model undertaken originally for the Army. Britain had focused on radial engines since 1919, and in 1921, the U.S. Navy began shopping for an air-cooled radial engine in the 200-horsepower range. The Navy's first carrier was, fittingly, the Langley, and the task of the federal Bureau of Aeronautics was to design a fighter plane to fly from it. The Navy had looked with favor on a nine-cylinder, air-cooled radial engine designed by Charles Lawrance, but Lawrance ran what Rentschler judged "a completely confused manufacturing operation."

Wright decided to purchase the Lawrance company, and Rentschler put the able George Mead in charge of redesigning its engine. Eventually, it emerged as the J-5, or Whirlwind, engine, which in 1927 would carry Charles Lindbergh from New York to Paris in 33½ hours in his *Spirit of St. Louis.* As an air-cooled engine, the J-5 was far lighter than its liquid-cooled counterparts, eliminating the weight of pumps, radiators and plumbing and, therefore, having fewer parts to malfunction.[53]

The J-5 propelled the Wright company into the first rank of airplane manufacturers, and yet Rentschler's days there were numbered. Comprising his board were mostly investment bankers, men who valued bottom-line profits above all. Rentschler found it increasingly difficult to convince them of the need to set aside substantial sums for research and development, expenditures that would not translate into company profits for five or 10 years. Eventually, finding himself unable to sell his managerial philosophy, Rentschler resigned. His loyalty to some of his key co-workers compelled him first to tell, among others, George Mead and Andy Willgoos. Mead offered to quit on the spot, but Rentschler urged him to stay on. The chance might yet come for them to work together again.[54]

Rentschler Plunges Ahead

Given the go-ahead in 1925 by Pratt & Whitney, along with its financial backing, Rentschler plunged into production. By December, 1926, it would produce the P&W Wasp, a radial engine which would become the stuff of legend. The Wright Company, which Rentschler had left, now responded with an engine of its own. What pleasure it must have given Rentschler to defeat Wright for his first U.S. Navy contract of 200 Wasp engines, which soon became the dominant engine used in Army and Navy Air Force fighters. When Wright countered with the 500-horsepower Cyclone, the battle was joined. Throughout the next three decades P&W and Wright would be commercial rivals. The two companies would supply engines for such powerful craft as the Fokker and Ford Trimotors and a series of airliners produced by Douglas, beginning With the DC-2.

Rentschler's vision, that air-cooled radial motors would be the engines of the future, proved correct. By the end of the 1930s, these monster engines could generate 1,500 to 2,000 horsepower. In the run-up to World War II, the U.S. armed services came to recognize the P&W R-2800 Double Wasp engine, with horsepower ranging up to 2,800, as the best fighter engine.[55]

The mushrooming growth Pratt & Whitney experienced during the ensuing years, however, owed as much to commercial as to military contracts. In 1926, William Boeing adopted P&W Wasps for his Model 40 planes, designed to carry U.S. mail. The government had a monopoly on airmail business but had decided to open it to private contractors. Together, Boeing and Rentschler began to envision a mega-corporation, which would rely on airmail contracts for a revenue base. This would give it the security to experiment with the harder task of building passenger business.

In 1929, Rentschler and Boeing merged their companies into United Aircraft & Transport Corporation, which would become a who's who of aeronautics. Gathered under the new umbrella were such resonant names as Rentschler friend Chance Vought, whom the Wright brothers had taught to fly in 1910; and Russian-born Igor Ivanovich Sikorsky, an airplane designer who fled the Communist Revolution in 1918 to come to America. Hamilton Metalplane of Milwaukee had been a Boeing subsidiary since 1921, and now United's leaders merged it with newly-acquired Standard Steel Propellers of Pittsburgh, forming the Hamilton-Standard Division. The holding company would ultimately become United Airlines.[56]

Rentschler and Vought, whose forte was aircraft design, went back together to 1917. Described as "tough minded, dapper, electric, farsighted and highly gifted," Vought cut a handsome figure, with overhanging eyebrows over piercing eyes, a full mustache and hair parted down the middle. He seemed somewhat surprised that Rentschler, having left Wright, wanted to get back into "the rat race." He said, "A man cannot develop ulcers and high blood pressure half as fast anywhere else as he could in aviation, and Rentschler damn well knew it."[57]

The same year, the Pratt & Whitney division moved from Capitol Avenue across the Connecticut River to a huge parcel of land that would accommodate its new headquarters in East Hartford. In 1931, the Wasp was used in Ford's Tin Goose and in the first amphibious aircraft designed by Sikorsky. Amelia Earhart crossed the Atlantic in a Lockheed Vega powered by a Wasp. By the company's 10th anniversary, it employed more than 2,000.

Rentschler had become the first president of United, but in 1934, an anti-monopoly fervor swept through Congress in the wake of corporate abuses that had helped lead to the 1929 stock market crash. New legislation required the breakup of holding companies, of which United was one. The fallout left Boeing, United Air Lines, and Pratt & Whitney Aircraft as separate entities. Under the P&W umbrella remained Chance Vought, Sikorsky, and Hamilton Standard.

During World War II, P&W produced 166,500 Twin Wasp engines, packing 1,350 horsepower. So prodigious had Rentschler's accomplishments become that by the end of World War II in 1945, P&W engines accounted for half of America's military aerial horsepower.[58]

Breaking the Sound Barrier

The Wright brothers had to strain to reach 30 miles per hour on their early flights. A measure of how far technology had come since then is that in 1957 — barely four decades after the Wrights' Huffman Prairie flights — legendary Chuck Yeager flew a

Bell X-1 above the speed of sound. The first production aircraft to break the sound barrier was the F-100 Super Sabre, powered by a P&W J57.

Heading into the very real challenge of peacetime, United Aircraft still contained under its umbrella Hamilton Standard, Chance Vought, and Sikorsky, as well as Pratt & Whitney. But a few years later, Chance Vought broke off and became an independent. In the competitive world of aviation, airframe builders had become skittish about revealing competitive information to United, that might find its way internally to the competing Chance Vought division.[59]

Chance Vought was not the only breakaway. Young Charles Kaman, who had served as chief aerodynamicist for Hamilton Standard , put together some of the newly-available postwar venture capital and founded his own company in late 1945. Yet his backing capital was not enough to attract the military business he sought, until he landed a Navy contract in 1947 to develop a rotor and went public a year later. The Navy work proved a foot in the door for the tenacious Kaman, who next succeeded in securing production contracts for training helicopters. In 1951, Kaman tested the world's first turbine-powered helicopter, Model K-225. By 1953, he opened a 155,000 square foot facility in Bloomfield, Connecticut.

Jet Engines and Aerospace

Pratt & Whitney threw itself headlong into the jet engine era. To test jet engines, it opened its Andrew Willgoos Gas Turbine Lab, to honor the engineer who could "think with his fingertips." On the production side, eight P&W J57 turbojets powered Boeing's B-52 Stratofortress in 1952. When Pan Am's Boeing 707 made its debut in 1958, JT3s powered its first flight from New York to Paris.

The advent of the Cold War signaled an era of defense preparedness, and Pratt & Whitney was positioned as one of five major engine producers, along with Wright, Westinghouse, General Electric, and Allison. Together they would supply a total of nine producers of military aircraft, a number that would shrink as that military stand-off continued.

On a parallel track, Sikorsky was making a name for itself in helicopters, both for the military and domestic markets. As historian Donald Pattillo notes, its S-56 during the 1950s was the world's most powerful and largest production helicopter, powered as it was by twin P&W 2,000-horsepower engines. Igor Sikorsky, the company's founder, would retire in 1957 but stay involved in research for the rest of his life.

The ensuing years would bring massive changes in the aircraft industry which are beyond the scope of this book to chronicle, as aerospace became an increasing source of business for aircraft producers and airline deregulation created new competitive opportunities and challenges for the industry. Yet still leading the pack of aerospace manufacturers in 1989, as Nos. 15 and 17 among Fortune 500 companies, were Boeing and United Technologies, the same companies started more than 60 years earlier by two determined young Midwesterners named William Boeing and Frederick Rentschler.[60]

Notes

Abbreviations Used

AGB	—	Alexander Graham Bell
AGB Papers	—	Alexander Graham Bell Papers, Library of Congress
OC	—	Octave Chanute
C-H	—	Chanute-Herring Diary
SPL	—	Samuel P. Langley
LM	—	Memoirs of Samuel P. Langley
WP	—	Papers of Wilbur and Orville Wright
GS	—	George Spratt
CDW	—	Charles D. Walcott
KW	—	Katharine Wright
MW	—	Milton Wright
OW	—	Orville Wright
WW	—	Wilbur Wright

1. The Battle Is Joined

1. Crouch, *A Dream of Wings*.
2. Crouch, *The Bishop's Boys*.
3. *Ibid.*, p. 140.
4. Howard, *Wilbur and Orville*.
5. Crouch, *The Bishop's Boys*, p. 256.
6. *Ibid.*
7. *Ibid.*, p. 143.
8. *Ibid.*, p. 144.
9. Culick and Dunsmore, *On Great White Wings*, p. 21.
10. Crouch, *A Dream*, p. 233.
11. *Ibid.*, p. 142.
12. *Ibid.*, p. 162.
13. Gunston, *Aviation — The Story of Flight*.
14. Crouch, *The Bishop's Boys*, p. 163.
15. Gunston, p. 38.
16. Crouch, *A Dream*, p. 176.
17. Crouch, *The Bishop's Boys*, p. 145.
18. Bruce, *Alexander Graham Bell and the Conquest of Solitude*, p. 363.
19. *Ibid.*, p. 364.
20. *Ibid.*, p. 365.
21. *Ibid.*, p. 360.
22. Crouch, *A Dream*, p. 153.
23. Lupiano, *It Was a Very Good Year*.
24. Crouch, *A Dream*, p. 279.
25. Crouch, *The Bishop's Boys*, p. 287.
26. *Ibid.*, p. 289.

27. McFarland, ed., *The Papers of Wilbur and Orville Wright.*

28. *Ibid.*, p. 332.

29. *Ibid.*, p. 337.

30. *Ibid.*, p. 346.

31. *Ibid.*

32. *Ibid.*, p. 354.

33. *Ibid.*, p. 364; Howard, *Wilbur and Orville,* p. 123.

34. McFarland, p. 390.

2. The Primal Urge

1. Hart, *Prehistory of Flight,* p. 24; Douglas, *Pictorial History of Aviation,* pp. 9–11.

2. Hart, pp. 28–9, 57.

3. *Ibid.*, pp. 58–9, 24, 45.

4. Douglas, p. 13; Means, *Aeronautical Annual,* p. 14.

5. Hart, p. 96.

6. *Ibid.*, p. 98.

7. *Ibid.*, p. 56.

8. *Ibid.*, p. 101.

9. *Ibid.*, p. 102.

10. Means, p. 15.

11. Ethell, *Frontier of Flight,* p. 12.

12. Douglas, p. 15.

13. Ethell, pp. 12–14.

14. Douglas, p. 21.

15. Morison, *Oxford History,* p. 893.

16. Means, p. 130.

17. Gunston, *Aviation,* p. 38.

18. Ethell, p. 14.

19. Gunston, p. 42.

20. Means, p. 23.

21. *Ibid.*, pp. 17–18.

22. Ethell, p. 14.

23. Douglas, p. 19.

24. Ethell, p. 16.

25. Means, pp. 19, 25.

26. Gunston, p. 39; Ethell, p. 14.

27. Ethell, p. 15.

28. Douglas, p. 17.

29. Gunston, p. 40.

30. Ethell, p. 15.

31. Morison, p. 894.

32. Gunston, pp. 42–3.

3. Not So Funny Anymore

1. Lupiano, *It Was a Very Good Year,* p. 183–5.

2. Crouch, *A Dream,* p. 160.

3. Crouch, *The Bishop's Boys,* pp. 137, 149.

4. Crouch, *A Dream,* p. 157.

5. *Ibid.*, pp. 160–174.

6. Goddard, *Colonel Albert Pope,* p. 144.

7. *Ibid.*, p. 10.

8. *Ibid.*, p.94.

9. Crouch, *The Bishop's Boys,* pp. 74–5, p. 95; Howard, *Wilbur and Orville,* p. 4; Culick, *On Great White Wings,* p. 17.

10. Crouch, *The Bishop's Boys,* pp. 25, 51.

11. *Ibid.*, pp. 55, 39.

12. Howard, *Wilbur and Orville,* p. 4; Crouch, *The Bishop's Boys,* p. 56–7.

13. Howard, p. 8; Culick, p. 17.

14. Howard, pp. 9–10.

15. Crouch, *The Bishop's Boys,* p. 20; Howard, p. 10.

16. Howard, p. 13; Culick, p. 18; Crouch, *The Bishop's Boys,* pp. 35, 46, 77.

17. Kingsford, *F.W. Lanchester,* p. 80.

18. *Ibid.*, passim, especially pp. 79, 80, 82–3, 85, 101.

19. Culick, p. 20; Stewart, *Conquest of the Air,* pp. 59–60.

20. Stewart, p. 60.

21. Crouch, *The Bishop's Boys,* pp. 138–140; Howard, p. 17; Kirk, *First in Flight,* pp. 10–11.

22. Crouch, *The Bishop's Boys,* p. 151; Goddard, *Colonel Albert Pope,* pp. 66–68.

23. Howard, pp. 9, 12; Crouch, *The Bishop's Boys,* p. 169.

24. Combs, *Kill Devil Hill,* p. 51; Crouch, *The Bishop's Boys,* p. 130–40; Howard, p. 102; Kirk, pp. 10–11.

25. Howard, pp. 19–20; Crouch, *The Bishop's Boys,* p. 141, 145.

26. Crouch, *The Bishop's Boys,* pp. 163–68; Howard, p. 13; Kirk, p. 20.

27. Howard, p. 17; Crouch, *The Bishop's Boys,* pp. 164–5.

28. Crouch, *The Bishop's Boys,* p. 169.

4. A Critical Mass

1. Howard, *Wilbur and Orville,* p. 210; Crouch, *The Bishop's Boys,* p. 351.

2. Bruce, *Alexander Graham Bell,* p. 365. Doc. 1952, N. 4, Thomas A. Edison papers, Vol. 5, Rutgers University, New Brunswick, N.J.

3. AGB papers, Box 1.

4. Crouch, *A Dream,* p. 133.

5. *Ibid.*, p. 136–7.

6. Langley, "The Flying-Machine," *McClure's Magazine,* p. 654–5.

7. Crouch, *A Dream,* p. 141.

8. *Ibid.*, p. 145.
9. *Ibid.*, pp. 148–9.
10. Lupiano, *It Was a Very Good Year*, pp. 197–8.
11. AGB papers, Box 1, Langley to Bell, 5/4/1896.
12. Crouch, *The Bishop's Boys*, pp. 138–9.
13. *Ibid.*, p. 141.
14. Crouch, *A Dream*, pp. 151–2.
15. *Ibid.*, p. 152.
16. Howard, *Wilbur and Orville*, p. 17.
17. Crouch, *A Dream*, p. 154.
18. AGB papers, Box 1, letter to editor of *Science*, 5/12/1896.
19. *Ibid.*, Box 1, letter to *Science*, 5/22/1896.
20. Crouch, *The Bishop's Boys*, p. 144.
21. *Ibid.*, pp. 144–5.
22. Bruce, p. 363.
23. Goddard, *Colonel Albert Pope*, p. 157.
24. Crouch, *The Bishop's Boys*, p. 129.
25. Goddard, *Colonel Albert Pope*, p. 10.
26. *Ibid.*, p. 148.
27. Langley, "The Flying Machine," p. 647.
28. *Ibid.*, p. 660.
29. *Ibid.*

5. A National Mission

1. Goddard, *Getting There*, p. 3.
2. "Chronology of the life of Charles D. Walcott," free-standing document in files of Collections and Research Division of the Smithsonian Institution.
3. *Ibid.*
4. Crouch, *A Dream*, p. 131.
5. *Ibid.*, p. 255.
6. *Ibid.*, pp. 130–1.
7. Yochelson, *Charles Doolittle Walcott*, p. 341.
8. Leech, *In the Days of McKinley*, p. 167–191.
9. *Ibid.*, p. 169.
10. *Ibid.*, p. 181.
11. *Ibid.*
12. Andrews, *The Flying Machine*, p. 84; Crouch, *The Bishop's Boys*, p. 260.
13. Crouch, *A Dream*, p. 257.
14. Diary of Charles D. Wolcott for March 24, 1898, Collections and Research Division, Smithsonian Institution.
15. *Ibid.*, March 25, 1898.
16. Crouch, *A Dream*, p. 257.
17. Yochelson, p. 343.
18. *Ibid.*, p. 344.
19. AGB Papers, Box 1, Langley to Bell, June 18, 1898.

20. *Ibid.*, Langley to Bell, June 13, 1898.
21. Crouch, *A Dream*, p. 264.
22. *Ibid.*, p. 263; Howard, *Wilbur and Orville*, p. 125.
23. Yochelson, pp. 342–3.
24. Crouch, *The Bishop's Boys*, p. 257.
25. Langley, *Memoir on Mechanical Flight*, p. 126.
26. *Ibid.*, p. 123.
27. Crouch, *A Dream*, p. 271.
28. Crouch, *The Bishop's Boys*, pp. 161–2.

6. The Chanute Factor

1. Howard, *Wilbur and Orville*, p. 19.
2. *Ibid.*, p. 20; Crouch, *The Bishop's Boys*, p. 153; Gunston, p. 39.
3. Kirk, p. 103.
4. Crouch, *The Bishop's Boys*, p. 146.
5. *Ibid.*, pp. 146–7. Donald O. Weckhorst, Interim Curator at the Octave Chanute Aerospace Museum Foundation, says Chanute's first name is pronounced "Oc-Tayve."
6. Kirk, p. 9.
7. Howard, *Wilbur and Orville*, p. 54.
8. Crouch, *The Bishop's Boys*, pp. 151–2.
9. Kirk, p. 10; Gunston, p. 39.
10. Howard, *Wilbur and Orville*, p. 19; Kirk, p. 9.
11. Crouch, *The Bishop's Boys*, p. 152.
12. Howard, *Wilbur and Orville*, p. 21.
13. Kirk, p. 12.
14. Crouch, *The Bishop's Boys*, p. 154; www2.crown.net/sspicer/Chanute/Chanute.html. p. 4.
15. Howard, *Wilbur and Orville*, p. 22; www2crown net/sspicer/Chanute/Chanute.html, Chanute diary, 7/4/1896. p.5.
16. Howard, *Wilbur and Orville*, p. 22.
17. *Ibid.*
18. *Ibid.*, pp. 23–24.
19. *Ibid.*, p. 24.
20. Attributed to President John F. Kennedy.
21. Crouch, *The Bishop's Boys*, pp. 154–5.
22. Kirk, p. 104; Howard, *Wilbur and Orville*, p. 26.
23. Kirk, p. 105.
24. www2.crown.net/sspicer/Chanute/diary.html. p. 11.

7. The Wright Stuff

1. Microsoft Encarta article on Smithsonian Institution.

2. National Public Radio's Weekend Edition segment on John Wesley Powell, 9/22/02.

3. Howard, *Wilbur and Orville,* p. 132.

4. McFarland, *Papers of Wilbur and Orville Wright,* pp. 4–5.

5. *Ibid.,* p. 5; Crouch, *The Bishop's Boys,* p. 162.

6. McFarland, pp. 7–8.

7. Kirk, *First in Flight,* p. 21.

8. *Ibid.,* pp. 22.

9. McFarland, p. 8. Dr. Tom Crouch offers another way to view the important three axes: "These axes can best be understood as three imaginary lines around which a machine in the air is free to rotate: Pitch (a horizontal line running from wingtip to wingtip); roll (a horizontal line running through the center of the craft from nose to tail); and yaw (a vertical line running directly through the center of the craft)."

10. Westcott, *Wind and Sand,* from foreword by Oliver Jensen.

11. In a biographical deposition after Wilbur's death, Orville Wright conceded he wasn't present at the time of the testing but contended he had discussed the principles involved previously with Wilbur.

12. McFarland, pp. 11–12.

13. *Ibid.,* p. 15.

14. *Ibid.,* p. 17.

15. Crouch, *The Bishop's Boys,* p. 171.

16. Gunston, *Aviation,* p. 64.

17. Crouch, *The Bishop's Boys,* p. 173.

18. *Ibid.,* p. 201; Kirk, p. 23.

19. McFarland, p. 17.

20. Crouch, *The Bishop's Boys,* p. 174.

21. *Ibid.,* p. 182; McFarland, p. 17.

22. Crouch, *The Bishop's Boys,* p. 179.

23. McFarland, pp. 21–2.

24. *Ibid.,* p. 23; Kirk, p. 25.

25. McFarland, p. 25.

26. Crouch, *The Bishop's Boys,* p. 187; Kirk, pp. 32–3. As of the writing of this book, a stone monument stands in the yard of what had been the Tate homestead near Kitty Hawk landing, commemorating the assembly in that yard of Wilbur Wright's first flying machine.

27. Kirk, p. 34.

28. *Ibid.,* p. 35.

29. *Ibid.,* p. 26, 35.

30. Crouch, *The Bishop's Boys,* p. 195.

31. *Ibid.,* p. 171. McFarland, p. 26.

32. McFarland, p. 27.

33. Kirk, p. 35–7; Crouch, *The Bishop's Boys,* p. 190.

34. McFarland, p. 31.

35. *Ibid.,* p. 33.

36. *Ibid.,* p. 37; Kirk, p. 42.

37. McFarland, p. 39.

38. *Ibid.,* p. 40.

39. Crouch, *The Bishop's Boys,* p. 165; Gunston, p. 40.

40. McFarland, p. 43.

41. Kirk, pp. 42–3; Crouch, *The Bishop's Boys,* p. 190.

42. McFarland, p. 28.

43. *Ibid.,* p. 46.

44. *Ibid.,* p. 47.

45. *Ibid.,* p. 49.

46. Crouch, *The Bishop's Boys,* p. 167.

47. Kirk, pp. 46–7.

48. www.flight100.org.

8. No Simple Matter

1. www2crown.net/sspicer/Chanute/diary.html. p. 12.

2. *Ibid.*

3. *Ibid.,* pp. 12–13.

4. McFarland, *The Papers of Wilbur and Orville Wright,* p. 53, WW to OC, 3/19/01, OC to WW, 3/26/01.

5. Combs, Harry. *Kill Devil Hill,* p. 126.

6. McFarland, p. 54. WW to OC, 5/12/01; Kirk, *First in Flight,* p. 57.

7. McFarland, p. 54. WW to OC, 5/12/01.

8. *Ibid.,* pp. 54–56, WW to OC, 6/19/01.

9. *Ibid.,* p. 57n.

10. *Ibid.,* p. 58, OC to WW, 6/29/01.

11. *Ibid.,* p. 61, Wilbur Wright on "The Horizontal Position During Gliding Flight," from *Illustrierte Aeronautische Mitteilungen,* June, 1901.

12. *Ibid.,* p. 65, OC to WW, 7/3/01.

13. *Ibid.,* p. 66, WW to OC, 7/4/01; Crouch, *The Bishop's Boys,* p. 207; Combs, p. 129.

14. Interview with local historian David Stick, 6/22/02.

15. *Ibid.,* p. 68n, from WW lecture 6/24/03 to the Western Society of Engineers.

16. Interview with U.S. Park Rangers at Wright Memorial, Kill Devil Hills, 6/21/02.

17. McFarland, p. 69, Chanute/Huffaker Diary, 7/18/01; Howard, *Wilbur and Orville,* p. 59; Combs, *The Bishop's Boys,* p. 131.

18. McFarland, p. 70, WW to OC, 6/26/01.

19. Kirk, p. 60; Crouch, *The Bishop's Boys,* p. 208; Combs, p. 132.

20. *Ibid.,* p. 62.

21. *Ibid.,* p. 66.

22. *Ibid.,* p. 67.

23. *Ibid.;* Crouch, *The Bishop's Boys,* p. 211.

24. Kirk, pp. 67, 70.

25. *Ibid.*, p. 77; Howard, *Wilbur and Orville*, p. 623.

26. Kirk, p. 74.

27. *Ibid.*, pp. 74–7.

28. Combs, p. 135.

29. Kirk, p. 75.

30. *Ibid.*, p. 76; Crouch, *The Bishop's Boys*, p. 211; Howard, *Wilbur and Orville*, pp. 64–5; McFarland, p. 71, WW to diary, 7/27/01.

31. Howard, *Wilbur and Orville*, p. 64.

32. *Ibid.*

33. McFarland, p. 72, OW to KW, 7/28/01; Combs, p. 133.

34. McFarland, p. 72–3, OW to KW, 7/28/01.

35. *Ibid.*, p. 74.

36. Crouch, *The Bishop's Boys*, p. 211.

37. *Ibid.*

38. McFarland, p. 81, C-H Diary, 8/9/01.

39. *Ibid.*, p. 82; Howard, *Wilbur and Orville*, p. 66.

40. Crouch, *The Bishop's Boys*, p. 213; Howard, *Wilbur and Orville*, p. 67; Combs, p. 147.

9. The Clock Ticks On

1. DeGregorio, *Complete Book of U.S. Presidents*, p. 367.

2. Leech, *In the Days of McKinley*, p. 601; McFarland, *The Papers of Wilbur and Orville Wright*, pp. 93–9.

3. Kipling, *Something of Myself*, p. 132–3.

4. Morris, *The Rise of Theodore Roosevelt*, p. 608.

5. *Ibid.*, p. 840, n75, 76.

6. Levine, *Billy Mitchell*, pp. 20–21; Morris, pp. 641–2.

7. Levine, pp. 20–21.

8. Langley, *Memoir on Mechanical Flight*, p. 124.

9. *Ibid.*, p. 125.

10. *Ibid.*, p. 147.

11. *Ibid.*, passim.

12. *Ibid.*, p. 126.

13. *Ibid.*, p. 133.

14. *Ibid.*, p. 156.

15. *Ibid.*, p. 157.

16. *Ibid.*, p. 140.

17. *Ibid.*, p. 142.

18. *Ibid.*, p. 147.

19. *Ibid.*

20. *Ibid.*, p. 176.

21. *Ibid.*, p. 218; Crouch, *The Bishop's Boys*, p. 257.

22. Langley, p. 218.

23. *Ibid.*, p. 219.

24. *Ibid.*

25. *Ibid.*, p. 220.

10. A New Lease on Life

1. McFarland, *The Papers of Wilbur and Orville Wright*, p. 84, OC to WW, 8/23/01.

2. *Ibid.*, p. 92, KW to MW, 9/3/01.

3. *Ibid.*, p. 93, WW to OC, 9/6/01.

4. Howard, *Wilbur and Orville*, p. 69.

5. McFarland, p. 100.

6. Howard, *Wilbur and Orville*, p. 71.

7. *Ibid.*, pp. 69–71.

8. McFarland, p. 118, WW to GS, 9/21/01.

9. *Ibid.*, p. 138, WW to OC, 10/18/01.

10. *Ibid.*, p. 142, WW to OC, 10/24/01.

11. *Ibid.*, p. 187, WW to OC, 12/23/01.

12. Crouch, *The Bishop's Boys*, p. 229.

13. McFarland, pp. 191, 203, OC to WW, 1/1/02, 1/13/02.

14. *Ibid.*, p. 205, WW to OC, 1/19/02; Crouch, *The Bishop's Boys*, p. 230.

15. McFarland, p. 213, WW to OC, 2/7/02.

16. *Ibid.*, p. 235, WW to OC, 6/2/02.

17. As Wilbur wrote, Admiral Peary was on the last leg of a four-year unsuccessful expedition to the North Pole, for which he had taken a leave of absence from the U.S. Navy. He fell short of his goal but succeeded in his last quest in 1908, although this triumph set off a bitter struggle with Dr. Frederick Cook, ship surgeon on an earlier Peary expedition, over who had reached the North Pole first.

18. McFarland, p. 198, WW to OC, 1/5/02.

19. *Ibid.*, p. 201, OC to WW, 1/8/02.

20. *Ibid.*, pp. 95–98.

21. Kirk, *First in Flight*, p. 97; Howard, *Wilbur and Orville*, p. 73; Crouch, *The Bishop's Boys*, pp. 221–2. Wilbur positioned the wing and plate so that if Lilienthal's tables were correct, when exposed to wind, the wing's lift would match the resistance of the plate. The brothers mounted the wheel horizontally in front of the bicycle's handlebars, where it was free to turn, and pedaled the strange contraption at a constant speed. Instead of the wheel remaining stable, as it would have had Lilienthal's tables been correct, the rim turned toward the plate. This showed the resistance of the plate exceeded the lift of the wing and validated what Wilbur had surmised — that Lilienthal had overestimated the wing's lift.

22. Crouch, *The Bishop's Boys*, pp. 222–4.

23. *Ibid.*, pp. 221–8; Howard, *Wilbur and Orville*, pp. 73–4.

24. Howard, *Wilbur and Orville*, pp. 74–5.
25. *Ibid.*, p. 159.
26. *Ibid.*, p. 185.
27. *Ibid.*, pp. 251–2.
28. *Ibid.*, p. 207.
29. Kirk, *First in Flight*, p. 116.
30. Crouch, *The Bishop's Boys*, p. 235.
31. *Ibid.*, p. 236.
32. Author's visit to Kill Devil Hills, 6/21/03 to 6/23/03.
33. Crouch, *The Bishop's Boys*, p. 238; Kirk, *First in Flight*, p. 111.
34. Kirk, *First in Flight*, p. 119; Crouch, *The Bishop's Boys*, p. 239.

11. The Invitation

1. Crouch, *The Bishop's Boys*, p. 240.
2. McFarland, p. 283, WW to OC, 11/12/02.
3. Crouch, *The Bishop's Boys*, p. 240; Howard, *Wilbur and Orville*, pp. 95–6; Kirk, *First in Flight*, p. 122.
4. Crouch, *The Bishop's Boys*, p. 277; McFarland, p. 282–3, WW to OC, 11/12/02.
5. Howard, *Wilbur and Orville*, p. 96; Kirk, p. 124; McFarland, p. 290, WW to OC, 12/11/02.
6. Howard, *Wilbur and Orville*, p. 96.
7. McFarland, pp. 279–281, OW to KW, 10/23/02.
8. Stick, *The Outer Banks of North Carolina*, p. 207.
9. McFarland, p. 285, OC to WW, 11/30/02.
10. *Ibid.*, p. 287, Wright Cycle Co. to numerous auto manufacturers.
11. Culick and Spencer, *On Great White Wings*, p. 56.
12. *Ibid.*, pp. 56–9.
13. Howard, *Wilbur and Orville*, p. 106; Stick, p. 207; Kirk, pp. 132–3; Combs, *Kill Devil Hill*, p. 176.
14. Combs, p. 177.
15. Kirk, p. 134.
16. Culick, p. 60.
17. Combs, p. 182.
18. Stick, p. 208; McFarland, p. 313, OW to GS, 6/7/03; Howard, *Wilbur and Orville*, p. 108; Combs, pp. 179, 186.
19. Howard, *Wilbur and Orville*, pp. 104–5.
20. *Ibid.*, p. 105.
21. Crouch, *The Bishop's Boys*, p. 245.
22. *Ibid.*, p. 246.
23. Howard, *Wilbur and Orville*, p. 98.
24. McFarland, p. 303, OC to WW, 4/4/03.
25. *Ibid.*, p. 308, OC to WW, 5/15/03.
26. *Ibid.*, p. 314, OW to GS, 6/7/03.
27. *Ibid.*, p. 306, WW to GS, 4/20/03.
28. *Ibid.*, p. 307n.
29. Goddard, *Colonel Albert Pope*, pp. 124–5.
30. *Ibid.*, p. 125.
31. *Ibid.*, p. 126.
32. Howard, *Wilbur and Orville*, p. 31.
33. *Ibid.*, p. 32; McFarland, p. 316, WW to OC, 6/18/03.
34. Combs, p. 187.
35. McFarland, p. 337, WW to OC, 7/2/03.
36. *Ibid.*, p. 346, WW to OC, 7/22/03.
37. *Ibid.*, p. 346, OC to WW, 7/23/03.
38. *Ibid.*, p. 354, WW to OC, 9/19/03.
39. Crouch, *The Bishop's Boys*, p. 251–2.
40. *Ibid.*, p. 252.

12. Down to the Wire

1. McFarland, *The Papers of Wilbur and Orville Wright*, p. 361, unidentified news clipping contained in letter from OC to WW, 10/7/03.
2. Crouch, *The Bishop's Boys*, p. 253–4.
3. McFarland, p. 353, OC to WW, 9/3/03.
4. Crouch, *The Bishop's Boys*, pp. 253–4.
5. McFarland, p. 353, WW to OC, 9/9/03.
6. McFarland, p. 355, WW to OC, 9/19/03.
7. *Ibid.*, passim.
8. *Ibid.*, p. 356, OW to KW, 9/26/03. The reference to Roanoke refers to the settlement of Britain's Sir Walter Raleigh, which vanished without a trace in the early 1600s.
9. McFarland, p. 357; Howard, *Wilbur and Orville*, p. 113.
10. It is uncertain whether the Wrights would have used the term "hangar" to describe the shed that housed the Flyer. *The American Heritage Dictionary of the English Language* says that the word is derived from Old French, "probably from Medieval Latin *angarium*, meaning a shed for shoeing horses."
11. McFarland, p. 358, OW Diary, 9/28/03; Crouch, *The Bishop's Boys*, p. 256, 258.
12. Howard, *Wilbur and Orville*, p. 114.
13. McFarland, p. 362, OW Diary, 10/11/03.
14. Kirk, *First in Flight*, p. 165.
15. Langley, *Memoir of Mechanical Flight*, p. 256.
16. *Ibid.*, pp. 258–63.
17. *Ibid.*, p. 260.
18. Crouch, *The Bishop's Boys*, p. 257.
19. *Ibid.*, p. 258; Howard, *Wilbur and Orville*, p. 127.
20. Howard, *Wilbur and Orville*, p. 127.
21. *Ibid.*, p. 128.

22. *Ibid.*, p. 129.
23. Langley, *Memoir*, p. 266.
24. *Ibid.*, p. 268.
25. Howard, *Wilbur and Orville*, p. 130.
26. Crouch, *The Bishop's Boys*, p. 258.
27. *Ibid.*, p. 257; McFarland, p. 364, WW to OC, 10/16/03.
28. McFarland, p. 364.
29. *Ibid.*
30. Howard, *Wilbur and Orville*, p. 117; Crouch, *The Bishop's Boys*, p. 259.
31. Crouch, *The Bishop's Boys*, p. 48.
32. McFarland, p. 367, WW to KW, 10/18/03.
33. McFarland, p. 367, WW to KW, 10/18/03.
34. McFarland, p. 372, OC to WW, 10/24/03.
35. McFarland, p. 377–8, OW diary, 11/6/03.
36. McFarland, p. 381, OW to KW and MW, 11/15/03; Crouch, *The Bishop's Boys*, p. 260.
37. Combs, *Kill Devil Hill*, p. 296.
38. McFarland, p. 377n.
39. *Ibid.*, p. 381, OW to MW and KW, 11/15/03.
40. Crouch, *The Bishop's Boys*, p. 260.
41. Combs, p. 186.
42. McFarland, p. 332.
43. *Ibid.*, p. 377, OC to GS, 12/2/03.
44. *Ibid.*, p. 381, OW to KW and MW, 11/15/03; Stick, *The Outer Banks of North Carolina*, p. 208; Combs, p. 193; Crouch, *The Bishop's Boys*, p. 256; author's visit to Kill Devil Hills, 6/21–23/02.
45. McFarland, p. 385n.
46. Kirk, p. 173.
47. McFarland, p. 384, OW Diary, 11/20/03.
48. Crouch, *The Bishop's Boys*, p. 261.
49. *Ibid.*; McFarland, p. 377, 378.
50. McFarland, p. 390, WW to GS, 12/2/03.
51. Crouch, *The Bishop's Boys*, p. 262.
52. McFarland, p. 390n.
53. Howard, *Wilbur and Orville*, p. 131; Crouch, *The Bishop's Boys*, p. 262.
54. Howard, *Wilbur and Orville*, p. 131.
55. *The Washington Post*, 12/10/03, p. 2.
56. *Ibid.*
57. *Ibid.*; Kirk, p. 193.
58. Kirk, p. 192.
59. Howard, *Wilbur and Orville*, p. 131.
60. Combs, p. 191.
61. Howard, *Wilbur and Orville*, pp. 126–7.
62. *Ibid.*, pp. 394–8.
63. *Ibid.*, p. 132.
64. McFarland, p. 391, OW Diary, 12/12/03; Combs, p. 201.
65. Kirk, pp. 141–5.
66. *Ibid.*, p. 138; Combs, pp. 202–3.
67. Combs, p. 204.
68. Howard, *Wilbur and Orville*, p. 134; Crouch, *The Bishop's Boys*, p. 264; Kirk, p. 177;

McFarland, pp. 392–3, WW to KW and MW, 12/14/03.
69. McFarland, p. 394.
70. Crouch, *The Bishop's Boys*, p. 265.
71. *Ibid.*, pp. 263–4; Howard, *Wilbur and Orville*, pp. 135–6.
72. Crouch, *The Bishop's Boys*, pp. 266–7.
73. Howard, *Wilbur and Orville*, p. 137.
74. McFarland, p. 395, OW Diary, 12/17/03; Crouch, *The Bishop's Boys*, p. 268; Kirk, p. 180.
75. Kirk, p. 151.
76. McFarland, p. 395, OW Diary, 12/17/03; Combs, p. 211.
77. McFarland, p. 396, OW Diary, 12/17/03; Combs, p. 219.
78. Crouch, *The Bishop's Boys*, p. 269.
79. Kirk, p. 182.
80. McFarland, p. 397, KW telegram to OC, 12/17/03.
81. Crouch, *The Bishop's Boys*, pp. 271–2.

13. Grudging Acceptance

1. Stick, *The Outer Banks of North Carolina*, p. 82.
2. Audiotape of 1960 interview of Mary and Spence Midgett and Carlos and Mary Dowdy, in archives of Outer Banks History Center, Manteo, N.C. The young interviewer was Bill Harris, who was mayor of Kitty Hawk at the time the present work was written.
3. Stick, p. 92.
4. *Ibid.*, p. 82. Also see p. 33.
5. Kirk, *First in Flight*, p. 184, quoting newspaperman Byron Newton from an article in the June, 1908 issue of *Aeronautics Magazine*.
6. Stick, p. 180–1. The Outer Banks had appeal to inventors other than the Wrights during the 1900–1903 period. Inventors of wireless telegraphy, the forerunner of radio, conducted important experiments in Hatteras and Roanoke Island. Reginald L. Fessenden, formerly an assistant to Thomas A. Edison, perfected a wireless telegraphy system earlier than Italy's Guglielmo Marconi, and his supporters say that he, not Marconi, invented the system that served as the basis for radio broadcasting.
7. Gunston, *Aviation*, pp. 43–4.
8. *Ibid.*, p. 44.
9. Howard, *Wilbur and Orville*, p. 152–5.
10. *Ibid.*, p. 156.
11. Walsh, *One Day at Kitty Hawk*, pp. 148–9.
12. Combs, *Kill Devil Hill*, p. 226.

13. Walsh, p. 150. McFarland, ed., *The Papers of Wilbur and Orville Wright*, p. 409, OW Diary, 1/4/04.

14. Kirk, p. 189.

15. Walsh, pp. 153–4.

16. *Ibid.*, p. 155.

17. *Ibid.*, p. 156; Howard, *Wilbur and Orville*, p. 150.

18. Crouch, *The Bishop's Boys*, p. 273.

19. Howard, *Wilbur and Orville*, p. 148.

20. Crouch, *The Bishop's Boys*, p. 274.

21. *Ibid.*, p. 280; Walsh, p. 159; Howard, *Wilbur and Orville*, p. 153.

22. Crouch, *The Bishop's Boys*, p. 275; Howard, *Wilbur and Orville*, p. 152.

23. Crouch, *The Bishop's Boys*, p. 276, 278; Howard, *Wilbur and Orville*, p. 150.

24. Crouch, *The Bishop's Boys*, p. 277.

25. Goddard, *Colonel Albert Pope*, p. 145.

26. Crouch, *The Bishop's Boys*, p. 277; Howard, *Wilbur and Orville*, p. 163.

27. Crouch, *The Bishop's Boys*, pp. 274–5.

28. *Ibid.*, p. 279.

29. Walsh, p. 160.

30. Kirk, p. 196; Combs, p. 238.

31. Crouch, *The Bishop's Boys*, p. 283.

32. Walsh, pp. 162–3.

33. *Ibid.*, p. 163.

34. *Ibid.*, pp. 163–4; Crouch, *The Bishop's Boys*, pp. 282–3.

35. Jennings, *The Century*, p. 9.

36. Walsh, p. 165; Crouch, *The Bishop's Boys*, p. 284; Howard, *Wilbur and Orville*, p. 160.

37. Walsh, p. 166; Howard, *Wilbur and Orville*, pp. 161–2.

38. Crouch, *The Bishop's Boys*, p. 285; Howard, *Wilbur and Orville*, p. 161; Walsh, *Ibid.*, p. 168–9.

39. Howard, *Wilbur and Orville*, pp. 157–8.

40. *Ibid.*, p. 159.

41. Walsh, p. 170; Howard, *Wilbur and Orville*, p. 162.

42. Howard, *Wilbur and Orville*, p. 163.

43. *Ibid.*, p. 163; Walsh, p. 172; Crouch, *The Bishop's Boys*, p. 286.

14. Aircraft for Sale

1. Kirk, *First in Flight*, p. 198.

2. *Ibid.*, p. 200.

3. Combs, *Kill Devil Hill*, p. 251.

4. *Ibid.*, pp. 202–3.

5. McFarland, Ed., *The Papers of Wilbur and Orville Wright*, p. 479, WW to OC, 3/2/05.

6. *Ibid.*, pp. 481–2.

7. Gunston, *Aviation*, p. 44.

8. Howard, *Wilbur and Orville*, p. 163; McFarland, p. 494, WW to OC, 6/1/05.

9. Howard, *Wilbur and Orville*, p. 164.

10. *Ibid.*, pp. 165–6; McFarland, p. 465, WW to OC, 11/5/04. Also p. 493, WW to OC, 5/28/05.

11. Howard, *Wilbur and Orville*, p. 166.

12. McFarland, p. 492, WW Diary, 5/23/05.

13. Howard, *Wilbur and Orville*, p. 169.

14. Combs, p. 248.

15. McFarland, p. 515, WW to Secretary of War, 10/9/05.

16. McFarland, p. 520.

17. *Ibid.*, p. 529.

18. *Ibid.*, pp. 530–3; Combs, p. 252.

19. McFarland, p. 532, WW to OC, 12/8/05.

20. Howard, *Wilbur and Orville*, p. 150.

21. Combs, p. 245.

22. Kirk, pp. 203–4.

23. McFarland, p. 490, WW to OC, 5/6/05.

24. *Ibid.*, p. 729, WW to OC, 10/10/06.

25. *Ibid.*, p. 205.

15. Their Just Deserts

1. Combs, *Kill Devil Hill*, p. 299.

2. Crouch, *The Bishop's Boys*, p. 350.

3. *Ibid.*, pp. 351–2.

4. Pattillo, *Pushing the Envelope*, p. 11.

5. Kirk, *First in Flight*, p. 207.

6. *Ibid.*, pp. 208–14.

7. Howard, *Wilbur and Orville*, p. 245.

8. *Ibid.*, p. 239; Kirk, pp. 216–7.

9. Kirk, pp. 217–9.

10. *Ibid.*, p. 224.

11. *Ibid.*, pp. 222–230.

12. Howard, *Wilbur and Orville*, p. 217.

13 Crouch, *The Bishop's Boys*, pp. 365–9.

14. Gunston, *Aviation*, p. 44.

15. Crouch, *The Bishop's Boys*, p. 362.

16. Gunston, pp. 44–7; Berg, *Lindbergh*, p. 62.

17. Berg, p. 61.

18. Howard, *Wilbur and Orville*, p. 259.

19. Crouch, *The Bishop's Boys*, pp. 371–2.

20. *Ibid.*, pp. 374–5.

21. Howard, *Wilbur and Orville*, pp. 266–8.

22. Crouch, *The Bishop's Boys*, p. 375.

23. *Ibid.*, pp. 375–6.

24. Pattillo, p. 6.

25. Crouch, *The Bishop's Boys*, p. 377; Howard, *Wilbur and Orville*, p. 271.

26. Pattillo, p. 8.

27. *Ibid.*, pp. 7–8.

Epilogue

1. Crouch, *The Bishop's Boys*, pp. 476–7.
2. *Ibid.*, pp. 448–9.
3. McFarland, ed., *The Papers of Wilbur and Orville Wright*, p. 1046.
4. Goddard, *Colonel Albert Pope*, p. 210.
5. Pattillo, *Pushing the Envelope*, pp. 9–10.
6. Berg, *Lindbergh*, p. 62.
7. *Ibid.*; Pattillo, p. 16.
8. Berg, p. 63.
9. *Ibid.*, p. 10.
10. Pattillo, p. 12.
11. *Ibid.*
12. *Ibid.*, pp. 13–14.
13. *Ibid.*, p. 15; Berg, p. 62.
14. Gunston, *Aviation*, p. 104.
15. Pattillo, pp. 16–17.
16. *Ibid.*, p. 17.
17. Goddard, *Colonel Albert Pope*, pp. 14–5.
18. Pattillo, p. 17.
19. Shulman, *Unlocking the Sky*, p. 45–6; Pattillo, p. 17.
20. Shulman, p. 42.
21. Howard, *Wilbur and Orville*, p. 394.
22. As a litigator for three decades, the writer speaks from experience.
23. Shulman, p. 44.
24. Crouch, *The Bishop's Boys*, p. 486; Howard, *Wilbur and Orville*, p. 394.
25. Shulman, p. 48.
26. *Ibid.*, p. 49; Pattillo, p. 19; Howard, *Wilbur and Orville*, p. 394.
27. Combs, *Kill Devil Hill*, p. 346.
28. Crouch, *The Bishop's Boys*, p. 419.
29. *Ibid.*
30. Pattillo, pp. 18–19.
31. Combs, p. 348.
32. *Ibid.*, p. 352.
33. *Ibid.*, p. 356.
34. *Ibid.*, p. 357; Crouch, *The Bishop's Boys*, p. 415.
35. Combs, pp. 351–6, 360.

36. Crouch, *The Bishop's Boys*, p. 480.
37. *Ibid.*, p. 482.
38. *Ibid.*, p. 483.
39. Shulman, p. 57.
40. Crouch, *The Bishop's Boys*, p. 491.
41. *Ibid.*, p. 483.
42. *Ibid.*, pp. 495–6.
43. *Ibid.*, p. 520.
44. *Ibid.*, p. 527.
45. United Aircraft Corporation, *The Pratt & Whitney Story*, pp. 15–18.
46. Goddard, *Colonel Albert Pope*, passim.
47. Pratt & Whitney Company, *Descriptive and Illustrated Catalogue, 1899*, passim.
48. Pratt & Whitney Company, *1860–1940*, pp. 44–5.
49. Rentschler, *An Account of Pratt & Whitney Aircraft Company, 1925–50*, p. 12.
50. United Aircraft Corporation, *Ibid.*, pp. 23–6.
51. United Aircraft Corporation, *Ibid.*, pp. 20–27.
52. Wilford, "Man and Craft Were One," p. F1.
53. *Ibid.*, pp. 28–30.
54. Gunston, *Aviation*, pp. 78–9.
55. Pattillo, *Pushing the Envelope*, pp. 77–79.
56. United Aircraft Corporation, *The Pratt & Whitney Story*, p. 32.
57. Pratt & Whitney Aircraft, *75th Anniversary Celebration Booklet*.
58. Pattillo, *Pushing the Envelope*, pp. 171, 182.
59. *Ibid.*, p. 200. By the mid-1950s, Douglas, Chance Vought, McDonnell, North American and Grumman manufactured attack aircraft and naval fighters, while North American, Northrop, Republic, Convair, Lockheed and McDonnell made air force fighters.
60. *Ibid.*, p. 331. In 1989, Boeing placed 15th and United Technologies Corp. 17th in the Fortune 500 listing of American corporations. In 2002, Boeing was 16th while United Technologies had fallen to 59th.

Bibliography

Aero Club of America, *Navigating the Air*. New York: Doubleday, Page & Company, 1907.

Andrews, Allen. *The Flying Machine: Its Evolution Through the Ages*. New York: Putnam, 1977.

Bacon, Gertrude. *Balloons, Airships and Flying Machines*. London: Dodd, Mead & Company, 1905.

_____. *How Men Fly*. London: Cassell and Company, Ltd., 1911.

Bacon, John M. *By Land and Sky*. London: Isbister & Company, Ltd., 1901.

Baldwin, Neil. *Edison: Inventing the Century*. New York: Hyperion, 1995.

Bell, Alexander Graham. Papers. Archives, Library of Congress, Manuscripts Division, Washington, D.C.

Berg, Scott. *Lindbergh*. New York: G.P. Putnam & Sons, 1998.

Berry, W.H. *Aircraft in War and Commerce*. London: J. Burrow & Co., Ltd.

Brown, Aycock. *Birth of Aviation*. Winston-Salem, N.C.: Collins Co., 1953.

Brown, C.L.M. *The Conquest of the Air*. London: Oxford University Press, 1927.

Bruce, Robert V. *Alexander Graham Bell and the Conquest of Solitude*. Boston: Little Brown, 1973.

Cable, Mary. *Avenue of the Presidents*. Boston: Houghton, Mifflin, 1969.

Cayley, Sir George. *On Aerial Navigations*. Brompton, England: 1809.

Chanute, Octave. *Progress in Flying Machines*. New York: The American Engineer and Railroad Journal, 1894.

Christy, Joe. *High Adventure: The First 75 years of Civil Aviation*. Blue Ridge Summit, PA: Tab Books, 1985.

Collier, Peter, and Horowitz, David. *The Rockefeller: An American Dynasty*. New York: Holt, Rinehart and Winston, 1976.

Combs, Harry, with Martin Caidin. *Kill Devil Hill: Discovering the Secret of the Wright Brothers*. Boston: Houghton, Mifflin Co., 1979.

Corbin, Thomas W. *Aircraft, Aeroplanes, Airships, Etc.* London: C. Arthur Pearson, Ltd., 1914.

Crouch, Tom D. *The Bishop's Boys*. New York: W.W. Norton, 1989.

_____. *A Dream of Wings: Americans and the Airplane, 1875–1905*. New York: W. W. Norton, 1981.

Culick, Fred E. C., and Spencer Dunsmore. *On Great White Wings: The Wright Brothers and the Race for Flight.* New York: Hyperion, 2001.

DeGregorio, William A. *The Complete Book of U.S. Presidents.* Avenel, NJ: Wings Books, 1984.

Donovan, Frank. *The Early Eagles.* New York: Dodd, Mead & Co., 1962.

Douglas, Donald W. *A Pictorial History of Aviation.* New York: Year, 1953.

Edison, Thomas Alva. Papers, Rutgers University, New Brunswick, N.J.

Ennis, William Duane. *Flying Machines Today.* New York: Van Nostrand Co., 1911.

Ethell, Jeffrey L. *Frontier of Flight.* Washington, D.C.: Smithsonian Books, 1992.

Evans, Harold. *The American Century.* New York: Knopf, 1998.

Ferris, Richard. *How to Fly, or the Conquest of the Air.* London: Thomas Nelson and Sons, 1910.

Foster, Genevieve. *The Year of the Flying Machine, 1903.* New York: Charles Scribner's Sons, 1977.

Foulois, Benjamin D. *From the Wright Brothers to the Astronauts.* New York: McGraw-Hill, 1968.

Freudenthal, Elsbeth E. *Flight into History: The Wright Brothers and the Air Age.* Norman: University of Oklahoma Press, 1949.

Friedlander, Mark P., Jr. *Higher, Faster and Farther.* New York: William Morrow, 1973.

Gibbs-Smith, Charles. *Early Flying Machines, 1799–1909.* London: Eyre Methuen, 1975.

_____. *Sir George Cayley's Aeronautics, 1796–1855.* London: Her Majesty's Stationery Office, 1962.

_____. *The World's First Aeroplane Flights (1903–1908).* London: Her Majesty's Stationery Office, 1965.

Gilbert, Martin. *A History of the Twentieth Century. Volume 1.* New York: William Morrow, 1997.

Goddard, Stephen B. *Colonel Albert Pope and His American Dream Machines: The Life and Times of a Bicycle Tycoon Turned Automotive Pioneer.* Jefferson, N.C.: McFarland, 2000.

_____. *Getting There: The Epic Struggle Between Road and Rail in the American Century.* New York: Basic Books, 1994.

Grahame-White, Claude. *The Story of the Aeroplane.* Boston: Small, Maynard & Company, 1911.

Gunston, Bill, consultant ed. *Aviation: The Story of Flight.* London: Cathay Books, 1978.

Hart, Clive. *The Prehistory of Flight.* Berkeley: University of California Press, 1985.

Hearne, R.P. *Aerial Warfare.* London: John Lane, 1908.

Howard, Frank, and Bill Gunston. *The Conquest of the Air.* New York: Random House, 1972.

Howard, Fred. *Wilbur & Orville: A Biography of the Wright Brothers.* New York: Knopf, 1987.

http://chrisbrady.itgo.com. *Richard Pearse: First Man to "Fly" a Mechanically Powered Aeroplane.* July 27, 2001.

http://library.thinkquest.org/18033/Langley.html. *Samuel P. Langley.*

Jackson, Donald Dale. *The Aeronauts.* Alexandria, Va.: Time-Life Books, 1980.

Jennings, Peter, and Todd Brewster. *The Century.* New York: Doubleday, 1998.

Johnson, Paul. *A History of the American People.* New York: HarperCollins, 1997.

Kelly, Fred. *The Wright Brothers: A Biography Authorized by Orville Wright.* New York: Harcourt, Brace, 1943.

Kingsford, P.W. *F.W. Lanchester: The Life of an Engineer.* London: Edward Arnold, 1960.

Kipling, Rudyard. *Something of Myself for My Friends Known and Unknown.* Garden City, N.Y.: Doubleday, Doran & Co., 1937.

Kirk, Stephen. *First in Flight: The Wright Brothers in North Carolina.* Winston-Salem: John F. Blair, 1995.

Lacey, Robert. *Ford: The Man and the Machine.* Boston: Little, Brown, 1986.

Langley, Samuel Pierpont. *Experiments in Aerodynamics*. Washington, D.C.: Smithsonian Press, 1891.

_____. "The Flying Machine." *McClure's Magazine*, June, 1897, pp. 646–660.

_____. *Memoir on Mechanical Flight*. Washington, D.C.: Smithsonian Press, 1911.

Leech, Margaret. *In the Days of McKinley*. New York: Harper & Brothers, 1959.

Levine, Don. *Mitchell, Pioneer of Air Power*. New York: Duell, Sloan & Pearce, 1943.

Lupiano, Vincent DePaul, and Ken W. Sayers. *It Was a Very Good Year*. Holbrook, Mass.: Bob Adams, Inc., 1994.

Mackenzie, Catherine. *Alexander Graham Bell: The Man Who Contracted Space*. Boston: Houghton, Mifflin, 1928.

Mackworth-Praed, Ben. *Aviation: The Pioneer Years*. London: Studio Editions, 1990.

May, Charles Paul. *Women in Aeronautics*. New York: Nelson & Sons, 1962.

McFarland, Marvin W., ed. *The Papers of Wilbur and Orville Wright, Including the Chanute-Wright Letters*. New York: McGraw-Hill, 1953.

McMahon, John R. *The Wright Brothers: Fathers of Flight*. Boston: Little Brown, 1930.

Means, James, ed. *The Aeronautical Annual*. Boston: W.B. Clarke & Co., 1895.

Meyer, Robert B., Jr. *Langley's Model Aero Engine of 1903*. Washington, D.C.: Smithsonian Institution, 1972.

Moolman, Valerie. *The Road to Kitty Hawk*. Alexandria, Va.: Time-Life Books, 1980.

Morison, Samuel Eliot. *The Oxford History of the American People*. NY: Oxford University Press, 1965.

Morris, Edmund. *The Rise of Theodore Roosevelt*. New York: Coward, McCann and Geohagan, Inc., 1979.

Mowbray, Jay Henry. *Conquest of the Air by Airships and Other Flying Machines*. George W. Bertron, 1910.

Park, Edwards. *Aviation Pioneers*. Washington, D.C.: United States Postal Service, 1992.

Parkinson, Russell. "Politics, Patents & Planes: Military Aeronautics in the United States, 1867–1907." Dissertation, Duke University, 1963.

Pattillo, Donald M. *Pushing the Envelope: The American Aircraft Industry*. Ann Arbor: University of Michigan Press, 2000.

Pratt & Whitney — In the Company of Eagles. Undated company publication.

Pratt & Whitney Division. *1860–1940, Pratt & Whitney Division*. Hartford: Niles-Bement-Pond, 1940.

Pritchard, J. Laurence. *Sir George Cayley*. New York: Horizon Press, 1962.

Rendall, Ivan. *Reaching for the Skies*. New York: Orion Books, 1988.

Renstrom, Arthur G. *Wilbur & Orville Wright: Pictorial Materials*. Washington: Library of Congress, 1982.

Rentschler, Frederick. *An Account of Pratt & Whitney Aircraft Company, 1925–1950*. Hartford: Francis S. Murphy Estate, Hartford Collection, 1950.

Ricketts, Harry. *Rudyard Kipling: A Life*. New York, Carroll & Graf, 1999.

Robson, William A. *Aircraft in War and Peace*. London: Macmillan & Co., 1916.

Roseberry, C.R. *Glenn Curtiss: Pioneer of Flight*. Syracuse: Syracuse University Press, 1991.

Shulman, Seth. *Unlocking the Sky: Glenn Hammond Curtiss and the Race to Invent the Airplane*. New York: HarperCollins, 2002.

Smith, Robert. *A Social History of the Bicycle*. New York: American Heritage, 1972.

Smithsonian Institution, Archival Division, Langley Aerodrome and Telescope File.

Spearman, Arthur Dunning. *John Joseph Montgomery, 1858–1911: Father of Basic Flying*. Santa Clara: University of Santa Clara Press, 1967.

Stewart, Oliver, and Bill Gunston. *The Conquest of the Air*. New York: Random House, 1972.

Stick, David. *The Outer Banks of North Carolina*. Chapel Hill: University of North Carolina Press, 1958.

Studer, Clara. *Sky-Storming Yankee: The Life of Glenn Curtiss*. New York: Stackpole, 1937.

United Aircraft Corporation. *The Pratt and Whitney Aircraft Story*. Harvard, CT: Pratt and Whitney Division of United Aircraft Corporation, 1950.

Villard, Henry S. *Contact! The Story of the Early Birds*. New York: Bonanza Books, 1953.

Walsh, John Evangelist. *One Day at Kitty Hawk: The Untold Story of the Wright Brothers and the Airplane*. New York: Thomas Y. Crowell, 1975.

Wescott, Lynanne, and Paula Degen. *Wind and Sand: The Story of the Wright Brothers at Kitty Hawk*. New York: Eastern Acorn Press, 1983.

Wilford, John Noble. "Man and Craft Were One, As a New Age Began." *The New York Times*, May 21, 2002, p. F1.

www.aeromuseum.org. Octave Chanute Aerospace Museum, June 30, 2001.

www.Fitzgeraldstudio.com. *Alexander Graham Bell — The Inventor*, June 30, 2001.

www2.crown.net. *Octave Chanute's Diary of his Visits to the Indiana Dunes in the Summer of 1896*, Jan. 2, 1902.

www.encyclopedia.com/articles/14020.html. *Orville Wright*.

www.flight100.org/history/wright.html. *Celebrating the Evolution of Flight*.

Wright, Orville. "How We Made the First Flight." *Flying* (December, 1913): 10–12.

Wright, Wilbur. "Experiments and Observations in Soaring Flight." *Journal of the Western Society of Engineers* (August, 1903): 400–417.

Yergin, Daniel. *The Prize: The Epic Quest for Oil, Money and Power*. New York: Simon & Schuster, 1991.

Yochelson, Ellis L. *Charles Doolittle Walcott, Paleontologist*. Kent, Ohio: Kent State University Press, 1998.

Young, Rosamond, and Catherine Fitzgerald. *Twelve Seconds to the Moon: A Story of the Wright Brothers*. Dayton: The Journal Herald, 1978.

Zahm, Albert Francis. *Aerial Navigation, a Popular Treatise on the Growth of Air Craft and on Aeronautical Meteorology*. New York: D. Appleton and Company, 1911.

_____. *Early Powerplane Fathers*. South Bend, Ind.: Notre Dame University Press, 1951.

Index